Why did Adam get the first fig leaf? *Because he wore the plants in the family.* • *Mother:* Billy, you just drove through a red light! Is this what you learned in Driver Education class? *Billy:* Gee, Mom, Bobby does it all the time. *Mother:* Now you're stopping at a green light! What's the idea? *Billy:* Bobby might be coming! • *Patient:* Doctor, Doctor, you've got to help me. I think I'm invisible. *Doctor:* Who said that? • *Dad:* Okay, who left the kids' Bongo Blaster in the driveway? *Mom:* Now, don't get upset, dear; that toy's supposed to be indestructible. *Dad:* It's indestructible, all right—it broke the car! • What do you get if you cross a kangaroo with a mint? *A hint with a pocketful of miracles.* • *Georgie:* Dad, what was the name of the train station we just left? *Dad:* Shhh, son, I'm trying to read the map. *Georgie:* Okay, but look for the name of that last stop, because Mom just got off there! • Knock, knock. *Who's there?* Recycle. *Recycle who?* Recycle around town on our bikes. • *Father:* I'll tell you something about happiness. Do you know what it means to come home to two adorable, well-mannered kids who are thrilled at the sight of you, hang on your every word, and think you're the smartest, strongest, best guy in the whole world? *Bachelor friend:* Well. . . *Father:* I'll tell you what it means—it means you're in the wrong house! • *Ralph:* My wife's a neat cook. *Ed:* Mine too. She's always offering seconds! • *Boy mole:* Did you go away with your parents this summer? *Girl mole:* Yes. *Boy mole:* Did you have fun?

3650 Jokes, Puns & Riddles

Why did Adam get the first fig leaf? *Because he wore the plants in the family.* • *Mother:* Billy, you just drove through a red light! Is this what you learned in Driver Education class? *Billy:* Gee, Mom, Bobby does it all the time! *Mother:* Now you're stopping at a green light! What's the idea? *Billy:* Bobby might be coming! • *Patient:* Doctor, Doctor, you got to help me. I think I'm invisible. *Doctor:* Who said that? • *Dad:* Okay, who left the kids' Bongo Blaster in the driveway? *Mom:* Now don't get upset, dear; that toy's supposed to be indestructible. *Dad:* It's indestructible, all right—it broke the car! • What do you get if you cross a kangaroo with a mint? *A pocketful of miracles.* • *Georgie:* Dad, what was the name of the train station we just left? *Dad:* Shhh, son, I'm trying to listen. *Mom:* *Georgie:* Okay, but look for the name of that last stop, because Mom just got off there! • Knock knock. *Who's there?* Recycle. *Recycle who?* Recycle around town on our bikes. • *Father:* I'll tell you something about happiness. Do you know what it means to come home to two adorable, well-mannered children who are thrilled at the sight of you, hang on your every word, and think you're the smartest, strongest, best Dad in the whole world? *Bachelor friend:* Well... *Father:* I'll tell you, it means you're in the wrong house! • *Ralph:* My wife is a real card. *Ed:* Mine too. She's always offering seconds! • *Boy mole:* Did you go away with your parents this summer? *Girl mole:* Yes. *Boy mole:* Did you have fun?

3650 Jokes, Puns & Riddles

By Anne Kostick,
Charles Foxgrover
and Michael J. Pellowski

Edited by
Michael Driscoll

BLACK DOG
& LEVENTHAL
PUBLISHERS
NEW YORK

Published by
Black Dog & Leventhal Publishers, Inc.
151 West 19th Street
New York, NY 10011

Distributed by
Workman Publishing Company
225 Varick Street
New York, NY 10014

Interior Design by Sabrina Bowers
Cover Design & Illustration by Daberko Design

Manufactured in the United States of America

ISBN-13: 978-1-57912-843-2

h g f e d c

Contents

High Technology   7

Word Play   17

Modern Romance   45

Bad Medicine   65

Not Smart   95

Mmm-mm...Food   127

Insults   153

The Supernatural   185

The Working World   195

Money   239

Games & Recreation   259

Music &
   the Performing Arts   287

Family Fun   299

Crime & Punishment   333

History   351

How Hot Was It?   357

Nature & the Farm   361

Animal Kingdom   375

Aging   409
TV, Movies & Pop Culture 415
Religion   429
Politics   437
Stop Me
  If You've Heard This One 449
Seasonal Laughs   453
Not Found in Webster's   461
Silly Signs & Slogans   477
Classifieds   485
Knock Knock...   491
Bonus One-Liners   533

HIGH TECHNOLOGY

· ·

Man's struggles with clocks, etc.

General: Why hasn't this rocket been shot into space yet?
Scientist: The crew is on its launch break.

How do you put a baby astronaut to sleep?
Rocket.

Rinky: Did you near NASA's planning to put 500 cows into orbit?
Dinky: Yeah, it'll be the herd shot round the world.

What did the baby light bulb say to its mother?
I wuv you watts and watts.

· ·

Systems analyst: It's time you upgraded your computer network.
Business manager: Oh, we can't get rid of this computer.
Systems analyst: With a new system, your operation will be faster. Why would you want to keep this old computer?
Business manager: It knows too much.

What does a baby computer call its father?
Data.

Critic: You say your new play is about launching rockets into space?
Author: Yes. And it uses three stages.

Why was the overstuffed mattress so happy?
It was time for spring training.

Mike: What do you get if you cross an automobile with a kangaroo?
Spike: A car that jump starts itself.

Why was Ms. Mattress so happy?
She was going to be a spring bride.

Mr. Lightbulb: Why are you going to see a doctor?
Mrs. Lightbulb: Because I keep having hot flashes.

What do you get if you cross a timepiece with a false friend?
A clock that is two-faced.

Nick: What do you get if you cross a camera with a firefly?
Rick: A shutterbug with a built-in flash.

What did the mommy train say to the little train at the dinner table?
Chew! Chew!

Little watch: Mom, I need your help right now to wash my face.
Mother watch: Wait a minute. I only have two hands.

Why should you never invite a watch to dinner?
They always ask for second helpings.

Computer teacher: Why are you bringing cheese into the computer room?
Little boy: You told me I was going to work with a mouse today.

Why did the telephone run away from home?
It wanted to join a three-ring circus.

Customer: My watch only runs every other day.
Salesman: It was probably made by a part-time employee.

Show me a small clock made by an old witch…and I'll show you a time hex watch.

Scientist: Where do you find the nerdiest place in outer space?
Astronaut: On the dork side of the moon.

What do you call a person who organizes car pools into the city?
A *commuter programmer.*

Engineer: It's a major breakthrough! A wheel-less, motorless, crash-proof automobile! Just one little problem left to iron out.
Executive: Which is…
Engineer: It won't move!

How do you slow down a speeding computer?
Use the disk brakes.

Captain Kirk: What's wrong with the engine of the Enterprise? It keeps knocking.
Mr. Scott: I need to change the spock plugs, Captain.

What do you get if you cross a grocery clerk with a scientist?
Market research.

Hal: I just invented a talking wristwatch that tells time and jokes.
Cal: Does it really work?
Hal: Of course. It's a laugh a minute!

Why don't fish go near computers?
They're afraid of getting caught in the internet.

Reporter: What's it like to be an astronaut?
Astronaut: It's a little weird. It's the only job in the world where you get fired before you go to work.

What is the favorite song of all electrical engineers?
Ohm on the Range.

Grandfather Clock: It's now 3:00.
Alarm Clock: You're wrong. It's 3:30.
Grandfather Clock: Don't tock back to me, young fella.

What did one important electrode say to the other?
Hey! Let's do a power lunch sometime soon.

Danny: What would you call a wristwatch worn in the 24th century?
Manny: Future-wrist-tick.

If athletes get athlete's foot, what do astronauts get?
Missile toe.

Office manager: I'm calling to complain about that Titanic computer you just installed here today.
Computer salesman: I don't know what you mean—I didn't sell you something called a Titanic.
Office manager: Oh, yeah? Well, it just went down!

What's a computer's favorite kind of cookie?
Chocolate chip.

Moe: I understand there might be a lot of computer problems in the year 2000.
Joe: True. But I'm not in the least bit worried about that.
Moe: Why not?
Joe: I don't own a computer.

Latest computer best-sellers
　　A Tale of Two CDs
　　Gates of Wrath
　　Gone with the Windows
　　War and PC
　　Moby Disk

Girl: My cat is so smart he has his own computer.
Boy: Does he use it much?
Girl: Yes. He's always playing with the mouse.

How do you make a car smile?
Take it on a joy ride.

Customer: If I buy a TV, do I get a free clicker with it?
Salesman: There's a remote possibility.

What do you get if you cross Ma Bell with a royal boy bee?
A touch drone phone.

Little girl: Scientists who launch rockets into space must be very intelligent.
Little boy: I don't think they're that smart. They can't even count correctly. They always get the numbers backwards.

What do you get if you cross a turnpike tollbooth with a clock?
A ticket tocker.

Silversmith:: What can I do for you?
Inventor: I made a new type of round cooking pot, but I haven't figured out a way to pick it up.
Silversmith : I'm sure it's a problem we can handle.

Where does a computer whiz keep his accounts?
In a data bank.

Al: I've invented the best automobile lubricant in the world. It's truly terrific.
Cal: What do you call it?
Al: Amazing Grease.

Which western hero was created in a science lab?
The Clone Ranger.

Reporter: What's the first thing you need to split an atom?
Scientist: A fission license.

Why did the android go to a psychologist?
He thought he was having a metal breakdown.

Fred: I heard you dropped out of computer school.
Ed: Yeah. I just couldn't hack the program.

How do you season a computer?
Use cyberspice

Customer: Every time I put a tape in my VCR the audio sounds scratchy.
Repairman: Maybe it has head lice.

What kind of snacks do computers munch?
Microchips.

Reporter: So, this year you'll be cracking down on illegal computer activities.
Federal Agent: Yes. We'll be taking a big byte out of crime.

What did the big floor lamp say to the little night-light?
"Wire you insulate?"

Inventor: I've got a great new invention that's ready to be patented just as soon as I work out one small problem. It's a lawn mower that actually flies!
Investor: But how can it cut the grass if it's flying?
Inventor: That's the small problem!

What happened when the Macintosh married the Epson?
They had a little laptop.

Rose: I just got one of those new washing machines that talks!
Violet: I'm holding out for the next model.
Rose: What next model?
Violet: The one that tells you what it did with the other sock!

WORD PLAY & RIDDLES

· ·

Twisting language to suit your comedy needs

Plumber: I can't finish putting in your bathroom fixtures until next month.
Homeowner: Now that's a shower stall if I ever heard one.

What do you get if you cross a chicken with test papers?
Eggsams.

Mechanic: Would you like me to winterize your car?
Tom: First summerize the cost.

· ·

A professional treasure hunter was diving for pirate treasure in an ocean cove. He searched for hours without any success. Finally he started toward the shore. When he was about knee deep in water he stumbled across an old strongbox. He scooped it out of the sea and yanked open the lid. The box was full of gold coins. "Well, what do you know," exclaimed the happy treasure hunter. "It just goes to prove that booty is only shin deep."

Nick: Did you hear the joke about the three deep holes drilled in the ground?
Rick: No, I didn't.
Nick: Well, well, well.

What do you get if you cross a memory expert and a conductor?
A person who never loses his train of thought.

Mary: I'd like to buy some goose feathers.
Brenda: Can you afford the down payment?

What did the jack say to the car?
Hey! I know you're in a rush, so don't let me hold you up.

Tailor: Would you like me to rent you a tuxedo, sir?
Customer: That'll suit me fine.

What did Mr. Fog say to Ms. Mist?
Let's dew lunch sometime.

Inspector: Why is that skyscraper sneezing?
Foreman: Maybe it has a building code.

What do you call a boomerang that won't come back?
A stick.

Anne: I crossed a talking bird with a clock.
Susan: Why did you do that?
Anne: I want to study polly-ticks.

What do you get when you cross an abalone and a crocodile?
You get a crockabaloney.

Sean: What did the Irish farmer say to his son when they went into the garden?
Pat: Hoe Danny Boy!

What do you get if you cross a kangaroo with a saint?
An animal that has a pocketful of miracles.

Teacher: George, what's the difference between ignorance and apathy?
George: I don't know, and I don't care!

How do you drive a baby buggy?
Tickle its feet!

Poet: How are things?
Tailor: Sew-sew. How about you?
Poet: Could be verse!

What is made of wood but can't be sawed?
Sawdust.

Sue: There's one word you always pronounce wrong.
Stu: What word is that?
Sue: Wrong.

How is a potato farmer like a baseball fan?
One yanks the roots; the other roots for the Yanks.

Boise: Is Helena Nome?
Montana: Idaho, Alaska.

Two army recruits are waiting in line to be inoculated. One turns to his pal and says: "Boy, what an outfit. We've only been in the army fifteen minutes and already we're presenting arms!"

Beach: How ya dune?
Ocean: Just swell!

What's the difference between a butcher and an insomniac?
One weighs a steak and the other stays awake.

Hokey: Do you file your nails?
Pokey: No, I throw them away.

What did Tennessee?
Same thing Arkansas.

Blair: I've got a bad case of snew.
Clair: What's snew?
Blair: Not much. What's snew with you.

Will February March?
No, but April May.

Farmer: Hey, neighbor—you can't take your sheep home that way.
Neighbor: I was just taking a shortcut across your frozen pond. What's wrong with that?
Farmer: Nobody pulls the wool over my ice.

When is a door not a door?
When it is a jar.

What's worse than raining cats and dogs?
Hailing a taxi.

Man: That's a nice wooden figure you've carved, fella.
Youngster: Thanks. Everyone says I'm a good whittle boy.

Why are you crying old Mr. Shoelace, can't you tie a bow?
No. I'm a frayed knot.

News Flash!
New bridge plan collapses due to lack of main stream support.

Cartoons: melodies to drive by

A boy opened his refrigerator and found a rabbit lounging in the butter dish.
Boy: What are you doing in there?
Rabbit: Isn't this a Westinghouse?
Boy: As a matter of fact, it is.
Rabbit: Well, I'm westing!

What's the difference between a teacher and a railroad conductor?
One trains the mind; the other minds the train.

What's the difference between a racehorse and a duck?
One goes quick on its legs; the other goes quack on its eggs.

At the photographer's studio:
Shutterbug: First we'll shoot you, then we'll blow you up, then you can go home and hang yourself.

What's the difference between a king's son, a monkey's mother, a bald head, and an orphan?
One's an heir apparent, the next is a hairy parent, the next has no hair apparent, and the last has nary a parent.

Attention weathercasters!
Wanted—a sunny forecast for the weekend. Don't try to cloud the issue!

How is the cop on the street like a bad architect?
They both have fallen arches.

Cannibal: Shall I boil the new missionary?
Chief: No, he's a friar.

What's the difference between a counterfeit bill and an irate rabbit?
One's bad money; the other's a mad bunny.

Tourist: Do you think the Seine will overflow with all these spring rains?
Guide: Do not worry, Monsieur. In France the water is always l'eau.

Why should you never tell secrets in the Rockies?
Because of the mountaineers.

George: Our new neighbor's getting to be a real pest.
Martha: Didn't you lend him your rake?
George: Yes, but he just came back for mower.

A rather innocent young man wandered into the wrong kind of massage parlor one day. He was ready to leave immediately but curiosity kept him glued to the floor, taking in all he could see. Finally the manager approached him, saying "Excuse me, sir—are you a member of this club?"

"Oh, no," said the young man, "I'm just aghast."

Best-sellers we'd like to see
   "Secrets of the F.B.I.," by Isadore Shut.
   "Court Cases," by Nita Lawyer.
   "Planning a Surprise Party," by Al B. Darn.
   "The History of Rock and Roll" by Tristan Shout.
   "Are You a Liar?," by I.M. Knott.
   "How to Lose Weight," by X. R. Sizemore.
   "Burglary Made Easy," by Jimmy DeLox.
   "Counterfeiting Exposé," by E. Z. Money.

Why is a bulldog like an auctioneer?
They both look for bidding.

Ebenezer: They finally got rid of that ghost over at the old Cabot place.
Jedediah: Yep—caught him haunting without a license.
Vampire: Let's do the town tonight.
Mummy: I can't. I'm pressed for time.

What did the island-gobbling sea monster say?
These islands aren't philipine me up; I want samoa tahiti!

Why did Zorro engage in so many sword fights?
He was leading a duel life.

What did one bumper car say to the other?
May I have the next dents?

Anne: What do you call a deer with no eyes?
Fannie: No eye deer.
Annie: What do you call a plaster deer with no eyes?
Fannie: Still no eye deer.
Annie: What do you call a plaster deer with no eyes and a hole in its sock?
Fannie: Still no darn eye deer.

Why does Santa Claus always go down the chimney?
He'll only do what soots him.

What did the jar of paste do on January 1st?
It made a Glue Year's Resolution.

What has four wheels, two claws, and a meter?
A taxi crab driver.

Postcard From Over the Edge
Dear Lorraine,

Yipes! I was Lyon around in the sun Toulon and got a bad Berne! But I won't let it Rouen my vacation. Getting ready to Chartres a Tours of the coast.

Au revoir,

Nancy

Al: What do you get if you cross a razor with a rifle?
Cal: A sharpshooter.

What kind of truck does a road hog drive?
An 18-squealer.

Gina: What do you get if you cross toothpaste with a newlywed woman?
Tina: A brushing bride.

What car is parked in the tower of a famous Paris cathedral?
The Hatchback of Notre Dame.

Ryan: Who are the toughest bugs in Scotland?
Sean: The Kilter Bees.

Why did the homeowner buy the new economy lawn mower?
It got good grass mileage.

Monster: Why are you so depressed today?
Ghost: It's a boo Monday.

What did the audio man say to the movie producer after his work was completed?
Sound check please.

Ed: My car engine sounds cold.
Fred: Maybe you have it in frost gear.

What did the farmer say to his compost pile?
Thank you very mulch.

Ed: My car is getting too old to run smoothly.
Ned: Maybe you should retire it.

How can you tell the difference between our legal system and a skating rink?
One is justice; the other's just ice.

Nel: Did you hear the riddle about the front door?
Mel: No, but I bet it's a knock-knock joke.

Why was Mr. B.B. Gun so happy?
Because his wife just had a B.B. boy.

Private: Hey, Sarge! Where do baby soldiers get their basic training?
Sarge: At bootie camp.

What's covered with soot and performs in silence?
A coal mime.

Hillary: What do you get if you cross a softball pitcher with a parrot and a clock?
Bubba: Underhanded polly-ticks.

Which officer is the butt of a lot of sailor jokes?
The rear admiral.

Rick: How did you get out of that camping supply store so fast? The checkout lines were really long.
Nick: I used the express lane for tent items.

What goes drip! drop! instead of tick! tock!?
A flood watch.

Anne: Why are all the cars honking their horns?
Charlie: It's Beep Year!

Why did the witch go out into the desert?
She wanted to try out some dry spells.

Tom: What does a bald artist use on his head?
Kevin: An air brush.

How do sailors get clean?
They throw themselves overboard and wash up on the beach.

Customer: I'm in the market for an exotic pet.
Pet shop owner: I recommend the mongoose. Loyal, cuddly, and a great help if you have a snake problem.
Customer: Terrific! I'll take two mongeese...uh, make that two mongooses...oh, heck, I'll just take one mongoose, and while you're at it, give me another one.

What's the difference between geography and biography?
Geography's about maps; Biography's about chaps.

Eb: I just built a bungalow.
Flo: You mean a tiny little house?
Eb: Not really—the builder bungled it and I still owe!

What's the difference between a cardboard paper towel roll and a Dutch comedian?
One's a hollow cylinder; the other's a silly Hollander.

Ted: My wife's taking a trip to the West Indies.
Fred: Jamaica?
Ted: Not at all, she wanted to go.

What do you get when you overfeed the British Navy and the American Navy?
You get too fat fleets.

Postcard From Over the Edge
Dear Helena:

Hi, Hawaii! I've been Suffern from a vague Malaysia from all this Russian around. I'm weak Indonesia and Congo on much longer. Otherwise, Havana good time. Alaska doctor about it when I return Nome.

Irish you were here, but Abyssinia soon!

Love, joy

Why are there no mausoleums in Prague?
Because the undertakers refuse to cache Czechs.

What's the difference between a panhandler and a pillow?
The panhandler's hard up; the pillow's soft down.

What do you get if you cross tons of bubblegum with the millennium?
The year chew 2000.

How do sailors get their clothes clean?
They throw them overboard and then they are washed ashore.

Inscribed on the tomb of Bugs Bunny:
Hare Today—Gone Tomorrow.

Inscribed on the tomb of R2D2:
Rust in Peace.

Inscribed on the tomb of a memory expert:
Gone but not Forgotten.

Inscribed on the tomb of a hairdresser:
The Good Dye Young.

If a red house is made of red bricks and a yellow house is made of yellow bricks, what is a green house made of?
Glass!

Seamstress No. 1: Should I put more stitches in this hem?
Seamstress No. 2: I think...sew.

Why did the bacterium cross the microscope?
To get to the other slide.

Producer: In this next scene you pick up a rod and reel and fling the lure into the river.
Actor: Someone better show me how to do that.
Producer: Quick! Send for the casting director.

"I just invented a new car that has a coffeemaker built right into the dashboard," said Mr. Morgan. "It makes driving in the morning rush hour a lot easier."

"Why is that?" asked Mr. Norton.

Answered Mr. Morgan, "You can perk the car anywhere."

Sarge: Why do you look so sad, soldier?
Private: I'm upset because I couldn't climb the wall on the obstacle course.
Sarge: Cheer up. You'll get over it.

Mr. Jones: I'm putting a new bay window in our breakfast area.
Mr. Smith: Is it a lot of work?
Mr. Jones: I'll say! It's a real pane in the nook.

Moe: I'm homesick.
Joe: Isn't that your home over there?
Moe: Yeah, but I'm sick of it.

Joe: I had a terrible nightmare last night.
Moe: How bad was it?
Joe: Real bad. I dreamt I was a muffler. I woke up exhausted.

Best-sellers we'd like to see
"How to Prepare Meals," by I. Ken Cooke
"How to Get in Shape," by Ron Daily
"How to Make More Money," by B. A. Counterfeiter
"How to Become a Gossip Columnist" by I. C. Rumors
"How to Start Your Own Business, " by Selma Products

What kind of humor do you like?
   "Sight gags," said the optometrist.
   "Slapstick," said the hockey player.
   "Dry humor," said the diaper maker.
   "Running gags," said the jogger.
   "Corny jokes," said the farmer.

What is the difference between a lighthouse keeper, a thief, and a pot of glue?
One watches over seas, one seizes watches, and as for the pot of glue? Ah, that's the sticky part.

Book review
The Wizard of Oz: A precious gem of a tale about a girl with a pearly grin who wears ruby slippers to the Emerald City. When she exposes the Wizard to be as fake as Cubic Zirconium, he yells, "Sapphire me!"

Real estate broker: I tell you this new house has no flaws at all.
Buyer: Then what do you walk on?

Minnie: Did you hear about the terrible accident? A pink cruise ship collided with a purple cruise ship.
Mickey: What happened?
Minnie: All the passengers were marooned!

Danny: My wife thinks we should get a used car.
Manny: What's wrong with that?
Danny: She likes to drive a tough bargain, but I think it's tough to drive a bargain!

Doris: Didn't your son join the Army?
Debby: Yes, but now he's a drop-out.
Doris: You mean he left the service?
Debby: No, he's a paratrooper!

Joan: Do you believe in intuition?
Jean: No, but I have a feeling I might someday.

Larry: I just read in the paper about a guy who jumped out of a window in Times Square. Now why would anyone do such a thing?
Harry: Probably wanted to make a hit on Broadway!

What's the difference between a hill and a pill?
A hill is hard to get up. A pill is hard to get down.

Ivor: I never mince words!
Igor: You should; it makes them easier to eat later on!

Sir Percy: Poor Sir Reginald! Went on safari last month and was never heard from again!
Sir Leslie: Pity...probably something he disagreed with ate him.

Betty: Where's Jake?
Letty: Oh, he's out on the porch with Clem, shooting the bull.
Betty: Well, I sure hope he knows how to cook it!

Why are you always welcome in the "Show me" state?
Because Missouri loves company.

First nudist: You're not dating Frank anymore?
Second nudist: No, we'd been seeing too much of each other.

What does a skydiving babysitter need?
An au-pairachute.

Donald: How was your trip to Helsinki?
Daisy: Terrible! All our luggage vanished into Finn Air!

Why are lost things always in the last place you look?
Because after you find them you stop looking.

Jack: What can you hold in your right hand that you can't hold in your left hand?
Benny: Your left elbow.

Show me a king with a sore throat…and I'll show you a royal pain in the neck!

Marge: Where'd you get all those bruises?
Vern: Oh, they threw a loud party downstairs last night.
Marge: So?
Vern: I was the loud party!

Jack: I haven't seen you around lately.
Zack: I had a growth removed from my head.
Jack: Oh my goodness. Were you in the hospital?
Zack: No, the barbershop.

What do you get if you cross a federal law enforcement officer and a pirate crew?
The F.B. Aye! Aye!

Billy: Gosh, everyone's so angry these days.
Millie: What makes you think so?
Billy: Today the Good Humor man yelled at me!

Bobby Ray: What're all those explosions I hear?
Fannie Fae: Oh, that's just Ida Mae in the backyard shelling peas!

What stands in New York Harbor, holds a torch, and sneezes a lot?
The Ah-Choo of Liberty.

Suzy: What a sale! I took three things that were marked down!
Annie: What?
Suzy: A blouse, a skirt, and an escalator!

Why did the Geologists Society hold its convention in New York City?
The members all wanted to see the Rockettes.

Ringmaster: The two acrobats just got married.
Clown: Was it love at first sight?
Ringmaster: Yes. They just flipped over each other.

Show me a hobo running for a freight train...and I'll show you a bum rush.

Little boy: Are you a pirate?
Capt. Morgan: I sure am.
Little boy: I thought all pirates had a ring in their ear.
Capt. Morgan: That's funny, I don't hear anything.

What kind of injury did Humpty Dumpty suffer when he fell off the wall?
Shell shock.

Angus: What did the Scotsman do when he couldn't find a pair of pants to wear?
Donald: He kilt himself.

Two cannibals were eating a clown, when one turned to the other and said, "This tastes funny."

Merman: Does King Neptune have throw rugs in his undersea palace?
Mermaid: No. He has whale-to-whale carpeting.

Why did King Neptune take shellfish to the gym?
He wanted to build up his mussels.

Sinbad: What did the cowboy yell to the sailor who was stuck out on the lake?
Pecos Bill: Hey pardner! Whoa, whoa, whoa your boat.

What do you get if you cross a chick and a tree with Danielle Steele?
A *peeperbark writer.*

Reporter: Did you see that new documentary about how skyscrapers are erected?
Movie critic: Yes. It was a riveting experience.

Show me a really insulting telegram…and I'll show you a barbed wire!

Alf: I was born in Australia in the late 1940s.
Ralph: Me, too, mate. I guess that makes us a couple of baby boomerangers.

Captain Morgan: What is a pirate's favorite letter of the alphabet?
First mate: I, I, Captain!

Mack: Look at this announcement for a meeting of the International Chair Haters Club. How ridiculous.
Zack: What's so ridiculous? I'm a member in good standing.

On what kind of road are you likely to get a flat tire?
On one with a fork in it.

Bruce: Watch me make this mud disappear.
Diane: No thanks. I'm not interested in dirty tricks.

Postman: Humph! These envelopes are stuck together.
Clerk: Gee. Talk about mail bonding.

Jack: You want me to put a hundred bay windows in your house?
Henry: Yes. I guess I'm just pane crazy.

Ken: That canoe gives me nothing but trouble.
Len: Your canoe sounds more like a woe boat to me.

Jim: What's the best thing to send to a couple who bought a house that has no water?
Slim: A get well soon card.

Dottie: Why is that skyscraper crying?
Pat: Too many sad stories.

Reporter: Who would I blame if California fell into the Pacific Ocean?
Geologist: It would be San Andreas Fault.

Corporal Glue: What did the glue say to the paste?
Sergeant Paste: I think it best if we stick together.

Pioneer: My house is too hot.
Scout: Maybe it has cabin fever.

Landlubber: Is the ocean messy?
Sea captain: No. It's a tide-place.

Mr. Morning Sun: Why are you so unhappy?
Mr. Mist: There's nothing to dew.

Lifeguard: The ocean is awfully quiet today.
Bather: Maybe it doesn't have much to spray.

Homeowner: My house is located in an earthquake zone.
Agent: Sorry. I can't help you. I only sell no-fault insurance.

Which part of a highway always freezes first?
The cold shoulder.

Soldier: I work at an Army camp.
Businessman: How's your base pay?

Tailor: Did you split your pants again?
Philip: Yes. Every time I bend over it's the seam old story.

What is the most dangerous part of a car?
The nut that holds the steering wheel.

What floats in the ocean but only at night?
A bat buoy.

Show me a non-commissioned officer who is an Army dentist...and I'll show you a drill sergeant.

Ron: I just saw an ocean liner that was stuck tight between two wooden docks.
John: Wow! Talk about pier pressure.

What do you get if you cross an acrobat with a novel?
A book that can flip its own pages.

Hobo: Every time I hitchhike I always get a ride.
Bum: You must have thumb luck.

What do you get if you cross a gym with a construction company?
Body builders.

Wife: How do you like my new jogging outfit?
Husband: I'm not sure. Run it by me again.

What did the kindling say to the lumberjack?
You gave me a splitting headache.

Cowboy: I once saw a bed 10 feet long and 10 feet wide.
Rustler: Ah, that's a lot of bunk.

Who makes sure railroads are always in shape?
The track coach.

Rocky: I went to a party last night.
Cliff: What kind?
Rocky: Oh, the kind where you drink beer and tell jokes.
Cliff: Must have been a real brew-ha-ha!

What's the difference between Goldilocks and a genealogist?
A genealogist is interested in forebears.

Violet: Watch out for Tex over there. He's a cowboy artist.
Rose: You mean he specializes in Western scenes?
Violet: No, he's always drawing a gun!

Lou: Whatever happened to that neighbor of yours who accidentally drank furniture polish?
Bud: He had a fine finish.

What happened when a gust of wind blew off the General's wig?
There was hell toupee!

Bob: How've you been since the big hurricane?
Bill: I've been living in a mobile home.
Bob: Oh, you moved?
Bill: No—before, it wasn't mobile!

Jamie: Did you hear about the accident down at the beauty parlor? Marge got her hair sucked into the dryer!
Mamie: My, that must have been very distressing!

Where is a good place to grow bad weather?
In a storm field.

Lady: Why is my mail so soggy?
Mailman: Postage dew.

Which letters of the alphabet were arrested for indecent exposure?
The naked "i" and the bare "s."

MODERN ROMANCE

....

Life, love and laughs

Daisy: Who was that gorgeous man I saw you kissing last night?
Maisie: What time was it?

They're a perfect match. She's a real bookworm and there's something fishy about him.

Mick: Why didn't you marry that gorgeous girl you were dating?
Keith: Things were going great until I told her about my rich uncle. Now she's my aunt.

....

Mrs. Green: My daughter's marrying a military man—a second lieutenant!
Mrs. Gray: So, she let the first one get away?

They're a perfect match. She's a timeless beauty with an hourglass figure and he enjoys watching time pass.

Ghoul: Who are you taking to the Halloween party?
Vampire: Oh, whomever I can dig up at the last minute.

"Pardon me," said a transatlantic traveler to his neighbor, "but I couldn't help noticing the diamond you're wearing on your finger."

"Thank you," replied the expensively dressed young woman next to him. "It's the Culbertson Diamond. You may have heard of it—it comes with a curse."

"What curse?" the traveler asked.

The woman sighed. "Mr. Culbertson."

First magician: Whatever happened to that red-headed wife of yours you used to saw in half every performance?
Second magician: Oh, we split up. Now she lives in New York and Seattle.

What happens when a salesman marries a saleslady?
They become sell-mates.

Young Miss Jones: I'm going out with Joe tonight, Mama.
Mama Jones: Joe again? If you like his attentions so much, why don't you marry him?
Young Miss Jones: Because I like his attentions.

Romeo: You won't go out with me? Big deal! I can get any girl I please.
Juliet: Maybe, but I bet you haven't pleased very many.

They're a perfect match. She's a geometry teacher and he has all the angles.

Adam: Do you really love me?
Eve: There's no one but you.

What did the snow guy say to the beautiful snow gal?
Do you believe in love at frost sight?

She: Am I the first girl you ever kissed?
He: Could be. Were you in Fort Lauderdale in 1965?

Miss Phiz: Officer, that man is annoying me!
Policeman: But he's not even looking at you.
Miss Phiz: That's what's so annoying!

Whom did Romeo Rocket love?
Flare Juliet.

Why were the girls who married Orville and Wilbur so happy?
Because they both married Mr. Wright.

Ann: Did you know that women are smarter than men?
Dan: No, I didn't.
Ann: See what I mean.

They're a perfect match. He's a night watchman and she's never worked a day in her life.

Boy pilot: Will you go out with me?
Girl pilot: No way, Ace.
Boy pilot: Shot down again!

Joey: I proposed to you last night, but I've forgotten whether you said yes or no.
Chloe: Oh, thank goodness. I knew I turned somebody down last night, but I just couldn't remember who it was.

They're a perfect match. He's stuck up and she's coming unglued.

George: Honey, let's not fight anymore about this. I've come to agree with you.
Martha: Oh yeah? Well, I've changed my mind!

Snobbette: I wouldn't go out with you in a million years.
Nerd: I've got a brand-new Porsche convertible and dinner reservations at Chez Chic.
Snobbette: My, how time flies!

We got married in a bathtub—my wife wanted a double ring ceremony.

Nino: Why won't you go out with me?
April: For three reasons: you're obnoxious, you're repulsive, and you haven't asked me yet!

Lancelot: Excuse me, I'm looking for a damsel in distress.
Guinevere: Fat chance, Lance; dis dress is one-of-a-kind!

Donald: Marry me, darling. I know I haven't got buckets of money like my friend Dan, or a hot film career like Dan, or Dan's good looks, youth, terrific sense of humor, or muscles, but I'm loyal and true and I love you.
Daisy: I love you too, honey…but first, tell me more about Dan!

They're a perfect matc. She has lots of cold cash and all of his assets are frozen.

Robin Hood: After we're married, would you live with me in the big forest near Nottingham?
Marion: Sherwood!

Her: Before we marry, there's something you should know about me. A long time ago, I...I practiced the world's oldest profession!
Him: You mean...you were a shepherd?

They're a perfect match. She's a mathematics teacher and he's a guy with a lot of problems.

Jenny: Aunt Isabel, why is it you never got married?
Aunt Isabel: Honey, I've got a dog that growls, a parrot that drops things on the floor, a chimney that smokes, and a cat that stays out late. Why do I need a husband?

Star No. 1: My dear, you look marvelous. Tell me how you keep your youth.
Star No. 2: Well first, darling, I never introduce him to other women.

Heather: Why did you break up with Michael?
Jessica: I found out his varsity letter was in tug-of-war. I mean, like, forget it! I told him, I'm not dating the school JERK!

They're a perfect match. She's a vegetarian and his face is as red as a beet and his hair is as bright as a carrot.

Fred: Vicki's a great girl. You've spent every evening at her place for the last 10 years; why don't you marry her?
Ted: What, and never go out again?

Fern: Congratulations on your marriage! What's your new husband's name?
Ivy: I call him Theory.
Fern: Because he embodies contemporary love and respect in an atmosphere of sexual equality?
Ivy: No, because he never works.

They're a perfect match. She's as straight as an arrow and he's bow-legged.

Fern: My friend the herpetologist is marrying an undertaker and I need to get them a wedding present.
Ivy: How about towels monogrammed "Hiss" and "Hearse"?

Josie: I can't marry you, Jack.
Jack: Why not? My candlemaking business is booming!
Josie: My mother told me never to marry a man who works on wick ends!

They're a perfect match. She's a geologist and he's got rocks in his head!

Why couldn't the book of poetry marry the romance novel?
'Cause she was from the trite side of the racks.

German boy: Can I have your phone number?
German girl: 999-9999
German boy: One "no" would have been enough.

Bill: Why do you go steady with Melanie?
Will: Because she's different than other girls.
Bill: How so?
Will: She's the only one who'll go out with me.

Jill: Did you hear about the cowboy who married a cowgirl?
Will: What kind of marriage is that?
Jill: Western Union.

They're a perfect match. Her social life stinks and he doesn't have a scent to his name.

Thelma: What did Miss Muffet say when the spider asked her for a date?
Selma: Ha! No whey!

Ken: I started to carve a heart for you out of wood, but the chisel slipped and it shattered.
Jen: Oh well, love is a many splintered thing.

Ted: I'm an incurable romantic.
Jane: Well go away, you're making me sick.

They're a perfect match. She sells balloons for a living and he's full of hot air!

Dolores: You look exactly like my third husband!
Horace: Is that so? How many times have you been married?
Dolores: Twice.

Betty: You're not going steady with Bill anymore?
Veronica: I should say not! I put an ad in the personals column and he answered!

A young woman entertained two proposals of marriage: one from a famous Broadway producer, the other from the town plumber. Which one did she marry?
She married the producer, because a full house beats a flush.

Bessie: I can't believe you dumped your last boyfriend! That makes seven so far this year.
Tessie: I can't help it. I'm just a curable romantic.

Ivy: You broke up with Harry? You told me he had that certain something.
Rose: He did, but he spent it.

They're a perfect match. She's a bank loan arranger and he never gets any credit.

Penelope: Your dating service stinks!
Manager: Let's see now…oh yes, you requested someone not too tall, who enjoys water sports, cool climates, and fancy dress.
Penelope: Yes, and you fixed me up with a penguin!

Nicky: Look at that couple over there arguing. Boy, he sure is henpecked.
Vicky: How can you tell? They're not speaking, they're using sign language.
Nicky: Yes, but just look; he can't get a finger in edgewise!

What did Mr. Yo-Yo say to Ms. Top?
Can I take you out for a spin?

Tom: My fiancé is an avid jogger.
Pat: When are you getting married?
Tom: Who knows? She keeps giving me the run around.

They're a perfect match. He's a chiropractor and she's a pain in the neck!

News Flash!
A male electrician falls in love with a beautiful woman who works for the electric company. It's the hot romance that sparked a shocking controversy. Tonight on *A Current Affair.*

Princess: You have to lose some weight, Lancelot.
Lancelot: But why, ma'am?
Princess: Because I need a knight lite.

Linda: Are you unattached?
John: No, I'm just put together sloppily.

Ann: My boyfriend complains a lot and then takes me out to eat.
Fran: At least he's whining and dining you.

They're a perfect match. He's a detective who never solved a case...and she's totally clueless.

Herb: Do you believe kissing is unhealthy?
Blanche: I couldn't say. I've never...
Herb: Never been kissed?
Blanche: Never been sick.

"I have to tell the truth," a young man said to his new girlfriend. "While we've been dating, I've been secretly seeing a psychiatrist."

"Don't worry about it," the girl told her boyfriend. "I've been secretly seeing a lawyer and a car salesman."

They're a perfect match. He's a podiatrist...and she's always putting her foot in her mouth.

Actress: I fell in love with my husband at second sight.
Gossip columnist: Don't you mean at first sight?
Actress: No. When I first saw him I didn't know he was a billionaire movie producer.

Madge: With Tom and me, it was love at first sight.
Mindy: Why didn't you get married?
Madge: I took a second look.

They're a perfect match. He's an airplane pilot...and she has friends in high places.

Madge: I hear Joyce gave her boyfriend the sack.
Mindy: Yep, but she kept the present that came in it.

Joe: Wow! Look at that beautiful woman over there! Do you know her?
Moe: Yes, I do. And she's got one more thing that's guaranteed to knock your eyes out!

Joe: Wow! What's that?
Moe: Her husband!

Joan: What happened to that boyfriend of yours?
Ginger: Oh, he lost all his money in the stock market.
Joan: That's too bad. You must feel sorry for him.
Ginger: Yes, he'll miss me terribly.

They're a perfect match. He's a fashion designer...and she's a model citizen.

Harry: The wedding's off!
Larry: I thought you two were crazy about each other!
Harry: So did I, until she told me she'd be true to the end.
Larry: Sounds good to me...
Harry: But I'm a quarterback!

Bill: I'm going to marry a widow.
Phil: I wouldn't want to be the second husband of a widow.
Bill: Better the second than the first.

They're a perfect match. The stories she tells never add up...and you just can't count on him.

TV interviewer: You were married four times: to a banker, to an actor, to a minister, and to an undertaker. Can you tell why?
Legendary actress: Well, it was One for the money, Two for the show, Three to get ready, and Four to go!

They're a perfect match. She's a breath of fresh air...and he's longwinded.

Holly: Can you imagine that dweeb in the orange polyester suit trying to put the moves on us?
Heather: Yeah, there's nothing I hate more than a wolf in cheap clothing!

Ted: How would you teach a girl to swim?
Joe: Well, I'd put my arm around her waist and gently...
Ted: Hey, this is my sister I'm talking about!
Joe: Oh, in that case, just push her in the water.

They're a perfect match. She's a redhead and he's a hothead.

Jeanne: I'm sorry I can't marry you, Joe, but my mother told me never to marry a watchmaker.
Joe: Why not?
Jeanne: She said you'd always be working overtime!

They're a perfect match. She's a cowgirl and he's full of bull!

Dena: Has anything changed in that messy affair of yours?
Lena: I'll say it changed! It went from a love triangle to a total wrecktangle!

Jenny: Why didn't you ever marry, Aunt Agatha?
Aunt Agatha: As a young woman I suffered from sleeping sickness, my dear.
Jenny: Sleeping sickness? What do you mean?
Aunt Agatha: I just couldn't keep my eyes open while some fellow was talking about himself!

Tillie: I heard the most amazing thing at June's wedding yesterday! A girl's allowed to have sixteen husbands!
Millie: I don't believe it! What did they say?
Tillie: Four better, four worse, four richer, and four poorer!

They're a perfect match. She's a statuesque beauty and he's a chiseler.

Jean: I can't believe you're marrying George—he's a pawnbroker.
Joan: Yes, but he has so many redeeming qualities!

Donald: Darling, why haven't you signed the prenuptial agreement?
Darla: Because, you worm, you didn't invite me to the party of the first part!

They're a perfect match. She's a real estate broker and he has lots to offer.

Amy: I've had three lovers in my whole life!
Jamie: You mean three all told?
Amy: No, one kept his mouth shut!

Elizabeth: We're through.
Richard: After all this time, you can't mean it! You always said my love was good medicine!
Elizabeth: Sure, but only if I follow the directions, "use well before shaking!"

Lance: A man is like fine wine; he improves with age.
Gwen: Then I suppose you'll be lying in the cellar for the next 20 years!

Abe: You know, I'm quite a catch! My boss says I have a lot of get up and go.
Ellie: Oh yeah? Prove it!

They're a perfect match. He's an auto mechanic and she drives everyone crazy!

Subway conductor: Why won't you be my wife? We've been meeting here on the platform every day for months. I love you!

Passenger: I'm sorry, my mother told me never to marry below my station!

Eric: I'm looking for ways to express myself!
Ariel: Why don't you try UPS!

They're a perfect match. He suffers from earaches...and her feet have corns.

Sheik of Araby: Marry me, darling! I'll make you the best husband in the world!
Desert Princess: Sorry, I've already found a Bedouin!

Donald: An Eagle Scout makes an excellent escort. Why, we're loyal, honest, helpful...
Daisy: Oh, go take a hike!

They're a perfect match. He's a funny old goat and she's a great kidder!

Tony: Will you go out with me tonight?
Cleo: Sorry, I'm busy. How about yesterday instead?

Mickey: A woman is like a flower, and man is the bee who...
Minnie: Oh, buzz off!

Tony: I guess I should go...
Maria: No, stay. I like being alone.

Sam: I'd go through anything for you.
Diane: Just the door will be fine.

Romeo: How can I ever leave you?
Juliet: How about taking the bus?

Rich: How was your date?
Mitch: Terrible! She didn't smile once all night!
Rich: Poker face, eh?
Mitch: No, but I wanted to.

They're a perfect match. He's a big shot and she just got fired from her job.

Ron: Marry me, darling! I know I'm not much to look at...
Nancy: Oh well, you'll be at the office most of the time, anyway.

Sam: Why do you want to go to the zoo?
Diane: I imagine you've never been there before—as a visitor, I mean.

It's a real dollars and cents wedding. He doesn't have a dollar...and she has no sense.

Fran: Did anyone ever tell you how wonderful you are?
Dan: Why, no!
Fran: Then where did you ever get the idea?

They're a perfect match. She loves presents, he's living in the past, and they have no future.

BAD MEDICINE

· ·

When the cure is worse than the disease

Psychiatrist: I see you're reading the telephone book. Are you enjoying it?
Patient: The plot is terrible, but what a cast!

Danny: Why so glum?
Gerry: I've got a bad case of shingles.
Danny: Did you see a doctor?
Gerry: Yeah, and he prescribed aluminum siding.

Did you hear about the podiatrist who ran for mayor? He was defeated.

· ·

Psychologist: Are you a popular fellow?
Patient: Are you kidding? I'm so popular, I have friends I haven't even used yet!

My doctor's always changing her mind...first she says she'll treat me, then she makes me pay.

Patient: Help me, Doc. Half the time I think I'm a teepee, and half the time I think I'm a wigwam!
Doctor: The problem is obvious—you're two tents!

Trixie: How's that wonderful boyfriend of yours?
Dixie: Oh, that's all over now. He was just a passing fiancé.

Patient: Doctor, I need help. I can never remember what I've just said.
Doctor: When did you first notice it?
Patient: Notice what?

Did you hear the one about the farmer who turned his south forty into an auto parts junkyard? Every year was a bumper crop.

Arnie: Are you still seeing that shrink?
Barney: Nah, all he did was charge a lot of money to ask me the same questions my wife asks me for free.

Doctor: I wouldn't worry about your habit of talking to yourself.
Patient: But Doc, I'm such a bore!

Did you hear about the girl with the split personality? She was always trying to have the last word.

Duke: My family always followed the medical profession.
Clint: Doctors?
Duke: No, undertakers.

Psychiatrist: Do you find you have trouble making decisions?
Patient: Well, yes and no.
Patient: Doc, all I ever dream about is baseball.
Psychiatrist: Don't you ever dream about girls?
Patient: What? And miss my turn at bat?

Psychiatry has helped me tremendously. Five years ago when the phone rang, I wouldn't answer it...today I answer it whether it rings or not.

Harold: My friend Ben got food poisoning eating salmon.
Florence: Croquette?
Harold: Not yet, but he's awfully sick.

Patient: Doc, I'm going crazy! I think I'm two separate people! Help!
Psychiatrist: All right now, calm down. Tell me everything. One at a time.

What's the first health rule of safe vacationing abroad? If you actually look like your passport photo, you definitely aren't well enough to travel!

Psychiatrist: What makes you think you have an inferiority complex?
Patient: Who am I to tell you that.

Show me a man who has braces on his teeth…and I'll show you a guy who put his money where his mouth is.

Psychiatrist: You'll never make any progress until you get over these phobias.
Patient: I was afraid you'd say that.

Fred: I'm going to quit trying to become an acupunturist.
Ed: Why?
Fred: Because everyone needles me on the job.

Attention podiatrists! When it comes to the care of patients, you are at the foot of the list.

Doctor: I can get rid of your nagging pain.
Wife: Really? I thought you were a physician, not a divorce lawyer.

What's the best vitamin supplement to take if you have straight hair?
Curling iron.

Pat: I'd better send this math test to a psychologist.
Matt: Why?
Pat: I just can't figure out its problems.

First psychiatric Patient: I'm not feeling myself today.
Second psychiatric Patient: That makes four of us!

Meg: I saw my doctor about this cough, and he told me I have walking pneumonia!
Peg: Did he prescribe any medicine?
Meg: Yes, I take one tablet every four miles!

Patient: I'm not feeling well and I'm really concerned.
Doctor: Don't worry, I've had the same illness myself.
Patient: Yeah, but you didn't have the same doctor.

Dentist: I can't understand why you say you need your dentures readjusted. They fit perfectly in your mouth.
Patient: Oh, they fit in my mouth all right. They just don't fit in the glass.

Elderly Patient: Doc, my leg aches all the time.
Doctor: Oh, that's just old age.
Patient: Well, the other leg's exactly the same age and it feels fine.

Millie: Did you see the doctor about your memory problem?
Billy: I certainly did.
Millie: Well, what did he do?
Billy: He made me pay in advance.

Patient: I'm a failure!
Psychologist: Now then, why don't you try the power of positive thinking.
Patient: All right—I'm positive I'm a failure!

Fred: Boy, is my wife a pessimist!
Gene: Why do you say that?
Fred: Her doctor told her she was perfectly well, and she decided to get a second opinion!

Patient: I have an appointment with Dr. Jones.
Receptionist: Dr. Jones has been called away on an emergency, but Dr. Fzzbzstrczywx can see you.
Patient: Which doctor?
Receptionist: Not at all! He's highly qualified!

Mary: Why are you eating your lunch sitting on the sidewalk?

Larry: My doctor told me to curb my appetite!

Patient: Help me, Doc, I've got this strange pain in my arm.

Doctor: Hmm. Have you ever had this pain before?

Patient: Why, yes.

Doctor: Well, you've got it again!

Mother: Hello, Doctor? I'm so upset! Georgie's swallowed a bullet! What should I do?

Doctor: Give him plenty of castor oil, and don't point him at anyone for 48 hours!

Patient: Doc, I've tried everything to stop smoking, really I have, but I just can't do it.

Doctor: I'll prescribe one of those new nicotine patches...

Patient: Oh, I tried that too, but I just couldn't keep the darn thing lit!

Joey: I haven't been feeling too well, so I called my acupuncturist.

Zoe: What did she say?

Joey: Oh, the usual. She told me to take two safety pins and call her in the morning.

Factory doctor: Mister, I know what's ailing you. It's plain laziness.
Employee: Great, Doc! Can you give it a long, fancy name so I can tell the boss?

Rickie: Do psychologists have their own union?
Lucy: Of course, silly: the United Mind Workers.

Bertie: My uncle had a terrible accident! He was run over by a steamroller!
Gertie: Oh, no! Is he in the hospital?
Bertie: City General, rooms 26, 27, and 28!

Patient: Doc, you gotta help me. I drank from a bottle marked "poison!"
Doctor: Why in the world did you do that?
Patient: Well, on the label it said, "Lye," so I didn't believe it!

What do you call an eye doctor who lives on an island in the Bering Sea?
An optical Aleutian.

Mark: I'd better stop taking those pep pills.
Clark: Why do you say that?
Mark: Last night I threaded my wife's sewing machine.
Clark: So what? I can do that.
Mark: While it's running?

Patient: If the psychologist can't see me immediately, I'm leaving.
Nurse: Calm down, sir. What's wrong with you?
Patient: I have a serious wait problem.

Cured patient to a psychologist: How can you tell me you don't want to see me anymore. I gave you the best years of my strife!

Mr. Jones: I'm an Army doctor.
Mr. Smith: Do you operate on officers?
Mr. Jones: No. I have a private practice.

Movie star: I just had all of my teeth capped.
Agent: That's putting your money where your mouth is.

Patient: Which two letters of the alphabet spell trouble for your teeth?
Dentist: D-K.

Joey: I feel terrible!
Chloe: You should visit my doctor—he gives discounts!
Joey: I don't believe it.
Chloe: It's true! When I had double pneumonia, he only charged me for one!

Patient: Help me, Doc. I keep making long distance calls to myself and I'm going broke!
Psychiatrist: Try reversing the charges.

Henry visited his doctor complaining that he saw spots before his eyes. The doctor informed him he had six months to live. Henry decided to spend his remaining days enjoying the finest things money could buy, beginning with a new, custom-tailored wardrobe. He went straight to Cedric and Cedric, where the owner himself attended to the fitting:

"Size 16 neck," announced Mr. Cedric.

"Oh, no, I've always taken a size 14," objected Henry.

"I don't advise it, sir," replied Mr. Cedric.

"Why not?" asked Henry.

"A size 14 collar might cause you to see spots before your eyes."

Psychiatrist: Why have you come to see me?
Patient: Oh, my family sent me here. They think I'm nuts because I love shoes.
Psychiatrist: How petty of them. Why, I myself am very fond of good shoes.
Patient: You are? Do you like them boiled or lightly breaded?

A little boy was sent to a psychiatrist because he refused to eat.

"Now, Henry," said the doctor, "you can eat anything you'd like. What'll it be?"

"Worms," replied Henry.

"That's fine," said the doctor smugly, and he sent the nurse out for a plate of worms.

"I only want one." Henry said. The nurse removed all but one worm.

"You eat half," demanded the boy. The doctor cut the worm into two pieces and gagged one down. The child burst into tears.

"What's wrong now?" asked the psychiatrist.

Henry sobbed, "You ate my half!"

Patient: Doc, you've cured me! I used to think I was a golden retriever, but you set me straight.
Psychiatrist: I'm glad to hear you're feeling better.
Patient: I sure am, Doc. Just feel my nose!

Research scientist: Eureka! I've found a cure!
Assistant: Congratulations! For what disease?
Research scientist: I haven't found that yet!

Patient: Doctor, my life is a mess. I just don't think I can go on this way anymore.
Psychiatrist: Yes, we all have problems. I can help you, but it'll take time. We'll start at four sessions a week. My fee is a hundred dollars an hour.
Patient: Well, that solves your problem. What about mine?

Smith, Jones, and White were driving to the train station to catch a train when the car blew a tire. By the time they arrived, the 10:21 was beginning to pull out, and they ran with all their might out to the platform. Smith and Jones managed to jump aboard, but White was a second too late.

The stationmaster patted him on the shoulder. "Too bad about that, but at least your friends made it."

White turned around and glared at him. "Yes, but they were just seeing me off!"

Doctor: You need to do something for your health. Why don't you take up jogging?
Patient: But Doc, I already jog.
Doctor: Oh. In that case, you'd better give it up.

Mark: My doctor told me to give up drinking, smoking, and fatty foods.
Clark: What will you do?
Mark: I think I'll give up my doctor.

Doctor: Gus, I'm discharging you from the hospital today—you're completely cured. I must tell you, it was your incredible will to survive that saved you.
Gus: Thanks, Doc. Just remember that when you write up my bill.

What do you give the man who has everything?
Antibiotics.

Psychiatrist: Well, George, you're making great progress, which is more than I can say for Stanley in Ward J. He keeps telling everyone he's going to buy the Vatican! Can you believe that?
George: No, I can't. After all, I've told him a million times I won't sell.

Why does a dentist always seem sad?
Because he looks down in the mouth.

Anne: Doctor, I'll never lose weight. All day long I see food passing in front of my eyes.
Doctor: Well, stop daydreaming.
Anne: Who's daydreaming. I'm a checkout clerk in a grocery store.

Times sure have changed. Years ago folks used to say "a penny for your thoughts." Today psychiatrists charge $200.00 an hour to learn what's on your mind.

Boss: Our new billing clerk needs to see a psychiatrist.
Secretary: Why?
Boss: She keeps hearing strange invoices.

Doctor: How are you sleeping now?
Patient: Much better since I stopped counting sheep.
Doctor: How did that help you?
Patient: I no longer have baa dreams.

Teacher: Is your father still in the hospital?
Boy: Yes. He's in the Expensive Care Unit.

A leopard went to see an optometrist because he thought he needed an eye exam. "Every time I look at my wife," he worriedly told the optometrist, "I see spots before my eyes."

"So what's to worry about?" replied the doctor. "You're a leopard, aren't you?"

"What's that got to do with anything?" replied the patient. "My wife is a zebra."

"Why did you run out of the operating room?" a hospital administrator asked a nervous patient.

The patient replied, "Because the nurse said, 'Don't be so jittery, an appendectomy is a simple operation.'"

"So?" said the administrator.

"So, she was talking to the doctor!" the patient explained.

How are you feeling?
   "I should have my head examined," said Mr. Cabbage.
   "I need my eyes checked," said Mr. Potato.
   "I feel run down," said Ms. Beet.
   "I hurt in the pit of my stomach," said Mr. Plum.
   "I have hay fever," said Mr. Bale.

Did you hear the one about the man who thought he was a rubber band?
His psychiatrist told him to snap out of it!

Nurse Brown: He has arthritis and she has rheumatism.
Nurse Green: They must have a lot of medical bills. How do they pay them?
Nurse Brown: They have a joint account.

Father: Cindy! If you don't stop practicing on that piano I'll go nuts!
Daughter: Too late Dad. I stopped an hour ago.

Doctor: You have bucket fever.
Patient: How do you know that?
Doctor: You're turning pail.
Patient: I need help, doctor. Everyone always takes advantage of me. How much will it take to cure me?
Doctor: How much do you have?

Patient: I think I need glasses.
Optometrist: What makes you think that?
Patient: Yesterday I went for a hike in the woods and I picked up a snake to kill a stick.

Where does a tornado go when it gets bent out of shape?
A *spiralpractor.*

Patient: Doc, can you cure me of compulsive lying?
Psychologist: Yes, if you have enough money to afford the expensive treatment.
Patient: No problem, I just won the lottery yesterday.

"For goodness sakes!" cried a dentist as he examined a new patient. "You have the biggest cavity I've ever seen! The biggest cavity I've ever seen!"

"Harumph!" grumbled the patient angrily. "You didn't have to repeat yourself."

"I didn't," replied the dentist. "That was an echo!"

Psychiatrist: Congratulations, Mr. Hill, you're finally cured of your delusion. How do you feel?
Patient: Terrible! How would you feel if one day you were President of the United States and then the next day you were nobody?

A middle-aged man took his car to an auto shop for a checkup. When he received the mechanic's bill, the man flipped. "Hey!" he yelled to the owner of the shop. "This bill is higher than the one I got from my doctor for a complete physical checkup."

The auto shop owner nodded. "I believe it," he said. "The difference is my bill includes the checkup and the replacement of worn out parts!"

Patient: Doctor, you've got to help me. I think I'm a toilet bowl.
Psychologist: Relax. You're fine, but you do look a little flushed.

Did you hear the one about the ear of corn that went to a psychiatrist?
It needed shuck treatment.

Patient: I'm here for my liver.
Doctor: Sorry. I don't have it.

Big Al: My doctor gave me a placebo to cure my illness.
Big Joe: A placebo is nothing but fake medicine. You were gyped.
Big Al: Not really. I paid him with counterfeit money.

What do you call an intern who gets sick from reading a medical textbook?
Ill-literate.

Hospital nurse: You're pretty banged up. How did this happen?
Patient: Well, you see, I used to be a window washer...
Hospital nurse: When did you give it up?
Patient: Halfway down!

Doris: Doc, it's my son...he just won't eat his rutabagas!
Doctor: Perhaps he doesn't like them?
Doris: Nonsense! Why, he liked them fine on Monday, Tuesday, Wednesday, Thursday, Friday, and Saturday... now, all of a sudden, he doesn't like them!

Lou: What happened to that cowboy who began hearing voices in the middle of the cattle drive?
Bud: He was deranged.

Randy: My doctor's always telling jokes.
Mandy: Well, they say laughter's the best medicine.
Randy: Can't be, or Doc would've charged me for it!

Harry: I've been seeing a shrink for years about my fear of failure.
Larry: But Harry, you are a failure.
Harry: Then I'm cured!

Dentist: Well, Tex, your teeth are in great shape.
Oilman: But I'm feeling lucky today, Doc, so why don't you go ahead and drill!

Joe: Why so sad, my friend?
David: My wife is pregnant, and our insurance policy is lousy!
Joe: You mean it doesn't cover you in case of pregnancy?
David: Oh, sure—mine!

A man hobbled slowly into the doctor's waiting room, bent almost double, grasping a cane in one gnarled claw.

Another patient looked on sympathetically.

"Arthritis with complications?" the patient asked.

"No," replied the man. "Do-it-yourself with cinderblocks!"

What do you get when you cross a hospital with a skunk?
A medical scenter.

Doctor: I've been practicing medicine for over 10 years.
Patient: Call me when you're done practicing and decide to get serious.

Greg: How did you break your leg, Bert?
Bert: See those steps over there?
Greg: Yes.
Bert: Well, I didn't!

Pediatrician: I think I've told you everything you need to do for your newborn. Oh, by the way, do you have the baby's formula?
New Mother: I sure do: Candlelight, Cabernet Sauvignon, and Ravel's "Bolero!"

Patient: Doctor, do you think sex over 55 can be dangerous?
Doctor: Absolutely! Pull over to the side of the road first!

Mother: Doctor, you've got to help my son. He thinks he's a smoke detector.
Doc: Calm down. There's no cause for alarm.

Mother: Doctor, help me. My wacky teenage son thinks he's a refrigerator.
Psychologist: Stay calm. I'm sure he'll chill out.

Doctor: I think you're suffering from paranoia, so I'm referring you to a specialist.
Patient: HA! You're only doing that because you hate having me for a patient.

Mother: Doctor, my loony son thinks he's a stick of margarine.
Doctor: Don't worry. I'm sure I can make him butter.

Nurse: Open your mouth. This medicine doesn't taste bad.
Patient: Do you really expect me to swallow that?

Nurse: Do you feel well enough to write some poetry today?
Sick poet: No. I feel verse than yesterday.

Did you hear the one about the young bone specialist?
He just opened his office and needed a break to get started.

Patient: Doctor, can you get these quarters out of my ear?
They've been in there for months.
Doctor: Good grief! Why didn't you come to me sooner?
Patient: Up until now I didn't need the money.

Berty: You should see my doctor—he's terrific!
Gerty: There's nothing wrong with me.
Berty: He's so good, he'd find something!

Doctor: Nobody lives forever.
Patient: I wouldn't mind trying!

Patient: Doctor, it's my son. He spends all his time making mudpies.
Doctor: That's nothing to worry about. It's quite normal at a certain age.
Patient: Well, I don't think it's normal, and neither does his wife.

Patient: Doctor, I have a terrible pain in my ear.
Doctor: Well, no wonder. There's a big bouquet of flowers in there. Where did it come from?
Patient: I haven't the faintest idea. Why don't you read the card?

Caller: Nurse, can you tell me how Joe Smith is doing?
Nurse: The doctor says he can leave the hospital tomorrow. Who's calling?
Caller: This is Joe Smith. That doctor won't tell me a thing!

Patient: Help me, Doc. I get this sharp pain in my eye every time I drink a cup of coffee. What can I do?
Doctor: Try taking the spoon out of the cup.

Patient: Doctor, I have an eggplant growing out of my ear.
Doctor: Yes, I see it. That must be very irritating.
Patient: Sure is, Doc. I planted radishes.

Woman: Doctor, you must do something about my husband. He thinks he's a dog.
Doctor: How long has he been feeling this way?
Woman: Ever since he was a puppy.

Patient: It's my ear, Doc. I bit it.
Doctor: How could you possibly bite your own ear?
Patient: I had to stand on a chair.

Patient: Help me, Doc, I've got a fish stuck in my ear.
Doctor: I'm referring you to a specialist. You've got a serious herring problem.

Doctor: This face lift will make a new woman out of you.
Patient: Great! Then your fee will be paid by the new woman.

Man: I want you to examine my wristwatch.
Psychologist: Why?
Man: It has a nervous tick.

Nurse: Mrs. Smith is here again with another contagious disease.
Doctor: That woman makes me sick.

Doctor: How bad is your insomnia?
Patient: It's bad. I haven't slept on the job in weeks.

Doctor: Your blood pressure is out of this world.
Man: That's okay. I'm an astronaut.

Lady: Why should I drink lemonade three times a day?
Doctor: It'll make you feel bitter.

Patient: I ate clams for the first time in my life yesterday and now I'm sick.
Doctor: Maybe they were bad. How did the clams look when you opened the shells?
Patient: Opened them?

Husband: Doctor, you've got to help me. My wife's difficult pregnancy was such a strain now I'm seeing double.
Doctor: Relax, you're the father of twins.

Doctor: How do you feel today, Mrs. Smith?
Patient: Not so good. It hurts when I breathe.
Doctor: Hum, we'd better try to stop that.

Patient: Hey Doc, so I need another appointment?
Physician: Yes. Make a date with my nurse.
Patient: I'd like to, Doc, but I'm a married man.

After finishing his examination, the doctor looked at his patient and said, "I can't find the exact cause of your trouble, Mr. Jones, but it's probably due to drinking too much."

The patient looked at the doctor and replied, "Gee, I'm sorry to hear that Doc. I'll come back when you're sober."

Doctor: The pain in your right leg is caused by old age.
Patient: But Doc, my left leg is the same age and it doesn't hurt.

Doctor: How's your insomnia?
Patient: Nothing helps, Doc. I'm exhausted.
Doctor: But I prescribed enough sleeping medication to sedate a horse!
Patient: Oh, I slept, all right, but I dreamed I was awake the whole time!

Doctor: I'm afraid there's no cure for your illness.
Patient: I'd like a second opinion.
Doctor: Very well, make an appointment to see me again next week.

Patient: It's been two weeks since my last visit and I still don't feel any better.
Doctor: I don't understand it. Did you follow the instructions on the pills I gave you?
Patient: I sure did. It said "Keep this bottle tightly closed."

Patient: Help me, Doc. I've had these terrible stomach pains, ever since that party last night.
Doctor: Overindulgence?
Patient: Nah, over in Jersey.

Doctor: Ever been in an accident?

Patient: Never.

Doctor: So, you've never been injured.

Patient: Well, there was that time I got kicked in the head by a mule.

Doctor: And you don't call that an accident?

Patient: Heck, no. That mule did it on purpose!

Lawyer: Whenever I stand up to speak in court I suddenly feel ill.

Doctor: It sounds to me like you're suffering from motion sickness.

Aging swinger: Gee, Doc, do I really have to give up wine, women, and song?

Doctor: Not at all. Sing as much as you like.

Patient: Doctor, I ate too much salmon and now my stomach hurts. What's wrong with me?

Doctor: Fishing bloat.

Teresa: Doctor, my son thinks he's a portable TV channel changer. What are the chances of curing him?

Doctor: Remote.

Patient: Doctor, Doctor, you've got to help me. I think I'm invisible.

Doctor: Who said that?

Patient: What's the best thing to do for a poor memory, Doc?
Doctor: Just forget about your problem.

Patient: Doctor, I insist that you give me a brain transplant.
Doctor: Then I'll do everything in my power to change your mind.

Doctor: What do you dream about at night?
Scott: Playing baseball.
Doctor: Don't you ever dream about anything else?
Scott: Of course not. Then I'd miss my turn at bat.

Doctor: I have a plan to make hair grow on bald men by feeding them natural cereal.
Scientist: Oh no! Another hair bran scheme.

Boy: I'm worried about what kind of gifts Santa will bring me. Is anything wrong with me?
Doctor: Relax. It's just present tense.

Patient: Doc, I'm calling long distance. I've been on this exercise program of yours for ten days now and it's just not working.
Doctor: I told you to run five miles a day. Have you lost any weight?
Patient: Sure, I've lost weight, but now I'm 50 miles from home!

Ralph: Did you hear about Dr. Klutzy, our dentist? He's changed specialties—now he's a brain surgeon.
Ed: How could he make a change like that?
Ralph: His drill slipped.

Doctor: You really should cut down on the drinking—alcohol's bad for you.
Patient: Yeah? Well, how come there are a lot more old drunks than old doctors?

Patient: Doc, I think I found a cure for my amnesia!
Doctor: Wonderful! What is it?
Patient: I forgot.

Doctor: I've never seen anything quite like these second-degree burns on both your ears. How did you get them?
Nora: Well, the phone rang and I picked up the steam iron by mistake.
Doctor: But what about the other ear?
Nora: They called back.

Patient: Doc, I feel lousy!
Doctor: You're not getting enough exercise. I recommend a day of horseback riding.
Patient: Why horseback riding? I've never ridden before.
Doctor: Because after a day of riding, you're sure to feel better off.

Doctor: How's that ringing in your ears—all gone since you took that medicine I prescribed?
Patient: Oh, yes, Doctor—now I just get a busy signal!

Doctor: I'm afraid your condition is fairly advanced.
Patient: Believe me, Doc, it was in its early stages when I sat down in your waiting room!

NOT SMART

....

Jokes for the loveable but slow-witted

Jeff: Isn't the plumber here yet? I've been plugging this leak with my finger for three hours!
Janet: Well, you can stop now—the house is on fire.

Did you hear the one about the bum who signed up for art classes? *All he could draw were flies!*

Postmistress: That package will need two dollars in postage stamps.
Miss Ditz: Oh, golly...do I have to stick them all on myself!
Postmistress: Heavens, no! Stick them on the package!

....

I like to get the most out of my mystery novels...I always start in the middle, so not only do I wonder how it'll end, I also wonder how it began.

Passenger: Driver, does this bus stop at the river?
Driver: Well, if you hear a really big splash, the answer is no!

Captain: Private, there's a squad of enemy soldiers hiding in that stand of trees. I want you to go in there and flush them out.
Private: Okay, sir, but if you see a bunch of guys running out of the woods, don't shoot the one in front!

Caller: Hello, may I please speak to Henry?
Answerer: I'm sorry, there's no Henry here. You must have the wrong number.
Caller: Are you sure?
Answerer: Have I ever lied to you?

Patroness: Will you paint me in the nude?
Artist: Okay, but I'll have to keep my socks on so I have someplace to put my brushes.

Caller: Fire Department! Come quick, there's a fire in my basement!
Dispatcher: Did you throw water on it?
Caller: Of course!
Dispatcher: Well, there's no use in our coming over, that's all we ever do.

Abelard: Are you buying Christmas seals this year?
Heloise: Certainly not. What would I feed them?

Customer: This Flak-ee Soap you sold me is dreadful! It doesn't lather at all, it doesn't float, it leaves a greasy film on my body, and it gave me a rash!
Salesclerk: Yes, but it's great company in the tub.

Shrimpo: Show me a tough guy and I'll show you a coward.
Bruto: Well, I'm a tough guy.
Shrimpo: And I'm a coward.

Chick: Boy, do I feel lousy. I've been on a train for three hours, riding backwards the whole time!
Chuck: Why didn't you switch seats with the person across from you?
Chick: I would've, but there was no one in the seat across from me.

Do-it-yourselfer: This prefab house is no good. I want my money back.
Salesman: There's nothing wrong with the house. You put it together upside down.
Do-it-yourselfer: No wonder I kept falling off the porch!

Teacher: Jimmy, name the greatest invention of the Phoenicians.
Jimmy: Blinds.

Billy: My daddy shot this moose and put its head on the wall.
Barbie: Can I go in the next room and see the rest of it?

Bill: I can't figure out why it's so hard, Phil, but my wife just doesn't understand me. Does yours?
Phil: I doubt it. She's never even mentioned your name.

Custom's agent: Do you have any pornographic literature?
Traveler: Gosh, I don't even have a pornograph!

Jenny: Where'd you get that watch?
Benny: It was a gift from Sylvia.
Jenny: Who's Sylvia?
Benny: I don't know, but that's what's engraved on the back.

Lady: Young man, will you call me a taxi?
Doorman: Certainly, Madam. You are a taxi.

Mother: Lucy, aren't you going to the birthday party?
Lucy: No, Mother. The invitation said three to six, and I'm seven.
Nora: We were right in the path of that tornado!
Cora: Was your house damaged?
Nora: We won't know until we find it.

Mrs. Fox: My dear, we had the most delightful vacation in the Caribbean.
Mrs. Wolf: Did you go by plane or boat?
Mrs. Fox: I'm not sure. My husband bought the tickets.

Hugh: How did you like the ballet?
Nicola: I don't understand all that toe dancing. Why don't they just get taller girls.

Suzie: My daughter is twenty-one years old today!
Annie: Now, how could you have a child that age?
Suzie: I didn't. When I had her she was just a baby.

Lady: I've heard a milk bath is good for the skin, so I'll need enough to fill the tub.
Grocer: Pasteurized?
Lady: Dear me, no. I think just over my knees will be sufficient.

IRS agent: What's this deduction for an umbrella?
Wayne: Well, it's overhead, isn't it?

Soviet auto mechanic: Your car needs a new transmission, but you'll have to wait for service. Will five years from next Thursday be all right?
Soviet citizen: Morning or afternoon?
Soviet auto mechanic: I'm talking about five years from now! What difference can it make?
Soviet citizen: The plumber's coming in the afternoon.

The City Zoo hired a trucker to pick up a shipment of penguins. When the truck broke down, the driver hailed a passing farmer and asked him to deliver the penguins in his pickup. The farmer agreed. Later that day, the truck driver spotted the farmer walking the penguins down Main Street.

"I thought you were taking those penguins to the zoo!" shouted the truck driver.

"I took 'em to the zoo," replied the farmer. "Now I thought I'd get 'em some ice cream."

Asylum inmate (reading the paper):
Here's a restaurant we should try. It ways they serve soup to nuts.

Blind date: Do you like Kipling?
Dumb Dora: I don't know. I've never kippled.

Arty: Why did you name your baby son Bill?
Marty: Because he came on the first of the month.

Diner: I'd like my coffee without cream.
Waiter: We're out of cream. Will you take it without milk?

Elevator operator: This is the fifth floor, son.
Child: How dare you call me son. We're not related.
Elevator operator: Humph! I brought you up didn't I?

Jack: Do you think you'll keep any of your New Year's resolutions?
Jill: Yeah, I think I'll keep them to myself.

Homeowner: How do you keep a house from freezing during the winter?
Painter: Paint it in the fall to give it an extra coat.

Irate passenger: This is the worst-run airline I've ever had the bad luck to travel with. I don't know why you even bother to publish a schedule!
Flight attendant: Well, we need something to base our delays on.

A man walked into a bar with a large carrot tucked behind his ear. The bartender noticed but decided not to say anything, figuring the man was just waiting to be asked about it. For 30 consecutive days the man came to the bar wearing a carrot. On the 31st day, the man entered the bar with a banana behind his ear, and the bartender broke down.

"Okay, I give up. WHY are you wearing a banana behind your ear?" he asked.

"Couldn't find a carrot today," replied the man.

Ben: Does your sister talk to herself when she's alone?
Jerry: I don't know. I've never been with her when she's alone.

Frank: I've finally found a foolproof way to come back from Atlantic City with a small fortune.
Dean: Tell me quick.
Frank: Go there with a large fortune.

Tenant: It's five degrees outside and there's no heat in my apartment! You never do a thing around this building!
Superintendent: I resent that! Didn't I fix your air conditioner just last week?

Farmer Brown: Why does it take you so long to care for your garden?
Farmer Green: I'm a remedial weeder.

Guy bee: Why is your hair so sticky?
Girl bee: Because this morning I used a honeycomb.

Man: Waiter, can you put this meal on my credit card?
Dumb waiter: Sorry, sir. I don't think it'll fit.

Father: What should you do when you see our flag waving?
Little boy: Wave back.

Caveman No. 1: I sprained my back hunting duck-tailed dinosaurs.
Caveman No. 2: What happened? Did one of the dinosaurs fall on you?
Caveman No. 1: No. I did it lifting the decoys.

George: Hey, I thought you were going bear hunting?
Jim: Well, I got as far as the Interstate.
George: What happened?
Jim: I saw a sign that said "Bear Left," so I came home!

Mother: I send you out for new clothes and you come back with a deck of cards?
Son: But Mom, the salesman said I could have four suits for a dollar!

Harry, a successful businessman, owed it all to his mother, now an elderly widow who still lived in the old neighborhood. For her birthday he decided to get her something really special—a trained parrot who could sing grand opera. The parrot cost a fortune, but what a wonderful companion for a lonely woman! He had the parrot sent right over. A day or two later he called: "Mom, how did you like the birthday present?" he asked.

"Delicious!" she replied.

Scoutmaster: How could you get lost? Didn't you have your compass with you?
Scout: Sure, but the needle kept pointing North when I wanted to go South!

Benny's car ran out of gas on a desert highway. He began to walk, but soon was crawling, dizzy with thirst. Finally a car stopped.

"Water, Water! gasped Benny.

"Gee, I'm all out," said the driver, "but I've got some beautiful ties for sale. Like to buy one?"

"Water, Water!" gasped Benny.

"Look, there's a restaurant about five miles on. You'll be okay," said the tie salesman, and he drove off. Benny crawled to the restaurant and collapsed at the maitre d's feet.

"Water, Water!" gasped Benny.

"Sorry," replied the maitre d', "you can't come in without a tie!"

Mrs. Dilly: My dear, our trip to the Orient was fabulous! We ate in hundreds of marvelous restaurants!
Mrs. Nilly: But did you see the pagodas?
Mrs. Dilly: See them? We had dinner with them!

Joey: I'm glad you finally made it to the party!
Chloe: To tell you the truth, I flipped a coin to decide whether or not to come.
Joey: Why did that make you late?
Chloe: I had to keep flipping until I got it the right way!

Rocky: I'm all set for our camping trip.
Cliff: Packed emergency supplies?
Rocky: Yep. I've got two bottles of brandy in case of snake bite.
Cliff: There aren't any snakes where we're going.
Rocky: That's okay. I've packed a couple of snakes!

Harry: I stay up late, but I don't need an alarm clock in the morning. In fact, I don't even own a clock.
Barry: What if you want to know what time it is?
Harry: Oh, then I just start playing my saxophone. One of my neighbors is sure to yell, "Don't you know it's 3 A.M.!"

Meryl: You really should get one of those cellular car phones, my dear.
Beryl: Oh, I had one for a while, but I sent it back. It was too much trouble running out to the garage to answer it!

Mayor Clifford was riding to work one morning when he noticed something odd. Along the edge of the highway, a workman was digging a row of holes. But as soon as he finished digging one hole, another workman would step up and fill it in again! The mayor had his driver pull over and sent his aide to investigate. The aide returned to the car looking relieved: "Nothing out of the ordinary, sir. They're usually a three-man crew, but the fellow who plants the trees is out sick today!"

Joe: I'd like to cash a check, but I don't have an account here.
Bank teller: Can you identify yourself?
Joe: Sure. Have you got a mirror?
Bank teller: Over by the door.
Joe (returning from the mirror): Yep, it's me all right!

Trixie: I dropped a quarter in the other room.
Dixie: So why are you looking for it in here?
Trixie: The light's better in here.

Two second graders were in a museum looking at a mummy. At the bottom of the mummy case was a sign that read "1286 B.C."

"What does that mean?" asked one student.

"It must be the license number of the car that hit him," said the other.

Bart: I'm dumber than you are.
Butthead: No. I'm really stupid.
Beavis: Hey! What is this, a dunce contest?

A beautiful but ditzy model knew that taking a milk bath was good for her skin so she ordered twenty gallons to be brought up to her hotel room. "Do you want it pasteurized?" the clerk asked. "No," she replied. "Just fill the tub up to my neck."

Tourist: A nice man just sold me the city of Cairo.
Guide: Egypt you!
A policeman stopped a motorist for driving down a one-way street. "Just where do you think you're going?" the policeman asked.

"I don't know," answered the confused driver. "But I must be late. Everyone else is already coming back."

Father: Where are you going with that watering can?
Little boy: Out to water my garden.
Father: But it's raining outside.
Little boy: Don't worry, I'll wear my raincoat.

A grandmother took her five-year-old grandson to the ballet. The boy had never seen a ballet before and watched the ballerinas prance around on their toes. After the show was over, the grandmother asked the youngster if he had any questions. "Yeah, Granny," said the boy, "wouldn't it be easier if they just hired taller dancers?"

Benny: A fool can ask more questions than a wise man can ever answer. Did you know that?
Lenny: Nope.

Customer: Can you clean these pants?
Dry cleaner: Well, Ma'am, these pants are satin...
Customer: I know that! I want you to remove whatever it was I sat in!

Dinah: I'm drawing a picture of God.
Mom: But nobody knows what God looks like.
Dinah: They will when I get this picture done!

Homeowner: Help! My house is on fire!
Fire Department: Okay, how do we get to you?
Homeowner: In your shiny red truck, I hope!

Waiter: Our pizzas are cut into eight slices.
Diner: Please cut mine into six slices—I really couldn't eat eight.

Barney: Hey, Mom! Look at this VCR I got!
Mom: Now, Barney, I told you we can't afford one of those.
Barney: It's okay, Mom. I traded the TV for it!

Usher: I'm sorry, son, you can't take your dog into this movie theater.
Little boy: It's okay, mister. He's over seventeen in dog years.

Scoutmaster: Joe, how do you treat someone who falls out of a tree?

Joe: Don't move him. Elevate his feet.

Scoutmaster: Right! Jimmy, what if your father burns his fingers while cooking dinner?

Jimmy: Hold them under cold running water.

Scoutmaster: Correct! Wayne, what if your brother swallows your house key?

Wayne: Oh, there's always a spare under the doormat.

Mary: What are you looking so mad about?

Gary: I need some light but all I've got is a box of candles and no matches!

Mary: That's no problem. Just take one candle out of the box.

Gary: How will that help? I still haven't got a match.

Mary: No, but it'll make the box a candle lighter.

Herbert: What do you think of Czechoslovakia?

Horace: Well, it's hard to say.

Sir Cecil: ... then after my ship went down, I survived a week in the open sea on just a can of sardines.

Lady Alice: Goodness, however did you keep from falling off?

Rich man: What's going on! I thought I told you to paint the porch white!
Handyman: I did paint it white. Now, how about teal green for the Ferrari?

Johnny: Do you know the difference between a taxi and a bus?
Jeannie: No.
Johnny: Okay, we'll take a bus.

Wyckoff boarded a city bus one morning and sat down next to a young man with a big duffle bag at his feet. Every time the bus pulled up to a stop, the young man would take a french horn from the duffle bag and give it a blast in C sharp.

"Why are you blowing that horn at every stop?" he asked.

"To keep the elephants from charging the bus," was the reply.

"That's ridiculous!" snapped Wyckoff. "There isn't an elephant for thousands of miles!"

"I know," the young man answered. "It's very effective."

Trudy: Judy, why are you still standing on the corner? Didn't I tell you to take the 14th Street bus?
Judy: Sure, but so far only ten have gone by!

Why did the silly person take sandpaper into the desert?
He needed a road map.

Bride: Darling, guess what! We've been married twenty-four hours!
Groom: Gee, it seems like only yesterday!

On the first day of summer camp, the director informed all the little campers that he expected them to put on a fresh pair of socks every day. Two weeks later, Johnny failed to appear at the morning flag raising. The director found him still in his cot.

"Why aren't you lined up with the other boys?" He asked.

"I can't get my shoes on over fourteen pairs of socks!"

Artist: I'll pay you twenty dollars if you let me paint you.
Young boy: I don't know...
Artist: Come on—it'll be easy.
Young boy: Sure, but how do I get the paint off afterwards?

Lucy and Ricky were off on a fabulous two-week vacation. As they entered the air terminal, Lucy became sad. "What's the matter, honey?" asked Ricky.

"Gosh, Ricky, I wish we'd brought our TV set with us."

"Are you serious? Why?"

"Because the plane tickets are on top of it!"

Judy: Dad, I had a little trouble with the car. There's water in the carburetor.
Dad: I never heard of such a thing. Where's the car now?
Judy: In the lake.

Jerry: Why on earth are you rubbing mashed potatoes in your hair?
Berry: Mashed potatoes? Oh, no! I thought it was cauliflower!

A guy walks into a bar, orders a beer, and then pulls out a caterpillar from his pocket and places him on the rim of the glass. The caterpillar leans over to sip some beer, and then launches into a passionate rendition of "Feelings." The bartender is awed.

"That's amazing!"

"Give me another beer and you can keep the caterpillar," says the man.

"Are you kidding?" asks the bartender. "How can you just give up such a wonder?"

"Because," replies the man, "that's the only song it knows!"

Charles: Check out this great camera I bought—I've shot over a hundred pictures already!
Douglas: I bet it'll cost a lot to develop all that film.
Charles: Film

Frank: I can't find anything I want to read in this library!
Librarian: We have thousands of books here. Do you mean there's not one book that interests you.
Frank: Nope. The covers are all too far apart.

Ella: What's today's date?
Gerald: Why don't you just look at that newspaper in your hand?
Ella: That's no good—it's yesterday's paper.

After a ship sank in the ocean, three men ended up stranded in a lifeboat. They floated around for days without food or water. One afternoon a bottle floated up to the boat. The men grabbed the bottle and when they pulled the cork out of the bottle, a genie appeared.

"I'll grant each of you a single wish," said the genie.

"I wish I was home," said the first man. Then, poof! He disappeared.

"I wish I was home, too," said the second man. Poof! He disappeared.

The third man looked around. "Gee, I'm kind of lonely," he said. "I wish my friends were here with me."

Megan: How do you like riding school?
Julie: It's great! My horse is very polite.
Megan: A polite horse! What do you mean?
Julie: Whenever we come to a jump, he lets me go first!

Brucie: Oh my goodness, I've gone deaf! I can't hear a word you're saying!
Lucie: I'm not saying anything, I'm chewing gum.

Passenger: I'd like a round-trip ticket.
Ticket agent: Where to?
Passenger: Back here, of course!

Harry: Someday I'd like to ride on a submarine.
Larry: Not me! I wouldn't set foot on any ship that sinks on purpose!

Percy: You have your shoes on the wrong feet.
Lucy: That's impossible. These are the only feet I have.

Why did 17 nitwits go to the movies together?
The sign said under 17 not admitted.

Chester: What are you doing?
Lester: I'm making a long distance call to myself.
Chester: Won't that cost a lot of money?
Lester: Nope. I'm calling collect.

Moe: If I doze off, wake me up at 10 P.M.
Joe: Why 10 P.M.?
Moe: That's the time I usually take my sleeping pills.

While in flight, an airplane catches fire. On board are five people—the president, the smartest man in the world, the pilot, a priest, and a kid—and four parachutes. The president takes a parachute and jumps because he has to run the country. The smartest man jumps because he has to help answer all the questions in the world. The priest says to the kid, "You can jump, I have lived my life." The kid says, "We can both jump. The smartest man in the world took my backpack!"

Nancy: You worry too much. Most of the things you worry about never happen!
Clancy: See how well it works?

Customer: I'm new in town. Do you know of a good garden club?
Florist: A rake handle's always worked for me.

Two bowling teams chartered a double-decker bus to go to Atlantic City for the weekend. One team sat in the bottom of the bus, and the other team sat in the top of the bus. The team down below was whooping it up when one of them realized he didn't hear anything from the top. He walked upstairs to see everyone clutching the seats in front of them, scared to death. "What the heck's going on?" he said. "We're downstairs having a grand old time."

Replied one of the guys from the second team, "Yeah, but you guys've got a driver."

Uncle Ezra: Just remember, my boy: Fools are always certain, while wise men hesitate.
Nephew: Are you sure, Uncle Ezra?
Uncle Ezra: Yes, I'm certain.

Two boys from the city were on a camping trip. The mosquitoes were so fierce, the boys had to hide under their blankets to keep from being bitten. Then one of them saw some fireflies and said to his friend, "We might as well give up, they're coming at us with flashlights!"

Herb: Sorry, I can't come to your party tonight. I'm going to see Romeo and Juliet.
Fred: That's okay. Bring 'em along.

A doctor approached his attorney friend and said, "Sam, I've got this problem. Whenever I'm at a social gathering, people always tell me about their ailments. I don't mind giving medical advice, but I feel like I'm getting cheated out of my fees. Would it be legal or ethical for me to bill them for this?"

"Absolutely," replied the attorney, "That'll be $200."

Moe: I have a photographic memory.
Joe: Humph! Then why do you forget so many things?
Moe: Hey! Can I help it if my mind isn't fully developed yet?

A farmer came home from working in the fields to find his lazy son in a chair on the front lawn watching a herd of cows graze.

"Didn't I tell you to cut the grass today?" the farmer asked his son.

"Oh, my mistake," apologized the lazy boy. "I thought you said to moo the front lawn."

Father: Why don't you put some fresh water in the fish tank?
Boy: The fish haven't finished the old water yet.

Harry's phone rang at 3 A.M. "What do you want?" he shouted into the receiver.

"Nothing," was the reply.

"Then why did you call in the middle of the night?" he asked angrily.

"Because the night rate is cheaper."

Con man: Would you like to buy the Brooklyn Bridge?
Foreign tourist: You must think I'm stupid. That bridge is in terrible shape. But do you know if the George Washington Bridge is for sale?

One morning, Mrs. Smith was taking care of her neighbor's little girl. She arrived in time for breakfast and was seated at the table.

"Mommy always has hot muffins for breakfast," said the little girl. Anxious to please, Mrs. Smith rushed into the kitchen and prepared a tin of hot fresh muffins.

"No thank you," said the little girl when they were brought to her.

"But I thought you said your mother always had muffins for breakfast," said the surprised woman.

"She does," said the girl, "but I don't eat them."

Housewife: Hello, Acme Plumbing? Come quick, I've got a huge leak in the basement!
Acme: Sorry, we can't get there for at least two days.
Housewife: Two days! What'll I do in the meantime?
Acme: Try teaching the kids to swim.

Scout leader: Georgie, what's the first thing you should do if you think you've contracted rabies?
Georgie: Grab a pencil and a piece of paper.
Scout leader: A pencil and paper? Why?
Georgie: To make a list of all the people I want to bite!

Johnny came home happily licking a big ice cream cone. "Where did you get that?" asked his mother.

"I bought it with the $1.00 you gave me," he replied.

"That money was for Sunday school," said his mother.

"I know," said Johnny, "but the minister met me at the door and got me in for free."

Herb: Why is your brother standing in front of the mirror with his eyes closed?
Blanche: Oh, he just wants to see how he looks when he's asleep.

Why did the stupid driver keep going round the block?
Because his turn signal was stuck.

Joe: Why did you put your watch in the bank?
Moe: I'm trying to save time.

Tim: You really should watch your drinking.
Tom: Oh, I do! I only go where there's a mirror behind the bar!

Lucy: I'm sorry, but I'm not going to do anything at all today!
Brucie: Why not?
Lucy: My fortune cookie disagrees with my horoscope!

Handyman: I need 36 two-by-fours.
Sales clerk: How long?
Handyman: Oh, a long time. I'm building a house!

Cliff: Why aren't you going to Joe's funeral?
Norm: He's not coming to mine, so I'm not going to his!

Sandy: Look, dear, I've shortened all the electrical cords!
Rocky: You did? Why?
Sandy: Well, you told me we should use less electricity!

Warden: Buddy, you're in big trouble now. I suppose you'll tell me you didn't see the sign?
Fisherman: That's why I'm here! It said "Fine for Fishing!"

Firefighter: Hey, Chief! There's a 1959 pumper truck being auctioned today. Let's buy it!
Fire chief: What in the world would we do with an old, broken-down fire truck?
Firefighter: Well, we could use it for false alarms!

Airline Pilot (to passengers): Folks, I've got good news and bad news. The bad news is that we seem to be lost. The good news is, we're ahead of schedule!

Elaine: I heard you just bought a two-story house.
Wayne: I'll say I did! The agent told me one story before I bought it, and another story afterwards!

Jack: Well, we made it to this party, but we got so lost getting here I don't know how we'll ever find our way home.
Jackie: It'll be easy. We'll just put the car in reverse.

Two bar regulars were walking home down the middle of the railroad tracks one night after closing time.

"Boy, this is the longest, steepest staircase I've ever walked down!" exclaimed the first.

"Yeah," agreed the second. "But it's these low bannisters that really make it tough!"

Mother: I see you've won a silver medal at camp! What's it for?
Daughter: It's for telling knock-knock jokes.
Mother: And what's this gold medal for?
Daughter: For stopping.

Dad: How was your first day of farm work?
Son: I dug up potatoes all day! What a waste of time!
Dad: Why?
Son: Well, if I'm just going to dig them up, why bother burying them in the first place?

Larry: I quit smoking cold turkey!
Barry: That must've been tough.
Larry: Not as tough as keeping that turkey lit!

Jean: Look at the sign in the window of that car—it says "For sale/phone number 555-3275."
Joan: Forget it. What would I do with another phone number?

Billy: Hey, I finished this jigsaw puzzle and it only took me 18 months!
Bobby: Boy, are you stupid! Nobody needs 18 months to finish a jigsaw puzzle.
Billy: Oh, yeah? The box said "3 to 5 Years!"

Visitor: If I'm in an earthquake here in Los Angeles, what should I do?
Native: Two things: first, stand in a doorway.
Visitor: And what's the second thing?
Native: Make sure the doorway's in Iowa!

Rose: I'm sending a cheer-up note to my mother.
Violet: But that envelope is empty.
Rose: Sure, but my mother always told me no news is good news!

Mr. Codger: Why, when I first came to this city, I was jobless, penniless, shoeless, and without a shred of clothing!
Interviewer: You mean ...
Mr. Codger: That's right! I was born here!

Why did the silly person write "TGIF" on the tops of his shoes?
To help him remember: "Toes Go In First!"

Travis: Hey, Matt, I know how to drop an egg three feet without it breaking!
Matt: How?
Travis: Just drop it from four feet up. For the first three feet, it doesn't break!

Postman: I have a package here for this address, but the name is obliterated.
McFee: Can't be for me, then: my name's McFee.

Youth counselor: You should listen to your conscience, young man.
Juvenile delinquent: Nah—my ma told me never to talk to a stranger!

George: Ouch! A bee stung me on the finger!
Alice: Which one?
George: How can I tell? All bees look alike!

Barfly: Did I spend a $50 bill in here last night?
Bartender: You sure did.
Barfly: Well, that's a relief. I thought I'd lost it.

Suzi: This cookbook is terrible!
Danny: What's wrong with it?
Suzi: They tell you to separate two eggs, but they don't tell you how far apart!

Bobby: Mom! I just went through all of volume M of the encyclopedia!
Mom: That's quite an accomplishment! What have you learned from it?
Bobby: Never hide a $10 bill in a big book without remembering the page number!

Passenger: Does this airplane fly faster than sound?
Flight attendant: It certainly does.
Passenger: Then would you ask the pilot to slow down? My friend and I would like to talk.

George: I'm going to have to let that new secretary go.
Henry: Don't you think he's learning word processing fast enough?
George: I don't think so. Too much White-Out on the monitor screen!

Aunt Sue: Johnny, it's not polite to take the bigger piece of pie. To be polite, I would take the smaller one for myself.
Johnny: What's the problem? You've got it!

Ranch visitor: This is the biggest ranch I've ever seen. How many head of cattle have you got over there?

Rancher: Can't tell. They're facing the wrong way.

Lillie: I hear you dropped out of beauty school because your looks weren't up to par.

Tillie: That's an ugly rumor.

Rose: I used to wear tight jeans, but I stopped.

Violet: Why did you stop?

Rose: Hindsight.

Millie: Boy, Tillie's a pessimist!

Willie: Why do you say that?

Millie: She wears a special bracelet that says "In case of accident, I'm not surprised!"

Andy: I'm a free spirit; I have absolutely no hang-ups!

Mandy: Well, that explains why your clothes are always on the floor!

Movie star: Just look at these photographs of me. They're terrible. The last time I posed for you the pictures were wonderful.

Photographer: Yes, but I was 10 years younger then.

Eddie: What would you like to do tonight?

Betty: I wanna go dancing in the worst way.

Eddie: Oh good, that's how I usually dance.

MMM-MM...FOOD

Tasty morsels to split your sides

Customer: Waiter, I see a bee in my soup!
Waiter: Of course U-C-A-B! It's alphabet soup!

Did you hear about the valedictorian of the cooking school? Passed her final exam with flying crullers!

Teacher: Eskimos usually eat whale meat and blubber.
Sam: I'd blubber, too, if I had to eat whale meat.

Diner: Waiter, your menu plainly states "country fresh eggs." Well, let me tell you, mister, these eggs aren't fresh and I'd like to hear what country they're from.
Waiter: They're from the old country.

What does an invisible baby drink?
Evaporated milk.

Diner: How hot are your hot tamales?
Waiter: Well, if more than three customers eat them at the same time the sprinkler system goes on.

What documents does a young man need to get a job cooking Asian foods?
Woking papers.

Waiter: May I tell you about our corn on the cob?
Customer: Yes. Give me an earful.

Customer: Why do you call these metric cookies?
Baker: They're gram crackers.

Diner: I'll have a hamburger and an ale.
Waiter: Pale?
Diner: No, no, a glass will be enough.

Author: Why did you give my cookbook an awful review?
Reviewer: I thought the recipes were in bad taste.

Waiter: Madam, all the food we serve is à la carte.
Diner: Then just wheel it in, sonny!

Mr. Margarine: My sister just got married.
Mr. Cream Cheese: What is her husband like?
Mr. Margarine: He's a typical butter-in-law.

Man: Why do you have a saddle on that large loaf of bread?
Cowboy Joe: It's my crusty steed.

What is the favorite song of green bread?
Mold Lang Syne.

Delivery man: Where do you want to store these shrimp?
Customer: Put them in my brine cellar.

Hal: I just crossed a pastry chef with a soft drink.
Cal: What did you get?
Hal: Baking soda.

Bill: Which breakfast cereal do cool rap singers eat?
Will: Cheeri—Yo-Yo-Yo's!

Lawyer: Congress is about to pass a law that makes baking rolls more difficult.
Baker: Oh no! Not another bun control law!

Hungry husband: Why are you cooking our meal slowly over low heat?
Wife: Because it's a simmer day.

Weather lady: What do you get when heavy thunderstorms go on a diet?
Weather man: Lite rain.

What do you call a nervous hotdog?
A *frank-fretter.*

Henny: What noise does Rice Chickies cereal make?
Penny: Snap! Cackle! Pop!

Fran: There's a new fad diet out. All you're allowed to eat are bugs and insects.
Ann: Yuck! I wouldn't eat bugs and insects.
Fran: See. That diet can't fail.

Why did the soda bottle go to college?
It wanted to be a fizz ed teacher.

Farmer: Where's the best place to keep these little ears of corn?
Farmer's wife: Put them in the corn crib.

Shopper: I'm looking for stewed tomatoes.
Clerk: Try the salad bar.

The trouble with buying health food is that its high price really makes you sick!

What kind of beer do couch potatoes like best?
Spud Lite.

Jan: The diet police just fined me for eating too much at lunch.
Ann: Did you get into big trouble?
Jan: No. They just gave me a meal ticket.

Diner: Waiter, this tea tastes like turpentine!
Waiter: Then it must be coffee. Our tea takes like dishwater.

Food For Thought
I had sea weedies cereal this morning. It's the breakfast of champion ships!

Sign in the window of a tavern:
Funtime Bar & Grill, where two pints make a cavort.

Waiter: What'll it be?
Exhausted shopper: A couple of soft-boiled eggs and a few kind words.
Waiter: Okay, here are the eggs. And here are the kind words: "Don't eat 'em!'

At the dining table
"Hey, Mom, this stuffing is great! How'd you get the turkey to swallow it?"

Waiter: Would you care for red or white wine?
Diner: It doesn't matter. I'm color blind.

Burger: What's the fruit salad all stirred up about?
Bun: Who knows? You can't raisin with them, they're always banana shape about something.

Gary: What sound do you get if you cross rice cereal with a kangaroo?
Barry: Snap! Crackle! Hop!

Waiter: Excuse me, sir, but you're reading that menu upside down.
Diner: Yes, and it's not easy, I can tell you.

What do you get if you cross clocks with steer?
Lots of minute steaks.

Customer: Waiter, why are you staring at my vegetables?
Waiter: Sir, you said check peas.
Customer: You idiot, I said check please!

Husband: My wife is a terrible cook, but she does wonderful things with leftovers.
Bachelor: What do you mean?
Husband: She throws them out.

Diner: I'll have what that man over there is having.
Waiter: Well, okay, but I don't think he's going to be very happy about it.

Fern: George is so argumentative about everything, it's driving me crazy!
Violet: Come on, he can't argue about everything.
Fern: Oh no? Why, he won't even eat food that agrees with him!

Customer: I want to complain about that turkey you sold me. It didn't have a wishbone.
Butcher: Lady, our turkeys are so plump and contented, they've got nothing to wish for!

Sonny: Mom, can we go to the movies instead of having Thanksgiving dinner?
Mother: Why would you want a movie instead of a Thanksgiving dinner?
Sonny: Oh, it wouldn't be instead—I heard a man on TV say if we wanted a turkey we could see one at the movies!

Food for thought
The Green Giant was an original member of the peas corps.

Diner: Does the chef have calf's brains?
Waiter: After what he just did to the soufflé, I don't think he has the brains of a flea!

Customer: What in the world is this creature?
Butcher: That's our Thanksgiving special—a cross between a turkey and a porcupine! When you're done eating, you can pick your teeth!

Mother: Eat your sandwich, Georgie! Why, if the Pilgrims at Plymouth Rock had that bread, there wouldn't have been a crumb left!
Georgie: Yeah, but it was fresh then!

Diner: For an appetizer, I'll take the caviar, but make sure it's imported.
Waiter: Yes, sir.
Diner: Now, don't forget—it must be imported!
Waiter: I understand.
Diner: I will only accept the caviar if its imported!
Waiter: Sir, why are you so concerned that I bring caviar that's imported?
Diner: Because I CAN'T TELL THE DIFFERENCE!

Customer: Young man, are you absolutely certain there are no chickens in these eggs?
Grocer: Yes, Ma'am. They're duck eggs!

Diner: Waiter, this soup must be ancient! Why, it's much too thick!
Waiter: It looks fine to me, sir.
Diner: It's not fine. When I stir it, the room goes around!

Bill: How was your camping trip?
Bob: A disaster!
Bill: What happened?
Bob: I was eating a lot of dehydrated food—then I got caught in a rainstorm and gained 125 pounds!

First man: Waiter, I'd like a cup of tea, weak, with lemon.
Second man: I'd like tea too, but strong, no lemon, and make sure that the cup is absolutely clean.
Waiter: Here we are. Now, which one gets the clean cup?

Diner: Miss, this coffee's much too strong.
Waitress: It's our regular brew. What's wrong with it?
Diner: I need both hands to dunk my doughnut!

Why do people dip bread into melted cheese?
Because it's fonduing it!

Diner: Waiter, I said I wanted this coffee with half-and-half.
Waiter: And I gave it to you—half in the cup, and half in the
saucer!

Ivan: What's the best way to prepare potatoes grown in Transylvania?
Igor: Monster mash them.

Frank: My new ties smell just like whiskey, rum, or bourbon.
Ed: Wow. I can't wait to tie one on.

French chef: How do our French dishes compare with your American ones?
American chef: They're about the same. If you drop them, they break.

Husband: What's for dinner?
Wife: Ham.
Husband: Good. I'm hungry enough to pig out.

Diner: Waiter, what's this insect in my soup?
Waiter: How should I know? I'm a waiter, not an entomologist.

Ted: I just spilled beer all over the stove.
Patsy: Oh great! Foam on the range.

Mr. Spigot: Can I borrow ten bucks from you, Mr. Keg?
Mr. Keg: Sorry. I'm tapped out.

Diner: Waiter, this apple pie tastes like glue!
Waiter: Then it must be peach pie. Our apple pie tastes like plaster.

Mother: This salad you made tastes terrible. Are you sure you washed these vegetables?
Patty: Of course. If you look hard you can still see the soap on them.

Diner: Do you think raw oysters are healthy?
Waiter: I've never heard one complain.

One worm to another: Follow me. I know a restaurant where we can eat dirt cheap.

Mrs. Smith: How did you make out at the church's pie-eating contest?
Mr. Smith: Not too well. Mr. Jones came in first and I came in sickened.

Diner: Waiter, this meal is the absolute worst!
Waiter: Sir, you are right. But there is an excellent restaurant just across the street.
Diner: Are you sure?
Waiter: But of course I am sure—I own it! I only come here to get customers.

Al: I'll trade you my hot dog for your hamburger.
Hal: Okay.
Cal: Hey! A swap meat!

Where's the best place to drive your car if you're on a strict diet?
In the fast lane.

Mr. Loaf: Two slices of bread are getting married.
Mr. Roll: Let's toast the happy couple.

Waiter: Why do you keep grunting?
Chef: I'm a snort-order cook.

What did the cake ingredients say to the blender?
Stop trying to mix us up!

Grocery store manager: I'm sorry we're not interested in buying your natural honey.
Farmer: Fine. I'll take my buzzness elsewhere!

Tom: I just won thirty days of free ice cream.
Jill: Wow! Talk about a month of sundaes.

Arty: Are we having ground beef for dinner?
Hazel: Yes. Dig in.

Shopper: Young man, I'm looking for some hot chocolate.
Grocery clerk: I'm sorry, ma'am. We don't sell stolen candy.

Bakery assistant: Oh no! I spilled a whole bowl of batter!
Baker: Quick! Grab a sponge cake!

Shirley: Why does your dish of ice cream have a miniature football on top of the whipped cream?
Jake: It's a super bowl sundae.

Bakery chef: How did you do on your pastry test?
Student: I passed with flying crullers.

When do peaches, apples, and grapes need to wear helmets?
When they play in a fruitbowl game.

Diner: Waiter! This farmer's cheese has a clump of dirt in it!
Waiter: What do you want for seventy-five cents—the whole farm?

Son: I won't eat eggs!
Mom: But darling, eggs are good for you!
Son: Oh yeah? Then why doesn't the chicken want them anymore?

Willie: You've been counting calories for months, but so what? You haven't lost any weight.
Millie: No, but my arithmetic is much better!

Waiter (calling after departing diner): Hey! What about a tip?
Diner: Oh, yes, I forgot…Don't ever eat here.

Teenager: I'll take forty-eight cheeseburgers to go, please.
Waitress: All for you?
Teenager: Heck, no! I've got a friend waiting outside in the car!

Rocko: I know a restaurant where you can eat dirt cheap.
Jocko: But who wants to eat dirt?

How do you kill tortellini?
Spray them with pastacide.

Archie: It's impossible to stay on this diet!
Reggie: What's so hard about watching what you eat?
Archie: It's not watching what I eat that's hard—it's watching what my friends eat!

Craig: Honey, why do we have to eat waffles all the time?
Leslie: Because, dear, you said you wanted to eat three squares a day!

Diner: Waiter, take back this salad! The dressing has pieces of brick in it!
Waiter: Of course, sir. You asked for the house dressing.

What can't you eat for breakfast?
Lunch and dinner.

Diner: Waiter, there's a footprint in my breakfast!
Waiter: Well, you ordered an omelet and told me to step on it!

A man walks into a restaurant, orders a cup of coffee, and when it arrives, pours the coffee into an ashtray and eats the cup and saucer, leaving only the handle on the table. He then calls the waiter over and order more coffee. As each cup arrives, he pours out the coffee and eats the cup and saucer. Pretty soon, there's nothing but a pile of china cup handles in front of him. He turns to the waiter and says, "You think I'm crazy, don't you?"

The waiter replies "Yes sir. The handle's the best part!"

Diner: Do you take orders to go?
Waiter: Certainly.
Diner: Then, go!

Army Doctor: You're looking pale, corporal. When did you eat last?
Corporal: 1959, sir.
Army Doctor: What? How could you survive so long?
Corporal: Well, sir, it's only 21:30 now.

Diner: Waiter! This London broil tastes like an asphalt shingle!
Waiter: Sorry, sir, meat prices have simply gone through the roof!

Old Dock Warren was a regular at Bob's Tavern. For the last 30 years he'd ordered the same drink—a walnut daiquiri. One day, Bob ran out of walnuts. He poked around and found an old package of hickory nuts. They would have to do.

Doc arrived as the clock struck six, sat down at his regular spot, and ordered his usual. When Bob put the cocktail up on the bar, Doc took one sip and made a face.

"What in tarnation—," Doc sputtered. "This isn't a walnut daiquiri!"

"I'm sorry," Bob said, shamefaced. "It's a hickory daiquiri, Doc."

Diner: Waiter, where should we sit to be served quickly?
Waiter: How about at the restaurant next door?

What do pirates set their tables with?
Long John Silverware.

Tim: What are you thinking about?
Jim: How to cook several Asian dishes.
Tim: You have woks in your head, pal.

Customer: How's your chicken soup today?
Waiter: It's pretty fowl.

Customer to waiter: "Quick waiter! Bring me an order of rabbit stew and hop to it!"

What do you call a frozen frankfurter?
A chilly hotdog.

Customer: Waiter, this soup is too weak.
Waiter: But sir, it's our best duck soup.
Customer: Oh no it isn't! It's watered down!

Joke-A-Thon 2000
What do you get if you cross a thousand years with a thousand chocolate cakes?
The start of a new millenni-yum-yum!

Chef: I just invented a new dish called Turkey `à la Tarzan?
Waiter: Why do you call it Turkey àß la Tarzan?
Chef: Because after you serve the bird it beats on its chest and knocks the stuffing out of itself.

Ice-cream store clerk: We call this the barber's sundae 'cause we lather it up with whipped cream. How do you like it?
Customer: It's okay. But could you take a little more off the topping please?

Customer: I'd like some coffee!
Waiter: How do you want it?
Customer: In a cup.

A diner was agitated that the waiter didn't bring him a spoon with his coffee. "This coffee," he said loud enough for most of the other patrons to hear,"is going to be pretty hot to stir with my fingers."

The waiter reddened, made a hasty retreat to the kitchen, and returned shortly with another cup of coffee.

"This one isn't so hot, sir," he beamed.

Ed: How's your new diet coming along?
Fred: I'm sneaking too many snacks.
Ed: Why do you say that?
Fred: Last week I spent so much time poking my head in the fridge, my nose got frostbite.

Editor: Did you hear? Aunt Jemima wrote a cookbook.
Agent: No. How's it doing?
Editor: It's selling like hotcakes!

Kelly: I'm on a strict diet that allows me to eat only tiny portions the size of a postage stamp.
Nellie: Well, stick to it.

Shopper: It's pretty hard to pay $7 a pound for good steak.
Butcher: If you paid $5 a pound, it would be a lot tougher.

Sea captain: How does our shellfish catch look to you?
Inspector: Your oysters are fine, your clams look good, but you need to firm up your mussels.

What does the hot dog say when he crosses the finish line?
"I'm the wiener!!"

Elaine: This is my secret recipe for the best meal in town.
Doris: But you're burning everything to a crisp.
Elaine: I know. When my husband comes home, he'll take me out to dinner.

Mr. Apple: Did that fortune-teller predict your future?
Mr. Banana: Yes. She said that I'd live to a ripe old age.

A man had to lose twenty pounds, so his doctor told him to eat nothing but rice cakes for a month. After thirty days he went back to the doctor, who was amazed to find that instead of losing weight, he'd gained ten more pounds. "What happened?" asked the doctor. "Couldn't you eat the rice cakes? Were they too bland?"

"At first they were," answered the man, "but they tasted much better after I started dipping them in melted chocolate."

Moe: Do you like codfish balls?
Joe: I don't know. I never got invited to any.

Why did the cookie visit the doctor?
He felt crummy.

Did you know?
There's a new alcoholic beverage on the market. It's called Bourbon Renewal. After a few drinks your old neighborhood starts to look a lot better.

Blanche: Yuck! Your breath smells like garbage.
Herb: It's not my fault! I had junk food for lunch.

Bob: I work in a factory that makes salt and pepper.
Rob: It sounds like seasonal work.

Which soft drink is half tree and half animal?
Birch Bear.

Apprentice chef: My hamburger was voted the best meal at my cooking school.
Waiter: Really?
Apprentice chef: Yep. It ended up on the honor roll.

Moe: I heard the price of alcoholic beverages is rising by 25%.
Joe: Wow! Now that's a sobering fact.

Scientist: I can take this ice cream and make an exact duplicate of it.
Little boy: Oh boy! Ice cream clones for all of us.

What does a tea kettle do when it's angry?
Blows off a little steam.

Customer: Waiter, there's a fly in my soup.
Waiter: It's possible. The cook used to be a tailor.

Slim: I think hot dogs taste a lot better than hamburgers.
Jim: Now that's a frank opinion.

Customer: What's the secret recipe for your delicious homemade bread?
Baker: Sorry. The recipe is classified on a kneed the dough basis.

Rancher: Why are you using milk to irrigate your fields?
Dumb farmer: I'm raising creamed corn and creamed onions.

Customer: Waiter, this plate is wet.
Waiter: That's your soup, sir.

Pedro: I grow the best jalapeño peppers in the country.
Juan: Ha! That's a hot one!

Customer: Waiter, do you serve crabs here?
Waiter: We'll serve anyone. Sit down.

Chef: Did you like your minute steak?
Diner: Yes, I'll have a second helping.

Which space vegetable uses the dark side of the force?
Darth Tater.

Holly: The doctor's helping me lose weight with these three pills. This red one's for before dinner. That green one's for after dinner.
Ivy: And what's the pink one for?
Holly: The pink one is dinner.

For what vegetable do you throw away the outside, eat the inside, eat the outside and throw away the inside?
Corn on the cob.

Diner: Waiter, I can't find one clam in this clam chowder!
Waiter: Oh, and I suppose you expect to find angels in your angel food cake too!

Lucy: You're going on a diet? Why?
Ethel: Because I'm thick, and tired of it.

Traveling salesman: Bring me some old, cold, reheated coffee in a chipped cup, last week's meatloaf with a bottle of ketchup on the side, and a couple of slices of store bread with the moldy parts trimmed off.
Waitress: Oh, a gourmand, huh?
Traveling salesman: No, just homesick.

Betty: Did you hear about this new diet where you fast for seven days?
Veronica: Oh, I don't think one should fast for seven days—it would make one weak.

Diner: I'll have café au lait, and make absolutely sure that the coffee is from a fresh pot, not the bottom of the old pot, and very hot, and that the milk is whole milk, not cream or half-and-half or skim, and that it's positively fresh this morning.
Waiter: One thing, sir: our cow's name is Betsy. Will that be all right?

Fern: Have you seen Al? He's been on a diet.
Ivy: How much weight has he lost?
Fern: Well, if he lost any more, we'd have to file a missing persons report!

Diner: Waiter, where is my order of escargots! I've been waiting an hour!
Waiter: Sorry, sir, but you know how snails are!

Ernie: I'm inventing a low-calorie hot fudge sundae! There's nothing in it that's fattening!
Gertie: Oh, you'll end up putting something fattening in it—a spoon!

Diner: Waiter, the music in here is much too loud!
Waiter: Oh, do you think so?
Diner: Not only do I think so, my lobster just put his claws up over his ears!

Shopper: You're supposed to be a full-service grocery store, but I ordered a dozen oranges and you only delivered ten!
Grocer: That's part of the service, ma'am; two of the oranges were so bad we threw them away for you!

Diner: I'd like a hamburger, and make it lean.
Waiter: Yes, sir. Which way, sir?

Sonny: Daddy, why do you keep calling the turkey "Napoleon"?
Dad: Because I always get the boney part!

Diner: Waiter, I don't see any chocolate cake on this menu.
Waiter: No, sir. I wiped it off.

John: I was winning the argument until she threw a glass of lemon juice in my face.
Lon: Wow! Talk about a bitter defeat.

Diner: Do you have lobster tails?
Waiter: Certainly, sir: Once upon a time, there was a little lobster…

Boat steward: Shall I bring your lunch on deck, sir?
Seasick passenger: Better to throw it overboard and save time.

Diner: Waiter, this steak is rare. Didn't you hear me say "well done?"
Waiter: Yes, sir. Thank you, sir!

Harry: I hid two bottles of beer in the back of the refrigerator yesterday and there is only one there now. Can you explain why?
Larry: Sure. I didn't see the one that's left.

Tarzan: This is a tough jungle.
Jane: How do you know that?
Tarzan: Instead of bunches, the bananas hang out in gangs.

Diner: Waiter, bring me a bottle of wine, please.
Waiter: What year?
Diner: This year! We'd like to drink it with our dinner!

Why did the banana go out with a prune?
He couldn't get a date.

Diner: Waiter, what is this dish?
Waiter: It's bean soup, sir.
Diner: Yes, but what is it now!

INSULTS

Witty quips to shock and offend

Randy: My family is in iron and steel.
Mandy: Yeah, your sister irons and your brother steals.

Oscar: I met your neighbor the other day.
Elmo: Oh yes, he's an excellent fellow.
Oscar: That's nice of you, since he said you were a dishonest old coot.
Elmo: Well, perhaps we're both mistaken.

Leo: Listen, I'm nobody's fool.
Cleo: Then why don't you get yourself adopted?

Mrs. Van Gelt: Darling, I have the feeling you weren't enchanted with our bridge partners, the Bohrs.
Mr. Van Gelt: Not at all, my dear, they're a perfect couple: she's a hypochondriac and he's a pill.

Boring guest: My goodness, it must be terribly late. I forgot my watch and I've no idea how long we've been talking.
Host: Hold on, I have a calendar right here on my desk.

Eb: Don't give me that dirty look.
Flo: I didn't give you a dirty look—you were wearing it when you came in.

Tracy: Wilhelmina's a lot older than she looks.
Stacy: Oh, I'd say she's approaching forty.
Tracy: But from which direction?

First teenager: I'm so confused!
Second teenager: Why?
First teenager: Half the grownups I know tell me to find myself, and the other half tell me to get lost!

Betty: I think your new baby's going to be a movie star when she grows up.
Wilma: Do you really?
Betty: Oh, yes. She's already a real clamor girl.

Billy: Mary's so outspoken.
Bobby: Not by anyone I know.

Ralph: Let me give you a piece of my mind ...
Alice: Are you sure you can spare it?

Airplane passenger: Well, here we go. Gee, I just love transatlantic flights, only I already saw the movie and I can never sleep on planes. I'm so glad I have a nice person next to me to chat with, I love to meet new people ...
Seatmate: Parlez-vous Français?

Sandy: How do you like me in my killer bee Halloween costume?
Mandy: Oh, buzz off.

Driver: Does this road lead to Brattleboro?
Vermonter: Don't know.
Driver: Well, do you know how I can get to a road going south?
Vermonter: Nope.
Driver: You sure don't know much, do you?
Vermonter: Maybe not, but I ain't lost.

Millie: Your hair looks nice, it looks like a wig.
Tillie: It is a wig.
Millie: Doesn't look it.
Jill: Why so low?

Jack: My shrink just told me I don't have an inferiority complex.
Jill: That sounds like good news to me.
Jack: No, he said I really am inferior.

Waiter: Tonight's special is snails.
Diner: And I see you have them dressed as waiters.

Texan: Back home on my ranch I can get in my car at dawn, drive all day, and it'll be dark before I reach the end of my property.
Vermonter: I had a car like that once.

Singer: I see my rendition of "My Old Kentucky Home" has moved you to tears. Are you from Kentucky?
Gentleman: No, I'm a musician.

Orville: You mean that quiet little wife of yours up and divorced you?
Wilbur: Yeah. She used to be pensive. Now she's expensive.

Fred: I like George.
Barney: Yes, but he's so lazy.
Fred: Oh, yeah? Give me an example.
Barney: He always goes through a revolving door on someone else's push.

Alice: Do you like my new coat? It's dyed muskrat.

Ralph: Yup, it died, all right.

Susie: Whenever I'm down in the dumps I buy myself a new pair of shoes.

Sallie: So that's where you get them.

Tourist: Does it matter which road I take to White River Junction?

Vermonter: Not to me, it doesn't.

Actress: Darling, I read your book, and it was simply divine. Do tell me, who wrote it for you?

Authoress: I'm so delighted you enjoyed it. Do tell me, who read it to you?

Bob: Your telephone bills are gigantic!

Susan: They can't be; I use AT&T.

Bob: That's just the problem—Always Talking and Talking!

Martha: Do you like my new outfit?

George: Honey, it's in a clash by itself.

Fred: How do you like my dancing!

Adele: Oh, it's great…except for two things.

Fred: What two things?

Adele: Your left foot and your right foot!

Kim: May I speak frankly with you?
Jim: Sure. Why not?
Kim: Okay. You're a big wiener!

Barry: I heard Sally joined your health club.
Mary: Yes, but she's not very athletic. The only thing coordinated about her when she works out is her outfit.
Clairvoyant: I'm a mind reader.
Wise guy: Oh yeah? Well, read my mind.
Clairvoyant: Sorry. I can't. The print is too small.

Jack: All work and no play makes Jack a dull guy.
Jill: Gee, you must be a very hardworking fella!

Mary: Jack is so dumb.
Chris: How dumb is he?
Mary: He's so dumb that he called information for the phone number of 911!

Ed: I can't think straight anymore.
Ned: I knew your mind was warped.

Bob: What did your blind date look like?
Rob: She had an hourglass figure.
Bob: That's great.
Rob: Not really. Time has stood still in all the wrong places.

Mrs. McCatty: My dear, I've just been wondering to myself why you weren't invited to Mrs. Whitney's party last week?
Mrs. McSharp: What a coincidence! I've just been wondering why you were!

Young writer: What do you think, sir? Should I put more fire into my stories?
Old editor: Or vice versa!

Annie: I can always tell when Johnny's lying.
Fannie: How?
Annie: His lips move!

An American was visiting Oxford University for the first time, and stopped a passing Oxford don to ask a question.

"Excuse me," said the American, "can you tell me if that's Trinity College I'm looking at?"

"You are probably unaware" sneered the don, "that you have just ended your sentence with a preposition. You may wish to rephrase your question."

The American began again: "Can you tell me if that's Trinity College I'm looking at, YOU JERK!"

Sammy: Why don't you like Judy? She never says anything bad about other people.
Tammy: Only because she's too busy talking about herself!

Bill: How do you like my poetry?
Phil: It could be worse!
Bill: That's a heck of a thing to say!
Phil: Okay, okay—it couldn't be worse!

Millie: George is the laziest person I know.
Tillie: Why do you say that?
Millie: He's always complaining that there isn't enough wind out on the porch to start his rocking chair!

Author: What's your opinion of my latest novel?
Critic: It's worthless!
Author: I know, but I'd like to hear it anyway.

Junior: I'm going to ask my dad to help me with my math homework.
Teacher: Now, you know that wouldn't be right.
Junior: Probably not, but at least I'd have something to hand in.

Guidance counselor: If Johnny becomes a cab driver after he leaves school he'll be rich.
Parent: Why?
Guidance counselor: Because he can't find the shortest distance between two points!

Teddy: My family says I'll never amount to anything!
Eddy: Why, that's not true! With your experience, you could be a wonderful terrible example!

Fern: My passport photo doesn't do me justice.
Ivy: You don't need justice, you need mercy!

Teacher: Cassandra, if I saw a man beating a donkey and I stopped him, what virtue would I be demonstrating?
Cassandra: Brotherly love?

Lillie: I can't decide which one I should go to, a palm reader or a mind reader.
Tillie: I think you should go to the palm reader.
Lillie: Why?
Tillie: At least you know for sure you've got a palm.

Ed: Want to see something stupid?
Fred: Sure.
Ed: Look in a mirror.

What dance do barbecue grills like to do?
The char-char.

John: I suggest we wage a battle of wits.
Ron: Personally, I think you're low on ammunition.

Private: Why are you throwing me out of the Marines, sir?
General: Because you're rotten to the Corps, soldier!

First art critic: This piece looks as if it was painted with cold cream.
Second art critic: Too bad it wasn't vanishing cream.

Lawrence: My performance of *Hamlet* left my audience open-mouthed!
Richard: Yeah, they couldn't stop yawning!

Madge: Do you think my new outfit will go out of style quickly?
Flora: Oh, no. It'll look the same for years to come—just awful.

Mrs. Swank: I'm terribly sorry, but I completely forgot about your cocktail party yesterday.
Mrs. Swell: Oh—weren't you there?

Horace: A person should always dress like a million bucks ...
Doris: Well, you're a good example—your suit's green and wrinkled!

Customer: I'd like a green scarf to match my eyes, or perhaps a romantic dress to reveal my soul ...
Clerk: How about a soft hat for your head?

Moe: I challenge you to a battle of wits!
Larry: I never fight an unarmed man!

Tom: I live by my wits.
Sally: It's no wonder you look like you're at death's door.

Ethel: If you were my husband, I'd put arsenic in your coffee.
Fred: If I were your husband, I'd drink it.

Madge: My boyfriend should have been named Geometry.
Flora: Why? Is he good at math?
Madge: No, he's just a square.

Herb: Ha! That's funny!
Blanche: What is?
Herb: Oh, I was just thinking.
Blanche: You're right, that is funny.

Ben: The circus is coming to town.
Len: Did you know I used to be in the circus?
Ben: Really? Which cage were you in?
Publisher: I've got good news and bad news for you.
Author: What's the good news?
Publisher: We just sold the one millionth copy of your book.
Author: What's the bad news?
Publisher: We still can't sell the other 999,999 copies.

Ingenue: I'd love to sing in your new musical. I just don't know what to do with my hands.
Producer: Hold them over your mouth.

Neighbor No. 1: Last night I dreamed that I saw something on your front lawn that made me very happy.
Neighbor No. 2: What was it?
Neighbor No. 1: A "For Sale" sign.

Herb: Drinking makes you look beautiful.
Blanche: I haven't been drinking.
Herb: But I have.

Pearl: It looks like it's going to storm. You'd better stay for dinner.
Shirl: Oh, I don't think it's bad enough for that!

Little boy: Ouch! I have a splinter in my finger.
Little girl: Scratching your head again?

Did you hear the one about the guy who is so conceited that every time he hears a clap of thunder, he runs to the window and takes a bow?

Blanche: My only sin is vanity. I look in the mirror each morning and think how beautiful I am.
Herb: That's not a sin—that's a mistake.

Joey: So, you're calling me stupid, eh? You'll be sorry!
Chloe: I've always been sorry that you're stupid!

Husband: I've half a mind to watch Monday night football tonight.
Wife: Then you've got everything you need.

Mickey: In my opinion, Wanda's a great singer.
Nickey: Yeah, she's waterproof!
Mickey: What do you mean?
Nickey: No one can drown her out!

Bert: My sister always sings in the shower.
Ernie: Mine too. She really should sing on the radio.
Bert: She's that good, eh?
Ernie: No, but then I could turn her off!

Sam: I'm at my wit's end!
Diane: And it didn't take you long to get there!

Henry: Why did you fire your secretary? I thought you said she had a mind like a blotter!
George: Exactly! She soaked up everything, but she got it all backwards!
Harry: Linda's such a pessimist!
Barry: Really? She always says she looks forward to the future.

Harry: Only so she can complain about how much better things used to be!

Mickey: I baked two kinds of bread today! Take your pick.
Minnie: No thanks, I'll use my hammer!

Writer: I haven't produced anything decent in months! My writing is getting worse!
Publisher: No, your taste is improving.

Martha: Why weren't you in the Army during the war?
George: Same reason you weren't in the Rockettes—couldn't pass the physical!

A commuter is getting on the train one morning when another passenger stumbles and bumps into him.

"Pardon me," said the passenger. "I'm a little stiff from rowing."

"How do you do," replied the commuter. "I'm from Larchmont, myself."

SCHOOL DAYS

....

Life was so much easier back then. And funnier.

Teacher: According to Archimedes, what happens when a body is immersed in water?
Henry: Usually the phone rings.

Mother: How was your history test, Lucy?
Lucy: Oh, I don't know ... the questions were easy.
Mother: Then what was the problem?
Lucy: The answers were hard!

Teacher: Davey, you must learn to write more clearly. I can hardly read your handwriting!
Davey: Oh, sure—then you'll complain about my spelling!

....

Grandma: How do you like kindergarten, Nicky?
Nicky: I hate it! I can't do anything there!
Grandma: What do you mean you can't do anything?
Nicky: Well, I can't read, I can't write, and they won't let me talk!

Teacher: Because it's Presidents' Day, children, I'd like you to make a list of nine great Americans. Billy, what's the problem?
Billy: I've got eight, teacher, but I can't come up with a shortstop.

Janie: Mom, how old is our car?
Mom: About five years old, honey.
Janie: And what kind is it?
Mom: A station wagon. Why all the questions about the car?
Janie: My teacher told us to write our autobiography!

Teacher: Veronica, you forgot the dot over the i.
Veronica: I didn't forget. It's still in the pencil.

Math teacher: Your homework assignment is the first 50 problems in Chapter Five, the next 10 problems in Chapter Six, the first 15 …
Student: Poor Dad!

Judy: My geometry teacher lost her parrot.
Carole: Gee, where's her polygon?

Teacher: Tiffany, why did you write in your essay that the moon is more important than the sun?
Tiffany: Well, if we didn't have the moon it would be too dark to see at night. But the sun only shines during the day when we don't need it.

Janie: Wow, Mom. It sure is lucky you named me Janie!
Mom: Why is it lucky?
Janie: Because that's what all the kids at school call me!

Teacher: Jeremy, please use "I" in a sentence.
Jeremy: I is—
Teacher: Don't say "I is." Say "I am."
Jeremy: Okay. I am the ninth letter of the alphabet.

Janie went to kindergarten for the first time. After an hour or two she began to cry.

"What's wrong, Janie?" said the teacher. "Are you homesick?"

"No," said Janie. "I'm heresick."

Jenny: Why didn't the physics teacher marry the biology teacher?
Penny: Their chemistry just wasn't right.

Student: I want to invent a better glue, but I'm having a difficult time.
Teacher: Stick to it.

Teacher: You'll get this comic book back at the end of the semester!
Susie: Will it really take you that long to read it?

Beryl: My son got an "A" for cutting class!
Meryl: How can that be? What school does he attend?
Beryl: Barber College!

Gym teacher: Today we're going to learn to jump rope.
Student: Oh boy! At last I get to skip class.

Fred: My daughter just graduated from law school!
Ned: My son didn't have to—he settled out of class!

James: What do you think of this new opening for my essay: "The gloom in the room gave Jim a sense of doom?"
Teacher: That's verse.
James: Okay. I'll try to make it better.

Marty: Ugh! Doing homework is for the birds.
Artie: Yeah, but if you don't do it you're a dead duck!

Principal: Why are you throwing away your class bulletin board?
Teacher: It's too tacky.

Jenny: Why is Georgie crossing the playground?
Benny: To get to the other slide!

Professor: I think you'll find that the course textbook, if assiduously perused, will do half your work for you.
Student: In that case I'm buying two copies!

Matt: Mommy, I learned how to count! Listen—One, two three!
Mom: Good! Go on!
Matt: You mean there's more?

Jim: Last night my dog tried to chew up the essay I wrote.
Teacher: What did you do?
Jim: I took the words right out of his mouth.

Mary: Why are you bringing a jump rope to school?
Terry: I'm going to ask the principal if I can skip a grade.

Art teacher: That's a nice well you painted. Is it finished?
Jane: No. I still have to draw water.

Bakery student no. 1: Yahoo! I got great marks in bread-baking class.
Bakery student no. 2: How do you know?
Bakery student no. 1: I just saw my name on the honor roll.

Teacher: Suzie, why didn't you do your history assignment?
Suzie: I'd rather let bygones be bygones.

Mother: Wake up, dear. Time for school!
Son: I'm not going. I hate school! I'm sick of school!
Mother: But dear, you must go to school.
Son: Give me one good reason!
Mother: You're the principal!

Teacher: Class, tomorrow you'll be taking an aptitude test.
Student: No fair! You didn't teach aptitude this semester!

Duke: Here are the royal math and science teachers, sire.
Little King Arthur: Ah, my favorite subjects.

Teacher: Henry, are you ready with your report on nitrates?
Henry: Yes, teacher. They're cheaper than day rates.

Mom: How was school today, Janie?
Janie: It was good. We learned how to make babies!
Mom: Is that so? And ... um ... how do you make babies?
Janie: It's easy. Just take away the 'y' and put on 'i,' 'e,' and 's'!

Teacher: George, can you name the four seasons of the year?
George: Football, Basketball, Baseball, and Vacation!

Marla: How did you do at modeling school?
Darla: I got high beauty marks.

Teacher: Janie, what's the difference between the North Pole and the South Pole?
Janie: All the difference in the world.

Astronomer (peering into a telescope): It's going to rain.
Grad student: What leads you to that conclusion, Professor?
Astronomer: My corns ache.

Teacher: Janie, why are you writing so fast?
Janie: I want to finish this essay before my pen runs out of ink.

Why did the little cave get sent to the principal's office?
It had a dirty mouth.

Teacher: This essay about your dog is exactly the same as your sister's.
Student: Well, it's the same dog.

Which is the stupidest letter in the alphabet?
The dumb S.

Teacher: If you had sixteen jellybeans and Jack asked you for ten, how many would you have left?
Sally: Sixteen.

Pat: My teacher talks to himself. Does yours?
James: Yes. But she thinks we're listening to her.

What did the student fish bring to school for his teacher?
A *crab apple.*

Math teacher: Why did you draw a heart in the middle of that isosceles triangle?
Rose: It's a love triangle.

Mother: Johnny, you've been working in our garden a lot this summer.
Son: I know. My teacher told me to weed a lot over the vacation.

Algebra teacher: And in conclusion, class, we finally learn that X is equal to zero.
Student: Humph! All that work for nothing.

Mother: My son's average grades in school are making me ill.
Doctor: It sounds to me like you're suffering from C-sickness.

Teacher: Edwina, can you give me an example of a coincidence?
Edwina: My mother and father were married on the same day!

Pat: What does your math teacher read on the weekends?
Pam: He reads the Sumday papers.

Student: If it was up to you would you penalize a person for something he didn't do?
Teacher: Absolutely not!
Student: Good, I didn't do last night's homework.

Aunt Fanny: Well, Judy, how do you like going to school?
Judy: I don't mind going, and I don't mind coming home. It's staying there in between that I hate.

Professor: Today I'm going to lecture on the heart, kidneys, liver, and lungs.
Premed student: Oh great! Another organ recital!

Sallie: My English teacher talks to herself.
Susie: Does she realize it?
Sallie: No, she thinks we're listening.

Teacher: Why do you want to be a geologist when you grow up?
Student: It would be cool to earn a living going to rock festivals.

Personnel manager: I see here that you paid for your education by playing in a band.
Student: Yes. I rocked my way through college.

Principal: Now, Amanda, did you really call your teacher a meany?
Amanda: Yes, I did.
Principal: And is it true you called her a wicked old witch?
Amanda: Yes, it is.
Principal: And did you call her a tomato-nosed beanbag?
Amanda: No, but I'll remember that one for next time!

Sunday school teacher: Some saints like Joan of Arc were burned at the stake.
Boy: Holy smoke!

Law student no. 1: Hey! Let's pretend we're in court and try a case.
Law student no. 2: Sorry. I'm not in the moot for it.

Driving instructor: Do you know what a green light means?
Teen student: It means go.
Driving instructor: Do you know what a red light means?
Teen student: It means stop.
Driving instructor: Do you know what a yellow light means?
Teen student: Yes. It means go fast so you don't have to stop.

Moe: How in the world could you fail an I.Q. test?
Joe: Easy. I didn't study for it.

Teacher: Is there any difference between a wild horse and a tame horse?
Student: Only a bit.

Professor: A liberal arts education will make your son well-rounded.
Parent: Yes, but shouldn't he be pointed at some end?

Student: Can I charge my graduate school classes?
Clerk: Sorry. No college credit allowed.

Teacher: Spike, tell me who shot President Lincoln.
Spike: I'm taking the Fifth, Teach!

Student: I enrolled at this college to learn how to be an astronaut.
Professor: Hummm. I thought you came here to take up space.

Teacher: I've asked you to come in, Mrs. Smith, to discuss Johnny's appearance.
Mrs. Smith: Why? What's wrong with his appearance?
Teacher: He hasn't made one in this classroom since September.

A foreign student came to America to study theology and had to learn how to speak English. After a while he had an interview with his college advisor. "I hear you're doing better in English," said the advisor. "Now how about syntax?"

"Goodness," lamented the foreign student. "I didn't know I had to pay one."

Teacher: This class is so noisy I can't hear myself speak!
Student: That's okay, teach, you ain't missing anything!

Dad: What is the meaning of this F on your report card?
Junior: Fantastic?

Teacher: Judy, I've had to send you to the principal's office every day this week! What've you got to say for yourself?
Judy: I'm glad it's Friday!

Father: Tell me you did well on your spelling test.
Son: I can't. Words fail me.

Teacher: Stanley, if I put a dozen marbles in my right pants pocket, fifteen marbles in my left pants pocket, and thirty-one marbles in my back pocket, what would I have?
Stanley: Heavy pants.

Why was the Green Giant so sad?
He did poorly on his Pea S.A.T.'s.

Student: The grade on my math test doesn't add up right.
Teacher: Hummm, there must be sum mistake.
Father: I certainly hope Junior's learning the three R's at State U.
Mother: From his grades, I'd say he's learning three R's all right: Rah, Rah, Rah!

Teacher: Georgina, spell "Mississippi"
Georgina: The river or the state?

One day Jimmy went down to the pond for a dip, but before he could dive in he spied his teacher, Mrs. Smith, emerging from a session of nude bathing. When Mrs. Smith saw Jimmy, she grabbed the nearest object—which happened to be an old wooden box—and held it in front of her.

"Young man, I know what you're thinking," she said.

"And I know what you're thinking," replied Jimmy. "You're thinking that box has a bottom on it!"

Teacher: Davy, if you had one dollar in one pocket and 75 cents in the other pocket, what would you have?
Davy: My hands in my dad's pockets!

Parent: This school stinks! I'm having my son transferred!
Principal: But your son is getting straight A's!
Parent: That's how I know the place stinks!

Teacher: Janie, I'll have to give you a low grade on your essay. How can you write that birds have three wings!
Janie: Come on, Teacher, it's just a difference of a pinion!

Son: I'm too tired to do my homework tonight.
Mom: A little hard work never killed anyone yet.
Son: Right. But why should I risk being the first.

Teacher: All right now, class; we've been studying the Great Lakes. Can anyone tell me which is the smallest body of water?
Georgie: Lake Inferior?

A college student walked into his ornithology class and found five birds with bags over their heads so only their feet showed. "What's this?" he asked.

"It's an exam," explained the professor. "Your job is to identify each bird by looking at its feet."

"What a stupid test," complained the student.

"What's your name?" demanded the angered professor. The student pulled up the legs of his pants and answered, "You tell me."

Chemistry teacher: What is the formula for water?
Student: H-I-J-K-L-M-N-O.
Chemistry teacher: What made you give a silly answer like that?
Student: You said it was H to O.

Annie: Why are you running?
Danny: I'm trying to prevent a fight.
Annie: Between whom?
Danny: Between me and that bully chasing me.

Teacher: Judy, can you spell "banana?"
Judy: I can start it, but I don't know when to stop!

Mr. Jones: My elementary school taught me a lot about investments.
Mr. Smith: What do you mean?
Mr. Jones: Everything I did in class aroused principal interest.

Teacher: Jimmy, can you name two responsibilities you have at home?
Jimmy: Get out and stay out?

Department chair: We're not renewing the new professor's contract.
Dean: Really? I thought his list of publications was vast!
Department chair: It is, but his teaching is only half-vast!

Teacher: Please name the little streams that run into the Nile?
Janey: The Juveniles?

Teacher: Jimmy, please recite Lincoln's Gettysburg Address.
Jimmy: Gee, I didn't know he'd moved!

Teacher: Georgie, I hope you're studying hard for the geometry test.
Georgie: Not to worry, Teach—I know all the angles!

Teacher: Georgie, name a product raised where the annual rainfall exceeds 40 inches.
Georgie: Umbrellas!

Teacher: Jimmy, what is the distance from New York to Philadelphia?
Jimmy: About 95 girls, ma'am.
Teacher: What kind of answer is that?
Jimmy: Well, yesterday you said a miss was as good as a mile!

Teacher: Susie, where is the ocean deepest?
Susie: At the bottom!

Kindergarten teacher: Can you tie your shoes well?
Paul: Knot always.

Teacher: See. You can enjoy yourself doing addition problems.
Alex: Yeah. Sum fun.

French student: Are you good in Spanish class?
Spanish student: Sí!
French student: Oh well, we can't all be "A" students.

Janet: Who calculates how many meals are served in the cafeteria?
Teacher: The lunch counter.

Karen: They had to evacuate the school library.
Teacher: Why?
Karen: Someone found dynamite in the dictionary.

Teacher: Johnny, do you use bad words?
Johnny: No, teacher.
Teacher: Do you disobey your parents?
Johnny: No, teacher.
Teacher: Come now, what do you do that's naughty?
Johnny: I tell lies.

Teacher: Donald, where's your pencil?
Donald: Me no got a pencil.
Teacher: No, no, Donald. Say, "I don't have a pencil; you don't have a pencil; he doesn't have a pencil; we don't have a pencil; they don't have a pencil." Do you see?
Donald: No. Where'd all the pencils go?

Teacher: Megan, what are the four main food groups?
Megan: Canned, Frozen, Instant, and Lite.

Professor: Why did you take my ornithology class?
Student: Just for a lark.

Teacher: Simon, what's thirty-five minus eighteen?
Simon: Seventeen, teacher.
Teacher: That's very good.
Simon: Good? It's perfect!

Teacher: All right, Ernie, let's hear you count to ten.
Ernie: One, two, three, four, five, six, seven, eight, nine, ten.
Teacher: That's fine, Ernie. Can you go a little higher?
Ernie: Jack, Queen, King!

THE SUPERNATURAL

....

Comedy from way out there

Martian No. 1: How do you hold up your space pants?
Martian No. 2.: I wear an asteroid belt.

What do you get when alien teens invade earth shopping malls?
Clothes encounters of the third kind.

Ted: Did you hear the new vampire joke?
Ed: Is it funny?
Ted: Not really. It's just a vein attempt at humor.

....

Why didn't Mrs. Skeleton leave Mr. Skeleton?
She didn't have the heart to break up with him.

Little ghoul: It's not fair! Why can you go to the Halloween party and I can't?
Grown-up ghoul: Because I'm the mummy, that's why!

What monster lives in the mountains and alters men's suits?
The Abominable Sewman.

Jules: How's it going at that progressive college of yours?
Jim: Terrible. I wanted to major in Witchcraft but I had to drop out.
Jules: Why?
Jim: I flunked Spelling.

What kind of telephones do mummies use?
Touch-tomb phones.

Mr. Elf: I watch a lot of television programs.
Mr. Hobbit: What's your favorite show?
Mr. Elf: Gnome improvements.

What is the Wolfman's favorite day of the week?
Moonday.

Ghoul: Aren't you afraid of getting sunburned if you haunt the beach?
Ghost: No. I always use sun scream.

What kind of television do you find in a haunted house?
A wide scream TV

Gus: I'll stop being frightened if you'll stop being scared.
Daisy: That sounds like a fear exchange to me.

What did the patent office head say when he first saw Edison's new lightbulb?
Okay. Whose bright idea is this?

Goblin: Are you all ready to go out?
Witch: One minute, I forgot to use scare spray!

Why did the two ghouls get married?
Because they loved each shudder.

Dracula: That witch doctor you sent me to is a quack!
Mummy: Why do you say that?
Dracula: He told me I didn't exorcise enough!

What's Frankenstein's favorite ice cream flavor?
Shock-a-lot!

Little boy: Why do you refuse to pull a rabbit out of your hat?
Magician: Because I just washed my hare and can't do anything with it.

What did Coach Ghost deliver to his fellow spirits the night before Halloween?
An inspirational screech.

First magician: Where's that pretty little wife you always saw in half during your act?
Second magician: She's not my wife, she's my half-sister.

Which toilet bowl cleaner do most magicians use?
Vanish!

Mamie: You must meet my friend. She's a medium.
Jamie: No, it'll only depress me. I'm a large.

What do witches like to put on their floors?
Magic carpeting.

Magician No. 1: I only paid a dollar for a vanishing chicken.
Magician No. 2: Wow! What a cheep trick!

What did the hobo vampire say to the rich man?
Can I put the bite on you for a free meal?

Sorcerer: How do you make a witch faint?
Magician: Use a dizzy spell.

What did the Mama Ghost say to the little ghosts before
they drove off in their car?
Fasten your sheet belts.

Invisible man: I auditioned for a starring role in a horror
movie.
Invisible girl: Did you get it?
Invisible man: No. The director couldn't see me in the part.

Where do wealthy vampires keep their valuables?
In the Swiss Blood Bank.

Ghost: Please let me join the Marines.
Recruiter: Why?
Ghost: I want to fright for my country!

What cable channel do leprechauns watch?
Gnome Box Office.

Igor: I know a witch who conjured up a work of fiction.
Boris: Wow! Talk about a spellbinding novel.

Why did the ghost become a sailor?
He wanted to haunt for buried treasure.

Lenny: Is it bad luck to have a black cat follow you?
Jenny: It depends.
Lenny: On what?
Jenny: If you're a man or a mouse.

Did you hear the one about the woman who spent all day and night learning how to cast spells?
She wanted to get witch quick.

Timmy: An alien creature just abducted the snowman I built.
Lynn: Now that's a close encounter of the frost kind.

Reporter: Why do you suppose aliens visit Earth?
Scientist: Perhaps they're looking for other intelligent life-forms in the usniverse.
Reporter: If that's so, why don't they make contact?
Scientist: Maybe they're still looking.

An out-of-work ventriloquist, deciding on a career change, bought a storefront fortune-telling business. He posted a price list and the first customer of the day inquired about it.

"I have three prices," the ventriloquist said. "For $10 you will hear a sound made by your dearly departed. For $15, you'll hear the voice of your dearly departed."

"How about for $20?" asked the customer.

"For $20," replied the ventriloquist, "you'll hear the voice of your dearly departed—while I drink a glass of water!"

Frankenstein monster: I don't feel like I have the energy to leave the office, doctor.
Mad scientist: I guess I didn't charge you enough.

What did Dr. Frankenstein say to his assistant, Igor, while he was sewing his monster together?
Give me a hand.

Hazel: I think someone cast a spell on me.
Witchie: Well, what the hex's wrong with you?

What is a werewolf's favorite televised sporting event?
Full Moonday Night Football.

Ghost: Wasn't that spirit an investment banker?
Specter: Yes.
Ghost: Why is he moaning like that?
Specter: He's reading the Wail Street Journal.

Three vampires sit down at a table in a bar and order drinks.
    The first vampire says "I vant some blood!"
    The second vampire says "I vant some blood, too!"
    The third vampire says "Just plasma for me, please."
    The waitress takes the order, walks over to the bar and yells "Two bloods and a blood lite!"

Ghost: What do you carve out of a stupid pumpkin?
Goblin: A jerk-o-lantern.

Why did the Wolfman go to the movie studio?
He heard they were having a Howlywood party.

Mrs. Ghost: Why are you so depressed?
Mr. Ghost: I've been job haunting all day and I can't scare up any work.

An American ghost went on vacation to Italy to scare people. The vacation turned out to be a dud. Finally he met an Italian ghost. "How do I have more fun?" the American ghost asked.

The Italian ghost replied, "When in Rome, boo as the Romans boo."

Author: Why didn't you like my new novel about witches and wizards?
Critic: It was a hex-rated book.

Why was the monster athlete so happy?
He won a ghoul medal at the Olympics.

Lil: I want to become a medium and contact ghosts for a living.
Bill: Doesn't the thought of that scare you?
Lil: No. I'm not afraid of success.

Did you hear about the wizard who directed a film?
He really made movie magic.

John: What is a ghost's favorite TV crime show?
Ron: America's Most Haunted.

How do you know the Invisible Man has no children?
Because he's not apparent.

Lou: What happened to that medium who used to hold seances with your departed relatives?
Bud: She became dispirited.

THE WORKING WORLD

···

Humor from the trenches

Ed: How's your job at the travel agency?
Ned: Terrible. I'm not going anywhere.

What do you call a person who makes miniature watches?
A *small-time operator.*

Ted: Why does the custodian always wait until 11:00 A.M.
to clean the floors on the weekend?
Ed: Because he likes to sweep late on Saturday mornings.

What did the oil delivery man say to the customer?
You're the first person I fueled today.

···

Employee: Why should I come to work for your coffee company?
Boss: We offer a lot of job perks.

Executive: Miss Davis, why are you soaking wet?
Miss Davis: I just came up from the secretarial pool.

Before they decide what kind of lumber to use on a house, carpenters usually get together and have a board meeting.

Consultant: Why did you buy that bottled spring water company?
Businessman: I believe in having liquid assets.

Show me a guy who makes his living washing cooking pots … and I'll show you a man who's an expert panhandler.

Businessman: I own two cookie factories.
Farmer: Big deal. I own thousands of food plants.

What is the worst time of the year for the owner of a cab company?
When it's time to pay his taxis.

Customer: What happened to that couch potato who used to sell furniture in this store?
Boss: He got sacked.

Why didn't the mailman pass his Civil Service test?
His postage marks weren't high enough.

Ed: How's your proofreading job at the history book publishing company?
Fred: Okay. But I don't see any future in it.

What kind of business did Mr. Gopher start up?
A hole-sale business.

Ken: How's your new job as a carpet installer?
Len: I just can't tack it anymore.

What did the ocean liner say to the tugboat?
Take this job and shove it.

Mack: Is it hard work planting shrubs for a living?
Zack: It sure is. I'm always bushed.

What happens to good hairdressers?
They dye and go to heaven.

Jack: What do you do for a living?
Bob: I sell boats.
Jack: Motor boats?
Bob: No, I'm in charge of sails.

Show me a celestial body that goes into footwear ... and I'll show you a shoe business star.

Mary: How's your job at the playing card company?
Larry: I just can't deal with the pressure.

Reporter: What's the secret of your success?
Perfume manufacturer: My company makes good scents.

If you're thinking of starting a grass cutting business, buy a lawn tractor and you'll get mower for your money.

Supervisor: You're fired!
Worker: I quit.
Mediator: Gee, isn't it nice when labor and management agree?

Jack: Why did you quit your job at the scissor plant?
Amy: They cut my medical benefits.

What is the biggest problem miners have?
They get coal feet.

Harry: How's your job at the hair club for guys?
Larry: Not so good. I had a falling out with the boss.

Mr. Biggie: I give the orders in this factory. I'm a captain of industry.
Mr. Small: Big deal. I'm a business major.

Jack: How's your job at the nudist camp?
Paul: I just couldn't bare it any longer, so I quit.

Reporter: What's your secret of success?
Hair Club President: I never ever keep a clear head for business.

Mr. Crow: I don't feel like going to work today.
Mrs. Crow: Well, caw in sick.

Jack: The management didn't have the factory walkway shoveled again. It's solid ice.
Henry: I guess it's time for a slip-down strike.

Why was the tugboat so mad?
He was docked a day's pay.

Customer: That used car looks like a huge top with wheels.
Salesman: Don't worry about how it looks. Just take it out for a spin.

Salesgirl: Which size dress would you like, ma'am?
Julie: I'd like a size 7, but I take a size 12.

Son: I'm going to sell light bulbs for a living.
Father: Now that's a bright idea!

Ted: What do you do for a living?
Fred: I'm a censor.
Ted: So you're the type of guy who sticks his no's in everyone else's business.

Lady: Why is that young clerk chasing flies around the store?
Manager: He's our best shoo salesman.

Boss: Do you have enough determination to transport trucks from coast to coast?
Employee: Yes. I'm full of drive.

What is the favorite cable channel of tailors?
HEM-TV

Al: Do you have to be smart to work in a perfume factory?
Val: No. But you need good scents.

What do miners eat for breakfast?
Coal cereal.

Commuter: I fell over 20 feet this morning.
Boss: Did you step in a hole?
Commuter: No, I walked through a crowded subway car.

Cara: How's your job at the diet plan company?
Tara: Bad. The chances for promotion are slim.

Farmer: I sent away for some baby chickens to be delivered by mail and they're not here yet.
Salesman: Relax. Your chicks are in the mail.

Tom: Jerry! Haven't seen you in ages! How's business?
Jerry: Couldn't be better, Tom, I'm looking at piles of money!
Tom: Really? What's your line?
Jerry: I'm a bank teller.

Harry: You really should hire Joe to represent you in this lawsuit.
Mary: Joe! Why, he graduated at the bottom of his law school class! I don't think he's ever won a case.
Harry: True, but he'll lose for you cheaper than anyone else in town.

Boss: You've got a lot of nerve asking for a raise. You never do any work.
Employee: Look at it this way. When I go on vacation, there's no extra burden on the others.

Ike: How's the job?
Mike: I had to quit due to illness and fatigue.
Ike: Oh. The boss was sick and tired of you, eh?

Restaurant manager: As a waiter, you're a flop. You've already broken more dishes than your week's salary. What am I going to do with you?
Waiter: I guess you'll have to give me a raise.

Chuck: How's your new job as a night watchman?
Pat: I'm really good at it. The slightest noise wakes me up.

Nicola: The Glamourland Salon is advertising a wash, cut, and blow-dry for only ten dollars.
Hugh: I've got a better deal than that at my salon. I offer a wash, cut, streak, perm, set, comb-out, and manicure for only ten dollars.
Nicola: You must lose a lot of money.
Hugh: Oh, no. I haven't had any customers yet.

Diner: Ask the chef if he has pigs' feet.
Waiter: Not me. I need this job.

Reporter: Sir, you've won the biggest lottery prize in history—one hundred million dollars! How do you think this will change your life?
Dishwasher: Well, first thing, I'll have a chauffeur drive me to work.

Employer: You're new here, I see. What's your name?
New hire: John Lewis.
Employer: You should say 'sir' when you speak to me.
New hire: Okay. Sir John Lewis.

Ted: Are you busy?
Julie: Am I busy! If anything bad happens today, I won't get to worry about it for at least two weeks!

Suzi: Working at this company is a real rat race.
Sally: What can we do about it?
Suzi: Well, first we're going to strike for more cheese.

Bob: What do you mean, business is lousy?
Bing: Let's just say we're doing about as well as a hat-check concession at a nudist colony.

In an elevator
One of those passengers: I guess your job has its ups and downs, heh, heh.
Elevator operator: I don't mind the ups and downs. It's the jerks I can't stand.

Huey: So, you're a night watchman. What do you watch?
Dewey: I don't know. It's so dark I can't see a thing.

George had been a waiter all his life. After he died, his wife returned to his restaurant with a psychic to try contacting him in the spirit world. The psychic went into a trance and soon the wife thought she could sense her husband's presence.

"George, George, is that you?" asked his wife.

"Yes, it's me," said a faint voice.

"Come closer, George, I can hardly hear you," she said.

"Sorry," came the reply, "that's not my table."

Benny: Remember our old pal Jack? Man, is he rolling in dough!
Lenny: What's his business?
Benny: He's a baker.

Customer: I'd like three dozen of those lovely anemones.
Florist: I'm sorry, we only have a dozen left. Won't you consider these unusually lush ferns that just arrived today? They'll make a spectacular arrangement.
Customer: They certainly will—I'll take them. With fronds like these, who needs anemones?

What part of their job do carpet installers hate the most?
Tacks time.

David: Do you like going to work?
Paul: Yes. And I like going home, too. It's the stuff in between that I hate.

Lou: We'll have to fire George, that new accounting clerk.
Bud: George? Not George! Why, he knows the job backwards!
Lou: Exactly!

Chairman: George, will you open this meeting with a reading of the minutes from the last meeting?
George: Certainly. First, the chairman spoke for 2 minutes; then Hank here spoke for 1 minute; after that, Judy spoke for 45 seconds ...

Elliott: Norm! Haven't seen you since high school! I suppose you're a big success today?
Norm: Am I ever! Why, I've got hundreds of people under me.
Elliott: Factory owner, eh?
Norm: Nope. Cemetery guard!

Customer: Do you honor any credit cards?
Clerk: Oh, we honor them all, but we only take cash!

Boss: I'm telling you for the last time—answer the phone when it rings!
Secretary: Why? It's almost always for you!

It was Sunday, when the brain surgeon discovered a huge leak in his basement pipe. He rushed upstairs and called the plumber.

"Triple-A Plumbing? This is an emergency! Get over here quick!"

"Okay, but I charge extra for Sunday emergency service," replied the plumber.

"Anything! Just stop this leak!"

The plumber arrived, took out a tiny wrench from his bag, and lightly tapped the pipe. The leak stopped. The plumber handed the relieved homeowner a bill for $500.

"What?" screamed the surgeon. "That's unbelievable! Why, I'm a brain surgeon and I don't make $500 for 5 minutes' work!"

"I know," agreed the plumber. "Neither did I when I was a brain surgeon!"

Bookstore clerk: May I help you?
Customer: I'm just browsing.
Bookstore clerk: Well, high browse is to the left; low browse is to the right.

Employment counselor: Any other job experience?
Job seeker: I used to be a security guard at a nudist colony, but I couldn't stand pinning on the badge!

Lou: I've had it with these useless, lazy temps! Call the agency and tell them to send me a man who can get his work done by Friday! Understand?
Bud: Sure. I'll just ask them to send over Robinson Crusoe!

Fern: I heard you're working as a maid over at the Johnson's.
Ivy: No, I had to quit. They were treating me like one of the family!

Boss: You're fired!
Employee: How can you fire me? I thought I was like a son to you!
Boss: That's right: lazy, insolent, and disrespectful!

Blanche: How's that brother of yours?
Nora: He's climbing the ladder of success.
Blanche: How nice. I suppose he's on Wall Street, or in advertising...
Nora: No, actually, he's a house painter!

Customer: Do you have any books on cloning?
Bookstore clerk: Try aisle four, "Duet Yourself."

How is a sailor like a sleazy merchant?
They both know how to rig a sale.

Bud: Whatever happened to that bald barber?
Lou: He departed.

Employee: Sir, I just heard that Jones, the supervisor over at Plant 22, died yesterday. I'd like you to consider letting me take his place.
Boss: Well, it's okay with me if it's okay with the undertaker!

Harry: I hear you got a regular 9-to-5 job at the racetrack! How is it?
Nathan: Oh, the job's lousy, but I like the odds!

Boss: If Mr. Brown comes into the office today, tell him I'm out.
Secretary: Yes, sir, anything else?
Boss: Yes. And don't look too busy when he shows up or he'll know you're lying.

Minnie: How was your day at work, dear?
Mickey: Just great! My boss told me I should try to see the big picture, so I spent the afternoon at the movies!

Boss: You've got to find a way to make fewer mistakes on the job.
Worker: Okay. How about if I come in later in the morning?

Mutt: I've hired a carpenter who hammers like lightning.
Jeff: He's that fast?
Mutt: No, he never hits the same spot twice!

Lou: Whatever happened to that bowlegged cowboy we knew?
Bud: He lost his job. Seems he couldn't keep his calves together.

Boss: You're always late!
Employee: I resent that! I get to work on time almost every day!
Boss: Sure ... almost on Monday, almost on Tuesday, almost on Wednesday ...

Business executive: The heat has been off in the communications department all day.
Secretary: Oh no. Guess we'll have to face the cold fax.

Jake: Look at that airplane pilot. Why is he grinning like that?
Anne: He's trying to accumulate frequent flyer smiles.

Employer: Would you like to work for me as an elevator operator?
Man: I may take you up on that offer.

Chester: I used to be a radio show host but now I wash plates for a living.
Lester: So, now you're a dish jockey.

Mr. Jones: What do you do for a living?
Mr. Smith: I investigate haunted houses for traces of ghosts.
Mr. Jones: I guess that makes you a boo-collar worker.

Ann: Let's have a group meeting on Friday.
Dan: Okay. I'll bring a table.
Fran: I'll bring a lamp.
Ann: That's great. Now who'll chair our committee?

Mary: I watch the stars for a living.
Larry: Are you an astronomer?
Mary: No. I'm a Hollywood gossip columnist.

What do you get if you cross a native of Maine with a cartoonist?
A Yankee Doodler.

Commercial pilot: I'm not sure I can fly a plane as well as I used to.
Psychologist: Try taking off a few days.

Mr. Chan: Do you like making Asian cooking pots?
Mr. Lee: Yes. And I take pride in my wok.

Ed: How did you get a job at the clock factory?
Ted: I told the boss I was an expert at making faces.

Don: I have a high paying job.
Ron: Are you a C.E.O.?
Don: No. I wash windows on skyscrapers.

Mr. Black: How's the carpet business?
Mr. Brown: Rugged.

Mr. Green: Why is that chimney sweep so happy?
Mr. White: It's flue season.

Young editor: I've read every great novel that's ever been written.
Publisher: Humph! Another story-eyed youth.

Reporter: Did your rubber ball factory go bankrupt?
Businessman: Yes, but I'll bounce back.

Boss: Jake, why aren't you working?
Jake: Gee, I didn't see you coming!

What game do retailers like to play?
Price tag.

Boss: You're requesting a high salary for someone with no experience in this field.
Applicant: Yes, but the job's so much harder when you don't know anything about it.

Consultant: According to these figures, you're losing a dime every time you sell something! How've you managed to stay in business this long?
Manufacturer: Well, it wasn't so bad when we started, but since we became a success, it's been murder!

Census taker: And how many people work in your factory, sir?
Factory owner: I'd say about one out of ten.

Boss: So, you'd like a job with our company. What can you do?
Applicant: Nothing.
Boss: I'm sorry, we have no executive-level openings right now.

Morris: Hey, I just saved our company five thousand dollars a year!
Doris: How?
Morris: I asked for a raise and the boss said no!

What did the beautician say to her client?
"I'll see you pretty soon!"

Mark: Man, you're sure hard at work.
Clark: Nah, I'm just fooling the boss. I'm carrying the same cartons in and out all day!

Barnum: George, the Human Cannonball, just resigned. How can we replace him in the grand finale?
Bailey: I don't know. It'll be hard to find another man of his caliber.

Customer: This lumber has holes in it!
Hardware clerk: Those are knot holes.
Customer: Look, buddy, if those are not holes, what are they?

Boss: Smedley, I'm told you went to a baseball game yesterday instead of coming to work!
Smedley: That's a lie, and here's the fish to prove it.

The foreman laughed when a tiny old man in a plaid shirt applied for a job as a lumberjack.

"So, you think you can be a lumberjack? What's your experience?" asked the foreman.

"I've felled a million trees, single-handed," said the lumberjack. "Ever hear of the Sahara Forest?"

"You mean the Sahara Desert," corrected the foreman.

"Sure...now!

Cheryl: It takes me an hour to get to work in the morning.
Beryl: Before or after you arrive?

Annie: Can you lend me ten dollars till payday?
Suzie: I'm not sure. When's payday?
Annie: How should I know? You're the one with a job!

Boss: This is a business office, not a rec room! Every time I come in here you girls are playing cards. Can't you think of something else to do?
Clerk: Well, there's always checkers.

Boss: The first thing you should know about the job is that it pays $50 a week.
Job applicant: Why, that's an insult!
Boss: But we only pay every two weeks, so you're not insulted as often.

Fran: I used to work at a chairmaking factory that paid low wages, but we forced them to raise our pay.
Anne: How did you do that?
Fran: We staged a sit-down strike.

Brad: Boss, the computer's down again.
Boss: What now!!
Brad: Someone dropped a rubber band into it and it's been making snap decisions.

Jewelry shop owner: How's business this morning?
Salesman: You won't believe this, sir, but I've sold five diamond tiaras already this morning!
Jewelry shop owner: Looks like a real tiara boom today!

Boss: I thought I told you to mail out those circulars.
Worker: I wanted to, but we were all out of round envelopes.

Show me a farmer who raises sheep for their wool…and I'll show you a shear cropper.

Boss: Did your supervisor tell you what to do?
New employee: Yes, sir, he told me to wake him up if I saw you coming.

Ed: Is being a fashion photographer easy?
Jed: It's a snap.

Boss: An hour late again! What's your excuse this time?
Barney: I was sideswiped by a crosstown bus!
Boss: And I suppose you're going to tell me that took an hour?

Hal: The boss made an anonymous donation to our charity.
Cal: What do you mean?
Hal: He gave me a check, but he didn't sign it.

Ted: I work the midnight shift as a short-order cook.
Ed: That sounds like a fry-by-night occupation.

Boss: Why did you pay this creditor twice?
Employee: You told me to double check the bill.

Jack: Mister, the dog you sold me was previously owned.
Cliff: What did you expect, lady, I'm a used cur dealer.

Hardware store owner: My ax sharpener just quit.
Customer: Why? Low pay?
Hardware store owner: No. His job was getting to be too much of a grind.

Bill: How's your job at the glove factory?
Will: Busy...the workload is a handful.

What do you get if you cross teamsters with morning mist?
Union Dews.

Customer: Can I pick out a watch?
Salesman: Sure. Just take your time.

Al: What do you do for a living?
Sal: I'm a peddler.
Al: What do you sell?
Sal: Nothing. I race bicycles.

Jill: What do you do for a living?
James: I press pants.
Jill: Do you ever worry about job security?
James: Nope. I have a lot of irons in the fire.

Rick: I sell pillows for a living.
Nick: Now that sounds like a soft job.

Manager: If you want to sell men's clothing you have to start at the bottom.
Job applicant: Okay, I'll work in the socks department.

Employee No. 1: Ouch!
Employee No. 2: What happened?
Employee No. 1: The edge of my check sliced my finger.
Employee No. 2: Now that's a real pay cut.

Zack: How do I apply for a job as a miner?
Mack: Send the owners of the mine a quarry letter.

Gal: What do you do for a living?
Guy: I remove address labels from envelopes.
Gal: Oh, you're a mail stripper.

A young businessman had just started his own firm. He rented a beautiful office and had it furnished with antiques. Sitting there, he saw a man come into the outer office.

Wishing to appear busy, the businessman picked up the phone and started to pretend he had a big deal working. He threw huge figures around and made giant commitments. Finally he hung up and asked the visitor, "Can I help you?"

The man said, "Sure. I've come to install the phone!"

Joe: I used to be a magician. Now I'm a professional fisherman.
Moe: Can you do any reel magic?
Which Swiss hero works in a bank?
William Teller.

Chester: I spend all of my hours at work drinking on the job.
Lester: And you haven't been fired?
Chester: Why should I get fired? I'm one of the best wine tasters in America.

Madge: Will you still be reading palms for a living in the new millennium?
Flora: Nah! There's no future in that line of work.

Sal: How did the job interview go?
Hal: The interviewer told me that they had an opening for a person of my ability.
Sal: Well, that's good.
Hal: Not really. She was referring to the exit door.

CEO: Where can I find the most enthusiastic workers in this furniture factory?
Manager: In our chairing section.

How's your job at the riding academy?
  "I'm saddled with a lot of responsibility."
  "I never have a free run."
  "People ride me at work."
  "The bucks aren't that good."
  "I never get to horse around."

Employee: I want to be a mattress maker. What do I have to do?
Employer: First you have to go for spring training.

Joe: I have a new job working for a pillow company. It lasts until the millennium begins.
Moe: What do you do?
Joe: I check the number of feathers stuffed into each pillow.
Moe: Oh! So you'll be counting down until the year 2000.

Worker on payday: I don't know why the company calls this a week's wages.
Paymaster: What do you mean?
Worker on payday: It only takes one day to spend it.

Guest: I'm a movie stuntman. I do dangerous tricks and take risky falls.
Host: That's cool. How'd you get your first break in show business?

Dora: What do you do for a living?
Flora: I'm a commercial pilot.
Dora: How did you land a job like that?
Flora: It was love at first flight.

"If you buy a built-in swimming pool from me," said the salesman, "I'll throw in a gas grill for free."

"Forget it," snapped the angry customer. "Everyone knows you can't use a gas grill underwater."

Customer: When's the best time to trim a beard?
Barber: Daylight shaving time.

Chief: Are you still instructing classes at the Firemen's Academy?
Man: No. After 40 years, I'm burned out.

Boss: Wake up, Simpson! If you want to snooze, why don't you leave work and go home?
Simpson: Oh no, sir. I can't get paid to sleep there.

Mr. Smith: I just opened my own tailor shop. Can I entice you to be one of my regular customers?
Mr. Jones: No, thank you. My old tailor suits me fine.

Show me a coal miner who wears a flashlight on his helmet, and I'll show you a guy whose work makes him light-headed.

Restaurant employee: Boss, when am I going to get a promotion to cashier?
Restaurant owner: Soon, but right now I'll have to keep you waiting.

Mel: I don't take good photographs because I can't concentrate on my subjects.
Nell: If you want to be a successful photographer, you've got to learn to focus.

News Flash!
Coal diggers around the world are demanding profit-sharing plans. They want to mine their own business.

Rich: Why do you work so hard?
Mitch: I'm too nervous to steal.

Boss: Why is everybody working so slowly today?
Employee: We're just following your orders.
Boss: What? I never said that!
Employee: Then who put up the "Conserve Energy" sign?

A store manager overheard one of his salesmen talking to a customer. "No sir," said the salesman, "we haven't had any for a while and it doesn't look like we'll be getting any soon."

The manager gasped and shouted after the departing customer, "Come back soon. We'll have whatever you want in a week or so." Then the manager turned to the salesman. "Never ever say we're out of anything to a customer," he said. "Tell them we'll have it in stock soon. Now what did that man want?"

"Rain," answered the salesman.

First lumberjack: So how's business?
Second lumberjack: Come see, come saw.

Lou: I used to work as a parking lot attendant. Then I got a job in a nightclub checkroom, but I had to quit.
Al: Why?
Lou: I was denting too many overcoats.

The shopper had looked at almost every suitcase in the store. Finally, she said, "Actually, I'm not buying one. I'm just looking for a friend."

"Very good, madam," replied the clerk.

"Would you like me to open up the last few to see if he's in one of them?"

Ditch digger: Hey, foreman! I don't have a shovel!

Foreman: We ran out of shovels, but what are you complaining about? You're getting paid anyway.

Ditch digger: Yeah, but all the other men have something to lean on!

Cabbie: Where to, Mac?

Businessman: Downtown: Bankruptcy Court.

Cabbie: You too, huh? lots of businesses going under—too bad.

Businessman: Yes, isn't it...well, here we are. You might as well come in with me.

Cabbie: Me? Why?

Businessman: Now you're one of my creditors!

Gloria: I'm going to have to let that new secretary go.

Betty: Oh, come on. He may be a little slow...

Gloria: A little! He's a month behind in his work, and he's only been here two weeks!

Employer: Your resume says you've worked about 45 years, but you say you're only 38 years old! How do you explain that?
Employee: Overtime!

Janice: Poor Henry has no sense of humor! The boss was telling jokes at lunch today, and everyone was laughing and laughing! Poor Henry just sat there—he didn't laugh once!
Jarvis: He doesn't have to laugh—he's quitting tomorrow!

Sally: So, you're in publishing. That's one of those glamor industries, isn't it?
Suzy: Oh, yes. You have to know what wine goes with Excedrin!

Why couldn't the shoemaker fix the torn shoe?
He didn't want to add insole to injury.

Lou: What happened to that electrician who stuck his finger in the live outlet?
Bud: He was delighted.

Worker: I'd like a raise.

Employer: Friend, in the monetary gridlock of this recession, it would be fiscally imprudent to escalate the underlying overhead of the productive infrastructure before maximizing the outflow contribution to the distribution network.

Worker: Huh? I don't get it.

Employer: Exactly!

A man and a woman were getting to know each other at a Hollywood party.

"Are you in the business?" asked the woman.

"Yes," replied the man. "I'm a stunt coordinator. You know, driving cars off bridges, jumping from cliffs, falling out of airplanes...things like that."

"Wow!" she responded. "How do you manage to stay alive?"

"I wait tables in Santa Monica," he answered.

Executive: My employees don't respect me.

Wife: You must be mistaken, dear.

Executive: No, I'm not. When I came to work this morning one of the secretaries said "Shhh. Here comes the B-O-S-S!"

Jenny: Whew! Your boss is certainly unpleasant!

Penny: Yes, but around here we like to think of him as the crank that makes the wheels turn.

Office manager: So, you'd like a clerical job here. Can you tell me about any skills you have?

Applicant: Well, I've won a lot of contests for writing slogans, solving puzzles, finding the hidden pictures...things like that.

Office manager: That's very interesting, but I was thinking more of skills that you'd use at the office.

Applicant: Oh, this was at the office!

Customer: What do you mean, you won't ship my order? I paid my last bill in three days!

Supplier: Yeah—Christmas, Easter, and the Fourth of July!

The beleaguered bank president had some good news and some bad news for the board members.

"Gentlemen," he began, "If this meeting had been held a week
ago, I would've had to report that our bank was teetering on the brink of the precipice. Today, however, I can say that we've taken a step forward!"

George: I think I've found just the person to fill the managerial slot.

Henry: Does he have a track record?

George: Well, he once started a profitable flea circus from scratch!

How is an undertaker like a bottle of Robitussin?
They both take away the coffin.

Boss: Have you ever worked before as a chef?
Chef: Oh, yes. I was at the CIA commissary in Langley for a few months, but it didn't work out.
Boss: Why not?
Chef: I kept spilling the beans!

Stan: I hear there's a new big gun in the executive suite.
Fran: And I bet he'll be doing a lot of firing!

A woman was shopping for fresh vegetables at a roadside stand. She picked up some ripe tomatoes and asked the price.

"Ninety-nine cents a pound," answered the owner.

"What? The stand down the road only charges seventy-nine cents a pound!" she exclaimed.

"Then why don't you shop there?"

"They don't have any."

"Well, when I don't have any I charge seventy-nine cents, too!"

Feeny: Do you ever worry your boss will replace you with a computer?
Sweeney: Nah. Where's he going to find a computer that grovels?

Customer: Hey, last week the clerk double-charged me over at that counter.
Clerk: Sorry, I can't help you.
Customer: Why not?
Clerk: Because now we're a discounter!

Interviewer: I see on your resume that you're a member of four different municipal unions! You must pay a lot of money in dues.
Applicant: Yes, but this way I'm usually out on strike!

Sam: Did you hear that Joe Smith died?
Janet: Didn't he own the movie theater?
Sam: Yes; the funeral's at 2, 4:30, 7, and 10.

Dave: I was out at lunchtime and heard something terrible!
Liz: What?
Dave: An editor over at the *Newsweek* building dropped twenty stories!
Liz: How horrible!
Dave: I'll say! Right into the wastebasket…and they were mine!

Cliff: Doing business with the Russians is really tough!
Rocky: What's so tough? You ship them the goods, they pay the invoice…
Cliff: Pay? All I ever hear is "NYET 30 days!"

Boss: You're recommending Jack for a raise? I can't believe it—he's the laziest worker on the line!
Foreman: Yes, but his snoring keeps the other workers awake!

Bartender: Boy, business is the lousiest. We might as well stop serving liquor and open a brothel!
Manager: That's ridiculous! If we can't get people in here to drink beer, they're certainly not going to come in for broth!

Reporter: To what do you attribute the phenomenal success of the Boerum Bakery Company?
Company president: Just basic business principles, young man: rising profits and shrinking turnovers.

Barbara: How was your first day as a supervisor, dear?
George: Honey, you wouldn't believe it! At 3 o'clock my men came to me and said they wanted to knock off early and go bowling!
Barbara: Goodness! What did you do?
George: I broke 200!

Boss: Well, well, well! Just what I like to see in my company, a bright young man ready for a challenging position. And you say you've just gotten out of Yale, my alma mater! Now, what was your name again?
Trainee: Yones.

Ethel: Listen, if you're too shy to tell the boss you're getting married, how are you going to get time off after the wedding?

Lucy: Oh, that's not hard. I'll just say my husband is going on his honeymoon, and I'd like to go with him!

Boss: You're quitting, after only four months on the job? For what reason?

Secretary: My reason will soon become apparent...and so will I!

Linda: I haven't seen you in the office lately.

Bob: I was out for the whole week.

Linda: Were you ill?

Bob: No, I stepped into an elevator at the World Trade Center right after a kid pushed all the buttons!

Customer: Look at this mangled package! Didn't you see that I wrote on the label, "Photographs—Do Not Bend"?

Postal clerk: Didn't you see that we wrote back, "They sure do!"

John: Our feather company's mascot used to be a goose. Now it's a duck.

Lon: It sounds to me like you're downsizing.

Al: This year's been a disaster for business! September was the slowest on record! October, I almost went into Chapter 11! November was even worse!

Sam: You think you've got trouble—my wife's divorcing me, my children are suing me, my club has ousted me...what could be worse than that?

Al: December!

Reporter: You look depressed. Do you want to talk about it?

Gossip columnist: That's the problem. There's nothing to tell.

Rental agent: This is a luxury apartment. From the bedroom you can see the sun rise.

Prospect: Yes, and from the living room I can see the kitchen sink.

Railyard boss: So, you want to be a switchman. Okay, what would you do if you saw two trains coming at each other at fifty miles an hour?

Henry: Why, I'd wave the flag at them.

Boss: And suppose they couldn't see the flag?

Henry: Then I'd flash the red light at them.

Boss: But what if they ignored the light?

Henry: Then I'd call my friend George.

Boss: Your friend George? Why?

Henry: I'd say, "Hurry down here, George, to see the biggest train wreck ever!"

A customer stormed into a jewelry shop and threw a watch down on the counter.

"You said this watch would last me a lifetime," he said angrily.

"Yes," replied the proprietor. "But you looked pretty sick the day you bought it!"

Salesman No. 1: That big ugly guy over there wants to buy some sod.
Salesman No. 2: Gee, he sure looks like a turf customer.

Efficiency expert: How many of your employees are approaching retirement?
Company president: Figure it out. None of them are going the other way.

Police Chief No. 1: Why are all these dry cleaning store owners gathered here?
Police Chief No. 2: They're holding a press conference.

Lester: Will you float me a business loan?
Chester: Can you guarantee me a quick return on my investment?
Lester: Sure. I'm opening a boomerang factory.

Job interviewer: Are you married, Ms. Dolan?
Applicant: No, but I'm engaged to a young man from Ireland.
Job interviewer: Oh really.
Applicant: No. O'Reilly.

A lady answered her front door to find a plumber standing there. "I'm here to fix the leaky pipe," he announced.

"I didn't call a plumber," said the lady.

"What?" huffed the plumber. "Aren't you Mrs. Snyder?"

"The Snyders moved out of this house a year ago," explained the lady.

"How do you like that," grunted the plumber. "They call
you up and tell you it's an emergency and then they move away!"

Moe: My boss is so lucky. Everything he touches turns to gold.
Joe: And you?
Moe: Everything I touch they make me put back!

Investor: I've heard the production of cars in Detroit is way down.
Broker: True, but they auto increase.

Millionaire: To make it big in business you've got to abide by two principles, honesty and wisdom.
Son: What do you mean, dad?
Millionaire: Always be honest in business. If you make a promise, keep your word even if you have to go bankrupt to do it.
Son: Okay, dad. Now what about wisdom?
Millionaire: Wisdom is simple to explain son. Never make any promises.

Company president: Do you know what the motto of our company is?
New employee: Yes, sir. It's Push!
Company president: Push! What gave you that idea?
New employee: I saw it printed on the front door when I came in.

Joe: I got mad at my boss and quit my job.
Moe: Why?
Joe: She said I stole $10.
Moe: Why didn't you make her prove it?
Joe: She did—that's what made me mad.

Boy: My father is a night watchman.
Girl: Does he work at a factory?
Boy: No. At an observatory.

How did you lose your job?
Comedy writer: "I got laughed out of the business."
Personal trainer: "I was handed my walking papers."
Lingerie saleslady: "I was given a pink slip."
Stop sign printer: "I was let GO."
Businessman No. 1: I bought stock in a company that makes three-piece suits.
Businessman No. 2: Me too. I have a small vested interest.

Customer: Remember me? I bought an electric razor from you last week.
Salesclerk: Certainly, sir: You chose the top-of-the-line model.
Customer: Yes, and am I angry! You gave me a lifetime guarantee and the darn thing's broken already! I hope you can explain yourself.
Salesclerk: Well, last week you weren't looking too good!

Personal clerk: What kind of work history do you have?
Applicant: I've been fired from every job I ever had.
Personnel clerk: There's not much positive about that.
Applicant: Hey! At least I'm not a quitter.

Salesman: Would you like to buy these speakers?
Customer: Are they a sound investment?

Employer: I'll pay you $8 an hour now and raise it to $10 an hour in three months. Now when would you like to start?
Employee: Three months from now.

What do you call the head of a corporation who makes a lot of business blunders?
A CEO-oh.

Employee: My job is fireproof.
Job applicant: What do you mean?
Employee: My father owns the company.

Employee: Boss, can I have Friday off? My wife insists that I paint the house.
Boss: Absolutely not. We're too busy. You'll have to paint your house some other time.
Employee: Oh thank you, thank you, boss. I knew I could depend on your help.

An angry motorist went back to a garage where he'd purchased an expensive battery for his car six months earlier. "Listen," the motorist grumbled to the owner of the garage, "when I bought that battery you said it would be the last battery my car will ever need. It died after only six months!"

"Sorry," apologized the garage owner. "I didn't think your car would last longer than that."

Tim: What do you do for a living?
Jim: I work with figures.
Tim: Accountant?
Jim: No. Fitness instructor.

MONEY

· ·

Nothing funny about it. (Except these jokes.)

I've got a terrific idea for saving money—I borrow a little every month and set it aside!

Financier: Young man, you've asked me for a dollar every morning for the last six months. Why don't you just hit me up for a hundred dollars and get it over with?
Panhandler: It seems imprudent to put all one's begs in one ask it.

I have some rich friends, but I don't hold it against them at all. The only time it gets to me is when they're summering in the country and I'm simmering in the city.

· ·

Charles: I'm selling my house.
Diane: Too far above town?
Charles: No, too far above my income.

What officer takes care of the Army's finances?
The Business Major.

Nancy: How much money do you make a year?
Jeff: Millions.
Nancy: Wow! What kind of job do you have?
Jeff: I'm a printer at the U.S. Mint.

Why was the yeti investor so mad?
The snow bank froze his assets.

Jeff: If we go out I'll buy you dinner on my gold card.
Lisa: Oh no. Another credit line.

Son: I just bought stock in a company that makes CD players.
Father: Now that's a sound investment.

How did the deceased millionaire reward Santa?
He put a Claus in his will.

Accountant: Why did you go bankrupt?
Fruit farmer: I kept making rotten business deals.

Frank: My uncle left money in the bank for his wife's old age.

Hank: Oh. I guess you could say he set up an auntie trust fund.

Who collects income taxes in Hades?
The Inferno Revenue Service.

Ed: Still own that party balloon company?
Ned: No. I couldn't keep up with the high cost of inflation.

Bank teller: That man is a self-made millionaire.
Loan officer: I'd say he's a guy who deserves a lot of credit.

Rudy: Does money really talk?
Judy: It does to me. Every time I go shopping my cash says: Good buy! Good buy!

Panhandler: How about a quarter, Mister?
Passerby: Don't you know panhandling's illegal here?
Panhandler: I'm not panhandling, I'm just practicing my hobby.
Passerby: Your hobby? What's that?
Panhandler: Coin collecting!

Ed: I heard your duck farm went bankrupt.
Ned: Yup. I had too many bills.

Teacher: Class, today we'll continue our study of national economics. Joey, can you tell me what follows after an investment?
Joey: An investigation!

Gina: They say you should wash your hands after handling money, because the bills are covered with germs.
Sophia: I'm not in any danger—even a germ couldn't live on the money I make!

Young upstart: You rich guys are all alike: born on Easy Street.
Mr. Moneybags: You're wrong, sonny—I was born without a penny to my name!
Young upstart: And what was the secret of your success?
Mr. Moneybags: I changed my name!

Barber: A haircut is ten dollars. A shave is five dollars.
Customer: Okay, shave my head!

Irate storekeeper: Sir, this unpaid bill is one year old! What have you got to say?
Deadbeat: Happy birthday?

Hank: How's business?
Frank: I'm working on my second million.
Hank: That's great!
Frank: Yeah…I had to give up on the first.

Lou: We'll have to fire the new accountant.
Bud: Why? He seems smart enough.
Lou: I don't know. He thinks Dun & Bradstreet is a downtown intersection!

Why is an empty coin purse always the same?
Because there's no change in it.

Nick: Now I know for sure that the economy's a mess.
Nora: Why?
Nick: That "Going Out of Business" store on the corner actually did!

Ted: I can't believe this. The check you wrote to the store came back!
Alice: Great! What'll we spend it on this time?

Why is a banker considered a good artist?
He knows how to draw interest.

Rickie: America's a land of untold wealth!
Dickie: Have you been peeking at my tax return?

Lucy: You just got a postcard from the Inflation Fighters.
Brucie: Oh yes, that organization I joined last month. Are they having a protest rally?
Lucy: No, they're raising the dues.

Rose: Where are you going on your vacation this year?
Violet: With prices the way they are, about all I can afford is to stay home and let my mind wander!

Diner: What's this "Recession Special" on the menu?
Waiter: Oh, that's just our "Businessman's Lunch," except you have to pay in advance!

Tim: Gosh, that Ted is really irresponsible. He's always broke.
Tom: Tried to borrow some money from you, eh?
Tim: No, I tried to borrow money from him!

Fern: Money can't buy happiness, you know.
Ivy: That's a relief! With prices what they are today, who could afford it?

Herbie: You may be 5 years old, but you are so dumb! You fall for that old "nickel or dime" routine from the grown-ups every time. When they offer you a choice, you always pick the nickel! Don't you know by now that the dime's worth more?
Harvey: Sure, I know. But if I started picking the dime, they'd stop offering!

Grandpa Al: I hid my retirement money in an old pot.
Grandpa Cal: It looks more like a pension pan to me.

Mr. Jones: I made a bet with the man who does our laundry and won a bundle.
Mr. Smith: I guess now you're not hard pressed for cash.

Neighbor: I heard your son went college to because he wants to be an author. Is he writing for money yet?
Father: Oh yes. Every other week he sends us a letter home asking for some.

Little boy: When I grow up I want to make millions and live in a mansion that has no bathtubs.
Teacher: Why do you want to live in a mansion with no bathtubs?
Little boy: I want to be filthy rich!

Mrs. Morgan: Were you nervous about asking your boss for an advance on your pay?
Mr. Morgan: No. I was calm and collected.

Rick: What university do all Internal Revenue agents graduate from?
Nick: I.O.U.

Trainer: I'll give you $50,000 for the thoroughbred you're riding.
Jockey: No thanks. It's not enough.
Trainer: I'll give you $100,000.
Jockey: Now you're talking horse cents.

A well-dressed man entered a fancy bar and ordered four very expensive drinks. The bartender served them all at the same time, and the man downed them in about a minute.

"Wow," said the bartender, "that sure was fast. Is everything okay?"

"If you had what I had," replied the man, "you'd drink them fast, too."

Leaning over, the sympathetic bartender asked, "And what is that?"

"Fifty cents," the man answered.

Ed: My insurance company paid me $2,000 because I fractured my arm and couldn't work for six months. Then they paid me $3,000 because I fractured my leg and couldn't walk for two months.

Fred: You always get all the lucky breaks.

Lawyer: How's your legal battle with the bank?
Chris: Not so good.
Lawyer: How will you keep them from repossessing your real-estate holdings?
Chris: I don't know. I keep losing ground.

Sally: Mom, can I have fifty cents for a man who's crying at the corner?
Mom: Why? What's he crying about?
Sally: "Ice cream, fifty cents!"

Customer: Hey, you gave me the wrong change!
Cashier: Sir, you stepped away from the counter. There's nothing I can do about it now.
Customer: Well, okay. Just thought you'd like to know you gave me five dollars too much.

Client: Listen, I need legal advice but I don't have much money. What's your minimum charge?
Lawyer: A hundred dollars for three questions.
Client: Gosh, don't you think that's pretty steep?
Lawyer: Not really. What's your last question?

Prince Charles is known to enjoy strolling through open-air markets, mingling with his subjects. One day he stopped at the stall of an old fish seller and asked the price of the mackerel.

"Fifty pounds each," replied the old woman.

"That's a lot of money. Are fish like these so hard to come by?" he asked.

"No," she said, "but princes are."

Upscale store owner: What a sweet child! Here's a treat just for you.
Upscale mother: What do you say to the nice lady?
Upscale tot: Charge it, please!

Harry: The economy's a wreck. If things keep getting worse we'll all be begging on the streets!
Larry: Yeah, but who from?

Office manager: What do you mean by charging me two hundred dollars to fix the copier! You were only here five minutes and all you did was kick it! I hope you can itemize your charges!
Repairman: Here's how I itemize it, lady: fifty bucks for kicking the copier; a hundred and fifty for knowing where to kick!

A man was walking down the street when he heard screams coming from an apartment window. A woman was calling for help—her little boy had swallowed a quarter! The man ran into the building and up the stairs to the apartment.

Grabbing the child by the ankles, he shook him up and down until the quarter fell out of his mouth and bounced on the floor.

"Thank goodness you were passing by!" cried the mother. "You must be from the ambulance squad."

"No, ma'am," he answered. "IRS."

Eb: Let's go to sleep, honey.
Flo: I think I'll stay up a bit longer. I'm reading a mystery.
Eb: Why, it looks like our tax return.
Flo: It is.

Customer: How much are these oranges?
Grocer: Two for a quarter.
Customer: How much is just one?
Grocer: Fifteen cents.
Customer: Then I'll take the other one.

Show me a guy who likes to buy old coins…and I'll show you a cash customer.

George: I can't even pay my bills! What've I got to be thankful
for?
Dan: You can be thankful you're not one of your creditors!

Two women were talking about their plans for the summer. "Your sister told me you can't afford to vacation in Paris," Anne said to Fran.

Fran shook her head. "You heard wrong," she told Anne. "That was last year. This year I can't afford to vacation in Rome."

George: Excuse me, sonny—can you direct me to the nearest bank?
Ronny: I'll tell you for five dollars.
George: Well, now…that's a lot of money, isn't it?
Ronny: Not for a bank director!

Claire: I never worry about money.
Beverly: Why not?
Claire: What's the sense in worrying about something I don't have.

Don: I plan to beat the inheritance tax.
Lon: How are you going to do that?
Don: I'm going to die broke.

News Flash!
People who have only liquid assets best watch out or all their investments might go right down the drain.

Mother: Why are you selling mud pies?
Little girl: I want to get filthy rich.

Jack: I earn extra money by piling up fallen leaves.
Jill: I bet you rake in the cash.

News Flash!
Invest in a dairy farm and you'll have lots of liquid assets.

Actor: My looks are my fortune.
Agent: Well, you're facing bankruptcy.

Farm agent: Why are you planting pennies in your field?
Farmer: My accountant told me I needed to raise a cash crop.

Will: They say you are what you eat.
Bill: Then let's order something rich.

Husband: Did you make a New Year's resolution for the year 2000, dear?
Wife: Yes. I promise starting the first of January I'll spend less money at the mall.
Husband: That's wonderful. Now, how would you like to spend New Year's Eve?
Wife: I want to go to the mall and shop like crazy until midnight.

Joe: A fool and his money are soon parted.
Moe: How did the fool get his money in the first place?

When a farmer noticed that his prize cow was missing from a field through which a railroad passed, he filed suit against the railroad company. A big-city lawyer was called in by the company and immediately tried to get the farmer to settle out of court. The farmer finally agreed to take half of what he was claiming to settle the case. After the farmer signed the release and took the check, the lawyer couldn't help but gloat a little over his success.

He said to the farmer, "I hate to tell you this, but I couldn't have won the case. I didn't have one witness."

The old farmer replied, "Well, I'll tell you, I was a little worried myself. That darn cow came home this morning!"

Boy: Hey, Grandpop! Why did you give me four quarters instead of a dollar bill?
Grandpop: Cause change is good for people.

Man: I'm a gentleman with a disposable income.
Woman: So why do you look so needy?
Man: My income has already been entirely disposed of.

Flo: My twenty-year-old cousin just married an eighty-year-old billionaire, and now he's deathly ill.
Joe: Maybe you should send her a get-will-quick card.

Clerk: Would you like to buy one of our new mountain bikes, sir?
Customer: I would, but the price is too steep.

A tax collector went to a tannery. "Why haven't you paid your taxes?" the collector asked the owner of the tannery.

"Business has been very bad," answered the tanner.

"Do you mind if I check around the place?" asked the tax man.

"Go ahead," invited the owner. "You'll see I have nothing to hide."

Bill: I heard a man jumped off the Brooklyn Bridge rather than pay his income tax.
Will: That must have been a debt-defying leap.

Mother: Where did you get that ten-dollar bill?
Boy: I found it.
Mother: Are you sure it was lost?
Boy: Absolutely. I saw a guy looking all over for it.

What kind of telephone does a nervous stock market investor carry?
A sell-phone.

Artist: I create statues for a living.
Art critic: How do you manage to make ends meet financially?
Artist: I just keep chipping away at the bills.

Madge: My brother finally figured out a way to save his money.
Mindy: Great. How?
Madge: He spends mine.

Joe: Boy, is my uncle rich.
Moe: How rich is he?
Joe: He's so rich he puts one of his suits away for the moths.

Did you hear the one about the company that produces ice cubes and ice cream?
All its assets are frozen.

Scientist: I can make a clone of anything.
Investor: Here's a hundred bucks. Double my money for me.

Blanche: My father made a million dollars selling glue and paste.
Herb: No wonder you're so stuck up.

Moe: I just crossed an automatic teller machine with a washing machine.
Joe: What did you get?
Moe: A money-laundering operation.

Daughter: Daddy, is it true that money talks?
Father: It's absolutely true.
Daughter: Well, can I have some to talk to me while you're at work so I won't get lonely.

Rick: Can you lend me five dollars?
Nick: Stop asking me for small loans all the time.
Rick: Okay. Can you lend me a thousand bucks instead?

Farmer Green: I need a cash advance before I bale my crop.
Banker: Go to a Hay-T.M. machine.

Which government agency collects taxes from snakes?
The I.R.Hiss.

School bully: How much money do you have?
Boy: I'm skunked.
School bully: What do you mean?
Boy: I don't have a cent and it stinks!

Two men meet on a train. They begin to talk about their occupations. "I'm in the investment business," says Mr. Brown. "My income is generated from stocks and bonds." "I'm a White House reporter," replies Mr. Green. "And my income is generated by capitol interest."

Wife: Let's go antiquing today. I'm feeling very Victorian.
Husband: Forget it: I'm feeling very baroque!

Travel agent: I've got one package tour for you that will fit your budget.
Client: Tell me about it.
Travel agent: Christmas in Alaska! Five nights and four nights!

Holly: I like your new coat! When did you buy it?
Heather: Within the next twelve months!

Why did the art collector keep his masterpieces in the vault?
To him it was Monet in the bank.

Wilma: Fred's so chintzy!
Betty: Why do you say that?
Wilma: Well, this summer I asked him for an air conditioner, and he brought home a videotape of *Psycho* instead! Said it would make my blood run cold just as well.

Earnest youth: Can you lead a good life in New York City on $5 a day?
Wise uncle: Boy, that's about all you can do!

Joe: In my experience, money talks.
Moe: In my experience, money doesn't: it just goes without saying.

Taxpayer: Are contraceptives tax-deductible?
Accountant: Only if you make an issue of it!

What did one raindrop say to the others?
Hey guys, let's get together and pool our resources.

Millionaire: Thanks for building me this elegant country estate.
Architect: Don't mansion it.

Did you hear the one about the freeloader who was so clean?
He was always sponging.

J. P. Morgan: I invested in a play called *The Cross Country Champion.*
N. Rockefeller: Is it doing well?
J. P. Morgan: Yes. It's expected to have a long run on Broadway.

Society dame (in a Rolls): Young man! Is this the way to go to Cold Spring Harbor?
Local yokel: Well, it sure beats walking!

Nelson: A leading economist is speaking at the Tuesday Rotary Club meeting. Want to go?
Franklin: Forget it. Why should I pay for some guy's meal and then hear him tell me there's no such thing as a free lunch?

GAMES & RECREATION

. . . .

Sporting humor

Salesman: Try this new toupee. You can swim, water ski, snorkel, or scuba dive with it on.
Bald customer: That's great! I can't do any of those things now.

Harry and Larry rented a rowboat for a day of fishing on the lake.
Harry: Boy, we're doing great! Let's mark this spot so we can come back here again.
Larry: I already did. See this "X" I drew on the bottom of the boat?
Harry: You idiot! What if we don't get this boat tomorrow?

. . . .

Did you hear about the Siamese twins at the golf club?
They wanted a tee for two.

Toddler: Mama, can we go to Belmont Park tomorrow?
Mother: Darling, whatever for?
Toddler: I heard on the radio they're having races for two-year olds!

Football coach: Now listen, son. What would you do if it were the fourth down with three seconds left to play?
Third-stringer: Slide over to the end of the bench where I can see better.

He was 26 over par by the eighth hole, had landed a fleet of golf balls in the water hazard, and dug himself into a trench fighting his way out of the rough, when the caddy coughed during a 12-inch putt. The duffer exploded.

"You've got to be the worst caddy in the world!" he screamed.

"I doubt it," replied the caddy. "That would be too much of a coincidence."

Janet: I can't see why you like professional sports so much.
Jeff: Look at it this way: Where else can I boo a bunch of millionaires to their faces?

Why are all tennis players crooks?
They're all racketeers.

Arnold: Guess what? Golfers aren't using golf clubs any longer.
Sam: They aren't? Why not?
Arnold: Because they're long enough now.

First fisherman: We haven't caught a thing and it's late. Let's go home.
Second fisherman: Oh, not yet. Let's let at least two more big ones get away before we give up.

Bridge player: I've never seen a hand played so terribly.
Partner: Really? How would you have played it?
Bridge player: Under an assumed name!

Reporter: Do your read all of your fan mail?
Pro athlete: I breeze through most of it.

Where does a train exercise?
On a jogging track.

Reporter: What position does that tough-looking pig play?
Football coach: He's a swinebacker.

Jackie: What do you call basketball nets in Hawaii?
Paul: Hula hoops.

Which TV sports program is less filling than most others?
Monday Lite Football.

Reporter: Why don't eggs make good quarterbacks?
Coach: When their protection breaks down they're too quick to scramble.

Reporter: That skinny player doesn't look strong enough to catch a football.
Coach: I know. He's my weak end.

What do quarterbacks like to eat at tailgate parties?
Hut-hut-hutdogs!

What video game is full of silly mistakes?
Blooper Mario Brothers.

Reporter: How's the football team this year?
Coach: Awful. Our players are so unfriendly they won't even talk to each other.
Reporter: Are they really that hostile?
Coach: Yep. We can't even make our ends meet.

Manager: What do you do with a naughty prizefighter?
Referee: Make him sit in a corner until he behaves.

How are baseball and pancakes alike?
They both depend on the batter.

Athlete: I'm going to write an article on jogging.
Editor: Fine. But don't use any run-on sentences.

Pitcher: What do I do if the Green Giant comes to the plate to bat?
Catcher: Throw a bean ball.

Salesman: Do you like this fishing gear, sir?
Fisherman: Yes. I think this is finally reel love.

What job did Dracula Junior have at the baseball stadium?
He was the bat boy for night games.

Why did the cook enter the poker game?
She wanted to win some pots.

What do wise golf clubs take when they go to a cocktail party?
A designated driver.

Spectator: Why does that guy look so mad every time he runs a marathon?
Coach: He's a cross-country runner.

Hal: We can't play golf now. It's pouring.
Cal: This is the perfect time to tee off. It's a driving rainstorm.

Jockey: My racehorse is named Flea Bag.
Bettor: Has he won many races?
Jockey: Nah! He keeps getting scratched.

Why did the baseball hurler take a job on a used car lot?
He wanted to develop a sales pitch.

Joe: When is fishing not a healthy way to relax?
Moe: When you're a worm.

Sports fan: Are baseball umpires good eaters?
Waitress: Yes. They always clean their plates.

Biff: I hear they're calling this new football team the "Cinderella team."
Jeff: Probably because they've got a pumpkin for a coach!

Show me the best rabbit wrestler in a tournament...and I'll show you a lot of hare pins.

Player: What's the first rule of practice on the tennis courts?
Coach: First come, first serve.

Which baseball team does George Stybrenner own?
The New Pork Yankees.

Lon: Did you hear about the Olympic swimmer who sank all of his money into a swimming pool company and went bankrupt?
Ron: No. What happened?
Lon: He got in way over his head.

Sal: Why do basketball players stay home so much during the season?
Al: They have to. Basketball players aren't allowed to travel.

Wife: Where are you going with your golf clubs?
Husband: To a tee party.

Why did Mr. Pig go into the gambling casino?
He wanted to play the slop machine.

Young goalie: But Coach, you've just got to pick me! Hockey is my whole world! I live hockey! I dream hockey! I eat hockey!
Coach: Yes, but you can't seem to play hockey!

Athlete: What's the best thing to drink during a marathon?
Coach: Running water.

Two lifelong New Yorkers took their first vacation in Southern California. On their first day they played golf. At the fourth tee, one turned to the other and said, "Boy, it's hot out here!"

"Well," replied his friend, "don't forget we're thousands of miles from the ocean!"

Dora: I won a bundle at the track on Slowpoke!
Nora: Slowpoke? Why, he came in last in the 6th!
Dora: Yes, but he was so slow he came in first in the 7th!

Reporter: Why is it so many of you Olympic long distance runners are from Kenya?
Runner: We have a truly unique training program.
Reporter: Cardiovascular? Smith-Ackerly?
Runner: No—Hungry Lion!

Ernie had just finished his first golf lesson, and his enthusiasm was boundless. His skill level was another matter. He teed up, gripped his driver, and fixed his eye on the ball. "I'm making this hole in two!" he shouted enthusiastically.

Ernie's mighty drive sent the ball a whopping four feet from the tee. Undaunted, he reached for an iron and strode out on the fairway: "And now for one hell of a putt!"

Which monks play in the National Hockey League?
The Philadelphia Friars.

Football player: Where am I on the depth chart, coach?
Coach: You're a sub.

Husband: I'm never playing golf with George again! Why, that cheat found his lost ball one foot away from the green!
Wife: Well, that could happen...
Husband: Not if I've got the ball in my pocket!

Why is it hard to drink soda pop at a double-header?
One team is bound to lose the opener.

Edna: Dear, you never play golf with George any more.
Frank: Would you play golf with a cheat who moves the ball and fools with the scorecard?
Edna: I should say not!
Frank: Well, neither will George.

A customer was explaining why he wanted to return the tennis racquet he'd purchased: "It's the racquet head—it just won't stay on."

"But this is our top-of-the-line, John McEnroe signature racquet," protested the clerk.

Replied the customer, "Just because his name is on it doesn't mean it has to keep flying off the handle!"

What's the difference between a chess player and a thief?
One watches pawns; the other pawns watches.

Bertie: I think these exercise classes are helping me lose weight!
Gertie: What makes you think so?
Bertie: I can touch my knees without bending the floor!

What do you call a hockey player who scored a lot and is under 18 years of age?
A goal minor.
First golfer: How's your game?
Second golfer: I shoot in the 70s. When it gets colder than that, I stop playing.

What did the Latin fishing rod say to the Latin fishing line?
Let's tangle!

Reporter: Why is that baseball player spinning around?
Coach: He's getting ready for the whirl series.

What did one football raindrop say to the other football rain-drops?
Hey guys! Let's puddle up!

Ben: Why did you try bungee jumping?
Len: I'm just a jerky guy.

Which bunny rabbit is the best professional basketball player in the world?
Michael "Hare" Jordan.

Zack: I took courses in how to fish and how to play blackjack.
Mack: That's an unusual combination.
Zack: Not really. Now I'm a reeler and a dealer.

What is the sports buzz in the Bronx?
New York Yankee Beesball.

Basketball player no. 1: We've been playing one-on-one for two hours and no one has scored. Shall we continue to play?
Basketball player no. 2: No. This game is pointless.

What did one bowling pin say to the other?
Do you have any spare change.

Al: I like the White Sox.
Hal: I like the Red Sox.
Mel: I like nylons. They get more runs.

Two gamblers were talking: "Last night I lost $200 playing cards," said one as he grinned from ear to ear.

"Well, you don't seem too upset about it," answered the other.

"I'm not," replied the first gambler. "I was playing solitaire."

Fan no. 1: Those two soccer players both hit the ball with their noggins.
Fan no. 2: Wow! A double header.
Amnesia victim: I think I used to be a long distance runner.
Psychologist: Enter a marathon. Maybe it'll jog your memory.

Why did the ocean liner sign up for an aerobics class?
It needed to get in shipshape.

Matt: Do you have to be a certain height to play for the school basketball team?
Pat: Nope. The coach doesn't care how tall you stand as long as your ears pop when you sit down.

Hunting guide: I've got some bad news, gents. We're lost.
Hunter: How can we be lost? You told us you were the best hunting guide in the state of Maine!
Hunting guide: Well, we're in Canada now.

Jimmy and Johnny were out bear hunting when they bumped into the object of their quest. Jimmy fired a shot, but the bear was only wounded and came after them at top speed. They fled, but Johnny stopped suddenly to get his running shoes out of his pack.

"What are you doing?" shouted Jimmy. "If you stop to put on those shoes, you'll never outrun that bear!"

"I don't have to outrun the bear," replied Johnny. "I just have to outrun you!"

Country squire: Wish you could join our fox hunt, old chap—I don't suppose you have a riding habit?
American: Sure, I've got a riding habit. My habit is to say "whoa!"

Mandy: You're a great shot! How do you manage to hit the bullseye all the time?
Randy: It's easy—I just try to avoid it.

Where do ferris wheels go in October?
To the whirl series.

Horace: George is a man you can trust.
Boris: Give me an example.
Horace: You can play dice with him over the phone.

Chris: Rollerblading isn't good exercise for me.
Terry: Why not?
Chris: I spend too much time resting on my backside.

Nick: I just saw a 7-foot chicken dribbling a basketball.
Rick: I'll bet that chicken plays in the Hen-B-A!

Coach: My pitcher has been on a hot winning streak.
Reporter: Gee, maybe he has baseball fever.

What do you call a person who makes up bad jokes as he jogs in a marathon?
A *cross-country punner.*

Mary Ellen: My husband is a couch potato during the football season.
Beth: Well, at least he roots for the home team.

Waiter: What will you have, sir?
Golfer: A club sandwich.

Friend: Why does your husband yell hut-hut before he goes ah-choo?
Wife: It's just football sneezin'.

Golfer No. 1: Look! That caddy isn't carrying anything.
Golfer No. 2: Quick! Let's club him!

Claire: Is it true that you're good at chess?
Mark: Check!

Why did the race horse go to a psychologist?
It had an unstable personality.

Matt: This canyon was discovered by football fans.
Pat: How do you know that?
Matt: They named it the Touchdown Pass.

Golf caddy: Get off the tee, kid.
Boy: But why, sir?
Golf caddy: You're not old enough to drive.

Father: Son, let me help you hit the ball.
Little leaguer: Dad, it's time for me to strike out on my own.

Judy: What do you do to keep in shape?
Jim: I go out in my canoe.
Judy: Oh! You do row impact aerobics!

Al: Did you hear about the baseball player who was having marital problems?
Sal: No. What happened?
Al: His wife threw him out at home.

What did one fishing lure say to the other?
Welcome to our cast.

Jed: Why do you always play golf with Ed. He's a sore loser.
Fred: Because I'd rather play with a sore loser than a good winner.

Crazy quote
Baseball player to TV cameraman: "I hope the camera captures my best slide."

Two men went bear hunting. While one stayed in the cabin, the other went out looking for bear. He soon found a huge one, shot at it, but only wounded it. The enraged bear charged toward him, and he started running for the cabin as fast as he could. He ran pretty fast, but the bear was just a little faster and gained on him with every step. Just as he reached the open cabin door, he tripped and fell flat. Too close behind to stop, the bear tripped over him and went rolling into the cabin. The man jumped up, closed the cabin door, and yelled to his friend inside, "You skin this one while I go and get another!"

Caddy: Sir, you've just aced the eighteenth hole.
Golfer: Wow! That's great!
Caddy: Not really. We're on the fourteenth hole.

Why did the football coach go to a hair salon?
He had too many split ends.

Fisherman: Hey, pal! You've been standing there watching me fish for three hours! Why don't you get a rod and reel and do some fishing yourself?
Onlooker: No, thanks. I don't have the patience for it.

Did you hear the one about the football game with the 0-0 score?
Never mind. It was pointless.

Duffer: I heard scary growling in that grove of trees on the golf course.
Golfer: Relax. It's just Tiger Woods.

New trade schools for blackjack dealers have just opened in Atlantic City, Las Vegas, and Reno. In order to enroll you have to be 21 or under.

Lady: Do you think I should take a chance on your miracle weight reduction program?
Trainer: Sure. What have you got to lose?
Lady: About thirty pounds.

Did you hear the one about the baseball umpire who became a bouncer at the local bar?
He was especially good at throwing people out.

Fisherman No. 1: Hey, did you catch anything?
Fisherman No. 2: Yeah, a whole lot of jellyfish.
Fisherman No. 1: Really? What flavors?

Trainer: Lift up that two hundred pound barbell.
Man: AAARGH! I can't. I don't have the strength.
Trainer: Why not? You lifted it easily enough last Saturday.
Man: I know. But today must be a weak day.

Mate: Do you think we'll catch enough fish to pay all of our bills on this fishing trip?
Captain: Cod willing.

Jordan: How is that new basketball camp you opened doing?
Rodman: Fine. Its reputation is growing by leaps and rebounds.

Did you hear the one about the marathoner who left his math homework at the starting line?
He thought he could run away from his problems!

Moe: I hear exercise kills germs.
Joe: That's silly. How do you get a germ to exercise?

A spaceship from Mars landed right in the middle of the Boston Marathon. An alien popped out of the UFO and shouted to a runner going by, "Take me to your leader."

Without slowing down, the runner replied, "I don't know who he is, but he's about two miles ahead of me."

Neighbor: How was your hunting trip?
Man: Terrible. That bird dog you said loves to hunt nearly ruined everything.
Neighbor: What? That's impossible.
Man: Oh, yeah? He knocked over my gun and blew a hole in the back of my pickup truck.
Neighbor: I said he loved to hunt. I didn't say he was a great shot.
Tim: My older brother was doing all right until everyone caught up with him.
Jim: Don't tell me your older brother is a crook.
Tim: No. He's a marathon runner.

Tina: I hired a handsome body builder to teach me how to lift weights.
Gina: Do you want to build up your muscles?
Tina: No, but I'm hoping a romance will develop.

John: I was about to land a giant fish when my line snapped.
Ron: Now that's reel disappointment.

Ann: How do you like being the golf pro at the country club?
Fran: The job suits me to a tee.

Jed and Zeke went to the theater to see a movie about horse racing. Jed said to Zeke: "I'll bet you ten bucks that the long shot, number eight, wins the big race." Zeke accepted the wager. The movie continued and number eight won the race. "I can't take your money," Jed said. "I saw this movie yesterday."

"That's okay," replied Zeke as he handed over the cash. "So did I, but I didn't think number eight could win two days in a row."

Sports reporter: What do you get if your receivers don't lift weights during Monday to Friday practices?
Football coach: Weak ends.

Mickey: Why are you wearing that silly hat to the ballpark?
Babe: I want to hit a few pitches into the stands.
Mickey: What's the hat got to do with round-trippers?
Babe: It's my homerun derby.

Uncle Pete: What position do you play on your Little League team?
Marty: Oh, I'm usually on the bench.
Uncle Pete: Oh, you're the designated sitter.

Why did the moron buy oversize playing cards?
He wanted to be a big deal!

Player: What's the first thing you have to know to manage in the Grapefruit League?
Coach: How to call a squeeze play.

Rick: I watched a prize fight last night and the champ really got clobbered.
Nick: Wow! I'll bet he was a sore loser.

What do golfers eat before they go out on the links?
A *fore-course meal.*

Rob: I bet on a horse named "Hangman" to win.
Bob: But that horse is a long shot.
Rob: I know, but maybe he'll win by a noose.

Husband: What did you think of my fish story about catching that trout?
Wife: It was reel interesting.

"The traps on this golf course are very annoying," said one golfer to another.

A third, who was trying to putt, looked up and added, "They certainly are. Now how about shutting yours!"

Yogi: Why did the rubberband go to the baseball stadium?
Casey: He wanted to enjoy the seventh inning stretch.

Joe: How come you know how to tie trout lures?

Moe: I'm a fly school graduate.

What do you call a chicken who skates for the Pittsburgh Penguins?
A hockey cluck.
Wife: Why do you always think about golf at bedtime?
Husband: It putts me to sleep.

A man was watching a fisherman at work. The fisherman caught a giant trout but threw it back into the river. Next the fisherman hooked a huge pike and threw it back. Finally the fisherman caught a little bass. He smiled and put the little bass in his bag.

"Hey!" yelled a guy who was watching. "Why did you throw back a giant trout and a huge pike and then keep a little bass?"

The fisherman yelled back, "Small frying pan."

Calm Ken: Why do you play golf instead of tennis?
Hothead Fred: I get more exercise playing golf.
Calm Ken: How is that possible?
Hothead Fred: There's more gear to break when I get mad.

Why do people who smoke cigars need lots of exercise?
Because they end up with big butts.

Bert: Boy, this ice fishing is a drag! I'm freezing, we haven't caught a thing all day, and those guys over there are hauling in one fish after another.
Ernie: Oh, sure, it's not hard to catch fish if you cheat! Look, they cut a hole in the ice!

Shorty: Gee, are you a basketball player?
Stretch: No—do you play miniature golf?

How are a skier and a wrestler alike?
They both love to go to Zermatt.

Fred: I'm going on a diet to improve my golf game.
Barney: How will losing weight help your game?
Fred: Because right now I can't see the ball if I put it where I can hit it, and I can't hit it if I put it where I can see it!

Cliff: Man, your face looks like a tomato! What happened to you?
Norm: It's a sports injury.
Cliff: Were you sacked in touch football?
Norm: No, I was reminded to pay my bookie.

Golfer: You're such a lousy caddy! When we get back to the clubhouse I'm going to see that you get fired.
Caddy: It's okay with me. By the time we get back to the clubhouse I'll be old enough to get a regular job!

Steve, a liquor salesman, encountered his friend Ed in a local bar at midday while making a sales call. He stopped to chat.

"I'm surprised to see you with a drink in your hand in the middle of the day. I hope you're celebrating." said Steve.

"In a way," answered Ed. "I put all my money on a sure thing at the track. It was the seventh horse in the seventh race, today is the seventh day of the seventh month as well as my son's seventh birthday, the horse's name was Septus, and the odds were seven to one."

"And the horse came in first!" exclaimed Steve.

"No, he came in seventh!" cried Ed.

Baseball manager: Kid, I'm taking you out.
Pitcher: You can't take me out now! Smith is up, and I've walked him twice and struck him out once!
Baseball manager: Yeah, but it's still the same inning!

Golf instructor: Okay, now let's just go through the motions without actually hitting the ball.
Student: But, that's been my problem all along!

Tom: Why am I so lucky at cards and so unlucky at the track?
Dick: Probably because they won't let you shuffle the horses!

Baseball coach: My god, Kirby, put some clothes on! You can't play center field stark naked!
Kirby: Center field? I thought you said centerfold!

Bud: I don't win at gambling because I'm lucky, I win because I'm smart!
Lou: Oh, yeah? Okay, if you can tell me how many quarters I have in my pocket, I'll give you both of them!

Airline clerk: Destination, sir?
Passenger: Well, this bag's going to Albany, the duffle is bound for Akron, and the set of golf clubs is heading for Altoona.
Airline clerk: Sir, we can't send your luggage to all those different places!
Passenger: Sure you can. You did it just last month when I flew to Atlanta.

Native: How was your trip to New York City?
Visitor: Terrible! We circled for hours!
Native: Yes, the airports are a problem...
Visitor: But we were in a car!

When can't sailors play cards?
When the captain is standing on the deck.
First fisherman: This lake any good for fish?
Second fisherman: Must be—I can't get any of them to come out!

Husband: Do you want to go to a lodge in Maine?
Wife: No.
Husband: How about a casino in Las Vegas?
Wife: No.
Husband: Then how about a beach hotel in Atlantic City?
Wife: Only as a last resort.

Barry: I heard the other kids at camp were going to push me out of the canoe and into the lake today.
Larry: How do you know?
Larry: I was tipped off.

Farmer: Say, you're a mighty brave guy to come down in a parachute in the middle of a hurricane.
Stranger: I didn't come down in a parachute! I went up in a tent!

Barnes took up skydiving as a hobby. On his first solo jump, he pulled the ripcord at the right time, but nothing happened; the parachute wouldn't open. He pulled the emergency chute, but it too was stuck. As he glanced down to see the ground rushing toward him, he noticed a man hurtling upward right at him.

"Hey!" Barnes yelled at the man, "Do you know anything about parachutes?"

"No!" the man called back. "Do you know anything about gas stoves?"

Madge: I went horseback riding today.
Flora: Oh? Sit down and tell me about it.
Madge: I can't.
Flora: You can't tell me about it?
Madge: No, I can't sit down.

A weary hiker stumbled upon another hiker deep in the North Woods. "Am I ever glad to see you," said the hiker. "I've been lost for three days."

"Don't be too relieved," answered the second hiker. "I've been lost for three weeks."

Hotel owner: Would you like to book a vacation at my island hotel?
Travel agent: Only as a last resort.

New Yorker: When you come to town, bring your camper.
Tourist: Why?
New Yorker: So you can have a place to eat and sleep while you look for a parking space.

Al: Why did you move to Hawaii?
Cal: So I could spend my vacations at home and still enjoy myself.

Recreation director: I'm jotting down some games we can use at our picnic.
Assistant director: Wow! You're a real play writer!

Fisherman: Where can I find the most fish?
Guide: Between the head and the tail.

In the middle of a chess tournament at a midtown hotel, the electricity failed and the contestants were forced to wait in the lobby while repairs were made. After some time had passed, the conversation among the players turned to past games. It seemed that each player had only triumphs and awesome feats of skill to his credit. The talk became louder and more raucous, until a passing guest stopped a bellman to ask what the commotion was about. "Oh, nothing much," replied the bellman. "Just chess nuts boasting in an open foyer."

MUSIC & THE PERFORMING ARTS

······································

Jokes in B-flat minor

At a symphony orchestra rehearsal
Concertmaster: Some conductor you are! You don't know your brass from your oboe!

What happens when you drop a piano into a coal mine?
You get A-flat minor.

At a recital
Music critic: This is the worst butchering of an aria I've ever endured.
Mrs. Critic: Now, have some sympathy. You know that this piece is extremely difficult.
Music critic: Difficult? I wish it were impossible!

······································

What did the Terminator say to Beethoven?
I'll be Bach!

Harry: Hey, Larry! Nice trumpet you've got there.
Larry: I borrowed it from my neighbor.
Harry: I didn't know you could play the trumpet.
Larry: I can't. And now, neither can my neighbor!

My friend's a real music lover. When he hears a soprano singing in the bath he rushes right over and puts his ear to the keyhole.

What song did the Beatles sing to the pig farmer?
I wanna hold your ham.

Bert: Why do you keep singing the same song over and over again?
Gert: The melody haunts me.
Bert: That's because you're murdering it.

What do you get if you cross MTV with flower beds?
Rock gardens.

First music critic: What do you think of the pianist's execution?
Second music critic: I'm in favor of it!

Which Beatles' song is about their favorite vegetable?
Peas Please Me.

Carole: Can you sing high-C?
Kim: No, I sing lou-sy.

How do you repair a broken tuba?
With a tuba glue.

Cave girl: Why are you hitting that boulder with a stick?
Cave boy: I want to hear some rock music.

What kind of dancing always leads to a riot?
Brawlroom dancing.

Conductor: Why is that stringed instrument smoking?
Musician: It has harp burn.

Why did MTV give Tutankhamen a music award?
He was the original king of wrap.

Mellie: Did you ever hear of Al Bee Jolson?
Kellie: No. Who was he?
Mellie: An insect who starred in the movie "The Jazz Stinger."

Did you know that Highland musicians who work in a Scottish band have a fife-day work week?

Jan: What is Elvis Monster's favorite hit song?
Fran: Love you too munch.

Why couldn't the turkey play in the rock band?
He forgot to bring his drumsticks.

Lisa: Those pop singers are sweet.
Bruce: They should be. They're candy rappers.

What's scary, wears cowboy boots, and loves country music?
The Phantom of the Grand Ole Opry.

Why did Diana Ross go to law school?
She wanted to work at the Supreme Court.

Mack: Those musicians seem to perspire a lot.
Zack: Maybe they're a sweat band.

What's tough and dances at Radio City Music Hall?
A Punk Rockette.

Boy: I'm going to New York City to continue with my trumpet lessons.
Girl: Sounds expensive. Where did you get the money?
Boy: The neighbors chipped in.

What did the CD player say to the bandleader?
Put me in, coach, I'm ready to play!

Freddie: I write great music, but I fail all my classes in school.
Eddie: Maybe you're just a song and dunce man.

Who is second in charge at the rock video channel?
The MTV P.

Rapper No. 1: What did the cool shark yell to the ocean marker?
Rapper No. 2: Yo! Home buoy!

What rock video channel does Dorothy watch in the Land of Oz?
Auntie Em TV

Customer: Where can I find an assortment of classical music?
Clerk: Go through the Bach door.

Show me a famous American western hero who travels with a rock band...and I'll show you Buffalo Bill Roadie.

Grace: I can't come to the concert with you.
Hope: Why not?

Grace: My mom says kids shouldn't be exposed to a lot of sax and violins!

What kind of music does MTV play on St. Patrick's Day?
Shamrock and roll.

Parent: What's the best thing to eat while watching rock videos on television?
Teenager: An MTV dinner.

What's woolly and plays really cool music?
A Dixie Lamb Band.

Fern: How's your singing career coming along?
Ivy: Great! I'm concentrating on songs of the South; my audience prefers them.
Fern: How do you know they prefer songs of the South?
Ivy: They're always putting cotton in their ears!

What do cool musicians use to stay dry?
Rock and roll-on deodorant.

Mary: My car radio only gets talk shows, no music.
Fred: It sounds like it needs a tune-up.

What was fat Elvis's favorite song?
Return to Slender.

Pat: I once sang the Star Spangled Banner nonstop for three hours.
Shannon: Big deal. I can sing Stars and Stripes Forever.

Which cat is a famous rock star?
Mewdonna.

Country agent: Your corn crop is fit as a fiddle.
Farmer: Thanks. That's music to my ears.

What is a herpetologist's favorite rock song?
Snake, Rattle, and Roll.

Fan no. 1: She's been singing the National Anthem for three hours straight.
Fan no. 2: I refuse to stand for this any longer.

What is the favorite music of Irish teenagers?
Sham-rock.

Highway policeman: You're driving a car and playing a saxophone at the same time! Do you know what a dangerous thing you're doing?
Driver: No, can you hum the tune?

Why couldn't Mozart find his teacher?
He was Haydn.

Lenny: I call this my millennium trumpet.
Jenny: What's it for?
Lenny: I'm going to blow it to celebrate the year toot thousand.

What do you call two bees, a hornet, and a wasp with violins?
A sting quartet.

Guard: Elvis is visiting the prison and he wants Chinese food for lunch. What should we do?
Warden: Quick! Somebody get the jailhouse wok!

Why did the trumpeter sign up for an algebra class?
He wanted to become a math tooter.

Pancho: My donkey sings to classical music.
Pedro: Really? What's the name of your donkey?
Pancho: Braytoven.

What kind of rock music do tough cows like?
Gangsteer Rap.

Parent: How's Janie coming along with her piano lessons?
Teacher: I've decided she should switch to the clarinet.
Parent: Why?
Teacher: Well, with a clarinet, she can't sing!

Who can cash checks while shooting an apple off of his son's head?
William Teller.

Betty: My son's majoring in music at college. He plays the tuba.
Hetty: Is he any good?
Betty: Good! Why, he's graduating Magna Cum Loud!

Fred: I come from a musical family.
Barney: I never knew that.
Fred: Oh, yes. Dad drummed his fingers, Auntie Mae blew her nose, and Grandpa fiddled with his beard!

What goes best with oyster butter?
Pearl Jam.

Katie: My neighbors are impossible! They must've had a fight last night—they were banging on the walls until three in the morning!
Tim: I guess it kept you awake.
Katie: No, I was up late anyway practicing my trombone!

What did the opera star say to the unexpected guest?
"If Aida known you were Carmen, I'd have made something to Nibeling!"

Passerby: Is that Bach you're playing?
Organ grinder: No, just a bit of handle.

Marty: I'm going to play a fisherman in a new movie about the ocean.
Artie: Is it a bit part?
Marty: Yeah. I only have one line.
Artie: Who cares! You still get to go to the cast party.

News Flash!
A local ballet school just merged with a parachute club. New students will be taught how to dance on air.

Box Office clerk: The orchestra seats are $50, the balcony seats $25, and the programs are $5.
Customer: Give me a program. I'll sit on it.

Musician: Which rock band do owls like the best?
Teenager: Whootie and the Blowfish!

What did the little chicks call their famous rock band?
The Red Hot Chili Peepers.

Heckler: Your jokes are stale. Don't you have any new material?
Comedian: No, I'm fresh out.

Agent: I have a new young comic with a machine-gun delivery. He fires joke after joke at the audience. Do you want to book him?

Club owner: No, thanks. I can't stand a performer who shoots his mouth off.

Critic No. 1: I had to leave the new play early. Did it have a happy ending?

Critic No. 2: I'll say! We were all glad when it was over.

Nick: Did you hear about the old lady who gave up knitting to take up trumpet playing?

Rick: You're darn tooting I did!

A cub reporter was sent to the circus to do a feature on the sideshow. When he knocked on the door of the midget's trailer, it opened to reveal an extremely tall man, well over six feet.

"Uh, I'm looking for Shorty O'Rourke, circus midget?" asked the reporter.

"I'm Shorty," the man answered.

"But...you're so...tall!" stammered the reporter.

"I know," replied Shorty. "It's my day off."

Club manager: Your last joke was so bad it put the audience to sleep. What do you plan to do about it?

Comedian: Copyright it and sell it as a cure for insomnia.

What's large, gray, and sings calypso?
Harry Elephante.

Producer: Didn't you write a play named Fireflies?
Writer: Yes. It got glowing reviews.

Author: I wrote a scene in my play where there's a big mob fight.
Critic: Oh. It's a riot act.

FAMILY FUN

....

Proving that all good humor starts at home

Horace is a model husband. Unfortunately, I married George.

Henry: Your husband seems lost in thought.
Alice: I wouldn't be surprised. He's a total stranger there.

Friend of the family: How's your mom? As pretty as ever?
Kid: Yeah. It just takes her a lot longer.

A woman encountered a friend walking down the street with her three grandchildren. She stopped to admire them.

"My, what beautiful grandchildren!" she said.

"That's nothing," replied the proud grandmother, "You should see the pictures!"

....

Jerry: I hear you named your sister's children.
Berry: Yes, I named the girl Denise.
Jerry: How about the boy?
Berry: Denephew.

Why can't a woman ask for help from her brother?
He can't be a brother and assist her, too.

Woman (on the phone): Doctor, come quick! Little Omar just swallowed my fountain pen!
Doctor: I'll be right there. What are you doing in the meantime?
Woman: I'm using a ballpoint.

Mrs. Higginbotham: I'm descended from a very long line...
Mrs. Jones: Yes, and your mother should never have listened to it!

Once there was a child who never spoke. His parents hired famous doctors to examine him, but none could find a reason for his silence. One day when he was eight years old he put down the glass of milk he'd been drinking and said quite clearly:

"This milk is sour."

"But, you can speak!" said his astounded parents. "Why haven't you ever spoken before?"

"Up until now," he said, "everything's been okay."

Census taker: Please list the names of all members of your household broken down by sex.
Householders: None, really—our family tends to have drinking problems.

Mother: Relax, Janie. Calm down, Janie. Take it easy, Janie.
Onlooker: You're a wonderful mother to keep your temper so well while little Janie is acting up.
Mother: Her name is Jennifer. I'm Janie.

Mindy: I'm worried about my son-in-law. He doesn't know how to drink and he doesn't know how to play cards.
Cindy: He sounds like a good man to me. Why are you worried?
Mindy: Because he does drink and he does play cards!

Little girl: Daddy, why is Mommy singing?
Daddy: So Baby will go to sleep.
Little girl: Will she stop singing when Baby is asleep?
Daddy: Yes, dear.
Little girl: Then why doesn't Baby just pretend to be asleep?

Junior: Mom, the new baby looks just like Rover.
Mom: Junior, don't say such things.
Junior: It's okay, Mom. Rover can't hear me.

~y, is Joe unlucky.

Ralph: You mean because he got divorced?

Ed: No, because he got custody of his wife's parents.

Tillie: My son's a big success today, and I'm responsible.

Millie: Why do you think so?

Tillie: He's so rich he can pay a psychiatrist $100 an hour just to listen to him, and guess who he talks about—ME!

Mom: You're not going to school with that lipstick on your mouth.

Daughter: But Mom, the teacher is giving me a makeup exam.

Morty: Did your son take his driving test today?

Shorty: Yes, and he did a bang-up job!

Mary: Work is the magic word around our house.

Ted: What do you mean?

Mary: When I say "work" my husband disappears.

Jack: My little brother stuck his head in our washing machine.

Jill: What happened to him?

Jack: He got brainwashed.

Husband: Being married to me gives my wife something to live for.
Wife: That's right. A divorce.

Boy mole: Did you go away with your parents this summer?
Girl mole: Yes.
Boy mole: Did you have fun?
Girl mole: No. It was a boring vacation.

Anne: All my husband does is watch TV
Lisa: Mine too, but now he gets more exercise.
Anne: How did you work that out?
Lisa: I hid the remote.

Why did Daddy Watch leave work early?
He wanted to spend some quality time with his offspring.

James: My wife spends all of her time at the mall.
Pat: My wife spends all of her time watching TV
James: Well, at least that doesn't cost money.
Pat: That's what you think. All she watches is the Home Shopping Channel!

Father: My teenage son took up jogging.
Uncle: That's good.
Father: No, it's bad. He keeps running away from home.

Nurse: Why are Mr. and Mrs. Number so happy?
Doctor: They're going to have a little one.

Wife: I hate it when you agree with everything I say. Will you please stop it!?
Husband: Yes, dear.

Lady: Why did you nickname your son Spud?
Father: He's a real couch potato.

Lady No. 1: I got married because I got tired of eating alone, watching TV by myself, and paying all the bills myself.
Lady No. 2: I got divorced for the same reason.

Neighbor: I hear you have a new baby at your house. Is it hard to take care of?
Big brother: Nah. You just keep one end full and the other end empty!

Mrs. Smith, mother of two, was observing her offspring playing in the backyard one wintry day. She called the oldest inside to speak to him.
"Johnny, I thought I told you to share your toys with your sister."
"I am sharing, Mom. She plays with the sled going up the hill, and I play with it going down."

Grown-up daughter: Mother, really! I'm absolutely shocked that at your age you bought yourself a see-through negligee!
Grown-up mother: Relax, dear. At his age, your father can't see through it anyway!

Father: Heather, you'll have to send your boyfriend home earlier from now on.
Heather: Sorry, Dad. Did the noise keep you awake?
Father: No, but the silences did!

Heather: How's your son doing at Agricultural College?
Holly: Great! He's so popular, the students voted him "Most likely to sack seed!"

Did you hear the one about the guy who moved to a penthouse? He wanted to make sure he kept a roof under his wife's feet.

Ernest: My wife says if I don't give up golf she'll divorce me.
Henry: That's dreadful!
Ernest: Yes, I'll miss her.

Rose: I can't get a baby-sitter who actually pays attention to the kids!
Violet: Oh, I solved that problem: I just put the baby on top of the TV!

Did you hear about the man on the flying trapeze? He caught his wife in the act!

Rose: When your daughter graduates college, what will she be?
Violet: At this rate, probably about 40!

Mother: Andrew, I'm tired of cleaning up your room. I've decided to charge you 10 cents every time I have to pick something up off the floor. So far, you owe me two dollars.
Andrew: Here it is, Mom, and keep up the good work!

Father: Junior, I've got to teach you the value of a dollar!
Son: You have, Dad; that's why I asked you to loan me 10!

Maisy: How's your son? He was such an unusual child.
Daisy: Henry's at Harvard.
Maisy: Really! What's he studying?
Daisy: Oh, he's not studying. They're studying him!

Father: When I was your age, I was too poor to eat lunch, and never had a holiday from my after-school job.
Son: Gee, Dad, I bet you're a lot happier now that you live with us!

Mother: I'm sorry, darling, we can't keep Rover in the house. Just think of the smell.
Junior: That's okay, Mom. Rover will get used to it.

Judge: Millie, I married you and your husband 15 years ago—now you have 10 children and you're here asking for a divorce! What possible grounds could you claim?
Millie: Compatibility, Your Honor!

June: Bad news, dear. The children are coming back early from visiting their grandparents.
Ward: But we sent them there to avoid the hurricane!
June: I know, but I just got a telegram from Dad. He says, "Returning kids. Send hurricane!"

Father: Joey, do you know about the facts of life?
Joey: I know about them, but I'm not sure if they're true!

Cliff: You're looking upset.
Rocky: My son took his driver's test yesterday. He stopped on a dime!
Cliff: Sounds like he passed with flying colors!
Rocky: Not exactly. The dime was in some pedestrian's pocket!

Dad: I think Junior's planning to become an astronaut.
Mom: What makes you think so?
Dad: He spends every day sitting in a chair staring into space!

Rose: My husband believes that marriage and a career don't mix.

Violet: Well, isn't that old-fashioned of him.

Rose: Yes, isn't it…when we got married, he stopped working!

Client: I hired you to follow my husband and his mistress, but this report isn't what I asked for at all!

Private investigator: Didn't you want me to find out where she sees him?

Client: No! I wanted you to find out what she sees in him!

Husband: Doc, you've got to examine my wife—I think her mind is finally gone!

Doctor: Why do you think so?

Husband: It must be—she's been giving me a piece of it every day for 20 years!

Rose: Even after all these years, Fran's still in love with her husband.

Violet: Why do you say that?

Rose: When he takes out the garbage, she goes with him!

Dad: Don't forget, Son, you have to set your alarm clock before you go to bed.

Son: It's okay, Dad I have my duck in my bedroom.

Dad: How will your duck take the place of an alarm clock?

Son: He'll wake me at the quack of dawn!

Fern: I just can't eat the way I used to without gaining weight.
Ivy: My husband eats like a horse and weighs just what he weighed 20 years ago—350 pounds!

Hester: It's too bad you and your wife divorced. You had such a long engagement.
Nestor: I try to put a positive spin on it—it shortened the marriage.

Joey: I've got a new baby sister at home.
Chloe: Is she nice?
Joey: No! She cries all the time.
Chloe: Maybe she needs to be changed.
Joey: We can't change her. We've lost the receipt.

Husband: Dear, must you spend so much money on food?
Wife: Sorry, darling, but you and the kids just won't eat anything else!

Why did Adam get the first fig leaf?
Because he wore the plants in the family.

Mother: Billy, you just drove through a red light! Is this what you learned in Driver Education class?
Billy: Gee, Mom, Bobby does it all the time!
Mother: Now you're stopping at a green light! What's the idea?
Billy: Bobby might be coming!

Dad: Okay, who left the kids' Bongo Blaster in the driveway?

Mom: Now, don't get upset, dear; that toy's supposed to be indestructible.

Dad: It's indestructible, all right—it broke the car!

Georgie: Dad, what was the name of that train station we just left?

Dad: Shhh, son, I'm trying to read this map.

Georgie: Okay, but look for the name of that last stop, because Mom just got off there!

Father: I'll tell you something about happiness. Do you know what it means to come home to two adorable, well-mannered children who are thrilled at the sight of you, hang on your every word, and think you're the smartest, strongest, best guy in the whole world?

Bachelor friend: Well...

Father: I'll tell you what it means. It means you're in the wrong house!

Ralph: My wife's a mean cook.

Ed: Mine too. She's always offering seconds!

Rocky: My son drives like lightning!

Cliff: You mean he's fast.

Rocky: No, he strikes trees!

George: How are you, Hank?

Hank: Just terrible. I've got this headache that won't go away.

George: Well, whenever I feel bad, I go home to my wife. She massages my forehead and sings to me, and pretty soon I feel a lot better. You should try that.

Hank: Sounds great! Do you think she's at home now?

Marriage counselor: Now, what seems to be the problem?

Husband: She's always threatening me!

Wife: I do not!

Husband: Do so! Why, even during the wedding ceremony, when I said "I do," you said, "You'd better!"

Tessie: Boy, am I absentminded.

Bessie: How absentminded are you?

Tessie: I'm so absentminded that this morning I walked out on my husband and kissed the porch good-bye!

Matt: Mom, which would you rather have happen to me— to be run over by a car or to have a bottle of glue spilled all over my new shoes?

Mother: What a question! Of course I'd pray that you got glue on your shoes.

Matt: Well, your prayers have been answered!

Rose: You're so lucky, dear; George is a model husband!

Violet: Yes, but not a working model!

How many spoiled brats does it take to change a lightbulb?
Just one—she holds it in the socket and waits for the world to revolve around her.

Marriage counselor: Please remember, Mr. and Mrs. Brown, that there are always two sides to every story.
Mrs. Brown: Fine. I'll tell you my side first; then I'll tell you his.

Little girl: My brother spends most of his time collecting fleas as a hobby.
Teacher: And how do you spend most of your time?
Little girl: Scratching.

A father was having trouble getting phone messages because his teenage son was always talking to girlfriends. Finally he had a private phone line installed.

One night the father came home and was astonished to find the boy using the family telephone. "Why don't you tie up your own phone?" the father shouted.

"No way, Dad," answered the son. "One of my friends might want to call me on it."

Mrs. Smith: My son is growing up.
Mrs. Jones: How do you know that?
Mrs. Smith: Now instead of asking me where he came from, he refuses to tell me where he's going.

Mother: Confess! Who got dirty fingerprints on the wall, Melanie or Martin?
Melanie: It was Marty, Mom. I saw him at the scene of the grime.

Father: Don't you want to be a traffic cop like I am, son?
Son: No, Dad. When I grow up I want to drive a garbage truck.
Father: Well, if that's what you want, son, I won't stand in your way.

Little Marty turned to his mother and said, "Mom, you woke me up for school this morning and now you're putting me to bed."

"Yes," said Marty's mom, "a mother works from son up to son down."

Ben: What did Mr. and Mrs. Emory Board do after ten years of marriage?
Jack: They filed for divorce.

Mrs. Smith: My grandson Johnny came home from school, threw a bucket of soapy water over me, and chased me around the house with a scrub brush—and it's all your fault!
Teacher: My fault! How?
Mrs. Smith: He says you told him to improve his grammar!

Pat: I filled my parents' waterbed with soda.
Shelly: And?
Pat: I jumped on it.
Shelly: And?
Pat: My parents now have a foam mattress.

Social worker: Mr. and Mrs. Plate are having marital problems.
Psychologist: Ah, a truly dish-functional family.

Teacher: As your children get older they cause more and more trouble.
Parent: Don't blame me for growing pains.

A husband and wife went to see a marriage counselor. "Here's the problem," the husband said. "We've been married ten years. For the last eight, we haven't been able to agree on anything."
The counselor looked at the wife. "Is that right?" he asked.
"Absolutely not," she answered. "We haven't been able to agree on anything for the last nine years."

Teacher: You have ten older brothers?
Mark: Yes.
Teacher: Does your mom holler at you a lot?
Mark: Nope. By the time she finishes hollering at my brothers and gets to me she usually has laryngitis.

First husband: I can never win an argument with my wife.
Second husband: I always have the last word.
First husband: How?
Second husband: I say, "Yes, dear!"

Father: Junior, what happened to you? You're a mess!
Junior: I challenged Joey to a duel!
Father: I see—very gentlemanly of you. I hope you gave him his choice of weapons.
Junior: Yeah, but who knew he'd pick his sister?

Wayne: I got a practically new BMW for my wife.
Duane: Wow! I'd like to make a trade like that!

Meg: My kids were giving me a headache, but I was fine once I followed the directions on the bottle of aspirin.
Peg: You mean you swallowed two aspirin.
Meg: No, I just followed the directions on the bottle. It says "Keep away from children."

Mother: I'll be going to the hospital soon so the doctor can deliver your baby brother or sister.
Janie: But Mother, that's what I don't understand.
Mother: What, Janie?
Janie: Well, if the doctor's going to deliver the baby, why do you have to go to the hospital?

George: Dear, did you know Junior's sitting in the refrigerator?
Martha: Yes, dear, I don't want him to get spoiled.

Patient: Doctor, since my husband divorced me I haven't had a decent night's sleep.
Psychiatrist: Yes, yes, a typical anxiety response...
Patient: No, no; he took the bed!

Father: Now, Charles, these grades of yours just aren't very good. Your friend Douglas doesn't get C's, does he?
Charles: No, but Douglas has very smart parents.

Fay: I never have any time to myself.
Saundra: I've got five kids, and I can be alone whenever I want.
Fay: How do you mange that?
Saundra: I just start doing the dishes.

Father: Wow, I'm impressed. You were on the phone for only thirty minutes. Most of your calls last two hours.
Teenager: Wrong number.

Charlie: Mom, remember how you always worried that I'd break your best teacups if I played with them?
Mom: Yes, I remember.
Charlie: Well, your worries are over.

Wilma: Doris treats her husband like a god.
Betty: What do you mean?
Wilma: Every evening at dinnertime she places a burnt offering before him.

Fannie: What's the latest dope on personal computers?
Annie: My husband.

Ed: Does this hot weather disagree with your mother?
Ned: It wouldn't dare!

It was a beautiful wedding, but the mother of the bride seemed to be taking it much too hard. Right after the ceremony, an old friend came up to console her.

"Don't cry so," said the friend. "They say girls marry men like their fathers!"

"I've heard that too," said the mother. "That's why I'm crying!"

Father: I pay your tuition at the Sorbonne, and when I ask you to show me what you've learned, you take me to a fancy restaurant and speak to the waiter in French. You call this a valuable education?
Son: Sure, Dad. I told him to give you the check.

Burglar's wife: You forgot my birthday again! What a lousy husband I've got; out every night, sneaks in at dawn—
Burglar: Honey, I tried to get you something at the jeweler's but when I got there the store was open!

Fred: The way George treats his wife I wouldn't treat a dog.
Barney: Why? What does he do?
Fred: He kisses her!

Wife: I'm homesick!
Husband: But you're at home!
Wife: Yes, and I'm sick of it!

Ivy: Why do you call your son Flannel?
Rose: Because he shrinks from washing!

Teacher: Jason, if you had a big apple and a small apple, and you had to share with your brother, how would you do it?
Jason: Do you mean my older brother or my younger brother?

Husband: Dear, would you marry again if I died first?
Wife: Possibly.
Husband: Would you cook his favorite meals for him?
Wife: I suppose so.
Husband: Would you give him my clothes?
Wife: Oh, I couldn't do that! He's a 42 long!

Billy: Where can I get hold of your husband?
Millie: It won't be easy—he's terribly ticklish!

Father: I'm keeping a record of your school years.
Son: In a scrapbook?
Father: No, in a checkbook!

An animal rights activist stopped a Park Avenue matron one chilly day and pointed to the lady's mink coat.

"Madam, do you realize some poor dumb beast suffered so that you could wear this coat?"

"How dare you talk that way about my husband!" she replied.

Husband: I just got a new car for my wife.
Wiseguy: Now that's what I call a great trade-in!

Tot: You're a bad mommy!
Mom: Why?
Tot: Because you always make me go to bed when I'm not sleepy, and you make me get up when I am sleepy!

Pam: Why did you name your only daughter Margarine?
Sam: Because we don't have any but her.

Sally: I'm leaving my husband because he's a rat.
Jane: I'm leaving my husband because he's a louse.
Judy: You two don't need a divorce lawyer, you need an exterminator!

Husband No. 1: My wife has down-to-earth looks.
Husband No. 2: My wife has plenty of dirty looks too.

Fred: Why did you decide to get married on Friday the 13th?
Ed: Well, if things don't work out at least I'll have something to blame the divorce on.

Man: My wife and I would have been divorced years ago if it wasn't for the kids.
Friend: Oh, you both refused to give them up?
Man: No, neither of us wanted to take them!

Cindy: My mother wants me married so badly.
Mindy: Why do you say that?
Cindy: Every time I bring a guy home she measures him for a tux.

A guy stood over his tee shot for a long time, looking up, looking down, measuring the distance, figuring the wind direction and speed. All this was driving has golfing partner nuts.

Finally his exasperated partner said, "Just hit the stupid ball!"

The guy answered, "My wife is up there watching me from the clubhouse. I want to make this a perfect shot."

"Forget it, man," said the partner. "There's no way you can hit her from here."

Hotel guest: Hello, room service. Send me up two burned eggs, undercooked bacon, cold toast, and weak coffee.
Hotel manager: Why do you want such a terrible breakfast?
Hotel guest: I'm homesick.

Bob: My wife and I used to sleep in a water bed. Now we're getting divorced.
Rob: What happened?
Bob: I guess we just drifted apart.

"Mary, you look stressed out," said Shelly. "What's wrong?"

Mary sighed. "This morning I woke up late and had to run downstairs to make breakfast. Then the dog got loose and I had to run after him. The kids forgot their lunch and I had to run after the school bus. Then I had to run to the train station."

Shelly shook her head. "You need a hobby to relax you," she said. "Maybe you should try jogging."

Wife: Golf! Golf! Golf! I think if you spent one Saturday home with me I'd die of surprise!
Husband: Stop trying to bribe me.

College student: Hey, Dad! I've got some great news for you!
Father: What, son?
College student: Remember that $500 you promised me if I made the Dean's list?
Father: I certainly do.
College student: Well, you get to keep it.

What's it like to be a mother?

"It certainly isn't child's play."

"I don't get to baby myself the way I used to."

"I had to learn to change things."

"I spend most of my day kidding around."

"There are other things I'd like to bring up, but I'm too busy."

"I'm ashamed of the way we live," a young wife said to her lazy husband who refused to find a job. "My father pays our rent. My mother buys all of our food. My sister buys our clothes. My aunt bought us a car. I'm just so ashamed."

The husband rolled over on the couch. "You should be ashamed," he agreed. "Those two worthless brothers of yours never give us a cent."

Wife: I just took some pregnancy tests.
Husband: Ha! Ha! And what grades did you get?
Wife: A-B-B.

Madge: I heard your husband left you. Are you drowning your sorrow in drink?
Mindy: No.
Madge: Why not? No liquor?
Mindy: No sorrow.

Duke: I'm a stuntman. I get paid to fall down the stairs and trip over things.
Little girl: Well, what do you know! All these years my clumsy brother has been performing for free.

Boy: I have three brothers and two sisters.
Man: Are you the oldest in your family?
Boy: Heck, no. My mother and father are a lot older than I am.

Husband: Great news, darling. I've finally saved enough money for us to go to Paris this year.
Wife: How wonderful! When are we leaving?
Husband: As soon as I've saved enough money for the return trip.

Phil: I didn't have a great infancy. The first month of my life my parents took me back to the hospital every day.
Will: Were you sickly?
Phil: No. They kept trying to exchange me.
Fred: What's wrong?

Ed: I tried to save money by keeping my thermostat very low all through the winter months. But my wife was cold, so I told her to wear something warm in the house.
Fred: Then why are you depressed?
Ed: She went out and bought a mink coat.

Sam got a little drunk at a party and started flirting with one of the women guests.

"Remind me to put a piece of raw steak on your black eye when we get home," said his wife.

"But I haven't got a black eye," replied Sam.

"You're not home yet," she responded.

Brother: Mom wants you to go into the kitchen to help her fix dinner.
Sister: I can't. Her cooking is beyond repair.

Why did Mr. and Mrs. Arithmetic go to a counselor?
They had marital problems to solve.

Lady: My husband bumped his head at work and now he thinks he's a giant pecan.
Lawyer: Oh no! Another nut case.

Madge: Your husband is so good looking, he must be the idol of the family.
Mindy: Yeah, idle for 20 years.
Blanche: Do you get along with your relatives?

Herb: I never speak to them.
Blanche: Is that right?
Herb: No, it isn't right, but I still don't speak to them.

Joe: I hear your mother-in-law's a real angel.
Moe: Yeah—she's always harping.

Madge: Husbands are such a worry.
Mindy: I didn't know you had one.
Madge: I don't—that's what worries me!

Mrs. Brown: Yesterday I broke an expensive vase my mother-in-law gave me.
Mrs. Green: What did your husband say?
Mrs. Brown: Ouch! What hit me?

Did you hear the one about the guy who kept his kid in the refrigerator?
He didn't want him to get spoiled.
Madge: I've been asked to marry thousands of times.
Mindy: Really? Who asked you?
Madge: My mother and father.

Wife: Stop trying to sugarcoat everything that bothers you.
Husband: Yes, sweetie.

Ken: I can't believe my mom let my aunt name my new twin brother and sister.
Len: What did your aunt name them?
Ken: Denise and Denephew.

Madge: My husband talks in his sleep.
Mindy: Why not get a cure from the doctor?
Madge: Are you kidding? It's the only time he talks to me.

The fathers of two teenage boys were talking. "My son Matt used to be late to school every day," said Mr. Smith. "I bought him a used car and that solved the problem."

"How did buying him a car solve the problem?" asked Mr. Jones.

Said Mr. Smith. "Now he gets to school early so he can find a parking place."

Jim: And how's the blushing bridegroom?
Tim: The honeymoon's over!
Jim: What? Last time I saw your wife, she was walking on air!
Tim: Sure, because I'd just carried her over the threshold; but then she decided to put her foot down!

April: I have ten children.
Mary: My goodness! Didn't you run out of names to call them?
April: No, but I ran out of names to call my husband!

Big sister: Mom says babies are expensive!
Big brother: Yes, but think how long they last!

Olive: It's my golden anniversary!
Angie: It can't be! You only got married in 1986.
Olive: Yes, but I count the time in dog years!

Wacky weather forecast
For Mothers-to-Be—Showers expected.

Mother: Now, dear, I never even held hands with a boy until I met your father. Will you be able to say that to your daughter?
Daughter: Yes, but maybe not with such a straight face!

Mrs. Snoot: Why did you let your maid go?
Mrs. Toot: Because my husband wouldn't!

Husband: Oh come on, honey; I hate to see you cry like this.
Wife: This is the only way I know how to cry!

Contestant: Yes, Bobby, my wife and I have been married for twenty wonderful years.
Game show host: I see. And how many miserable years?
Sue: I hate being married. Steve hasn't so much as kissed me since the wedding!
Jill: Have you thought about divorcing Steve?
Sue: Why? I'm not married to Steve!

Lady: What a cute little boy. What's your name, sweetheart?
Little boy: Connor.
Lady: Can you tell me your full name?
Little boy: Connor Stop That!

Rose: With the house, the family, and everything, I don't have a second to go to the gym!
Violet: I always exercise. Why, every morning I bend over and touch the floor fifty times picking up the kids' clothes!

Teenager: Dad, I got a very small scratch on the fender of your new car.
Father: Oh, no! Let me see! Where is it?
Teenager: In the trunk.

Frank: Well, you're certainly coming up in the world, playing golf with two caddies!
Ted: Oh, it was my wife's idea.
Frank: Your wife?
Ted: Yeah. She thought I should spend more time with the kids.

Rose: So, you're expecting your seventh child! What do you think you'll call it?
Violet: I think I'll call it Quits!

Child: Mom, where were you born?

Mother: In Boston, honey.

Child: How about Dad?

Mother: He was born in Chicago.

Child: And where was I born?

Mother: You were born in New York. Why?

Child: Oh, no reason. Just that it's sure lucky we all got together!

Betty: This cookbook shows you how to serve balanced meals.

Veronica: Oh, I'm already doing that. One day my husband complains, and the next day the kids complain.

Fern: Oh, I wish I'd listened to my mother!

Ivy: Why? What did she tell you?

Fern: I don't know! I didn't listen!

Abby: My son is home from college, I think.

Suzy: You think?

Abby: Well, he hasn't called me in a week, and the car's missing!

Hostess: Now Jenny, when you serve the guests at dinner, be careful not to spill anything.

Jenny: Not me! I won't say a word!

Fern: I've finally invented something that'll make my fortune! It's this small metal band that cures headaches!
Ivy: And you fit it over you forehead?
Fern: No, over your child's mouth!

Doris: My child is so honest, she simply cannot tell a lie.
Dolores: You're lucky. My kid can tell a lie the minute I open my mouth!

Bank teller: May I help you, ma'am?
Depositor: Yes. I have a joint bank account and I'd like to make a withdrawal from my husband's side.

Rose: This is my fourth wedding anniversary.
Violet: You and Joe have been married four years, eh?
Rose: No. Joe's my fourth husband.

Bartender: It's getting late. Isn't your wife wondering where you are?
Barfly: Not at all. She thinks I'm taking a sketching class.
Bartender: How'd you come up with that one?
Barfly: It just happened. One night I phoned her from here, and she heard someone yell, "Draw one and put a head on it!"

Mother: What did your father sleep in during the camp-out?
Boy Scout: A pop tent.

Romeo: You're calling me an idiot? After fifteen years of marriage?
Juliet: You're right. I'm sorry. I shouldn't have waited so long.

Violet: Does your daughter spend a lot of time on the phone?
Rose: I'll say! When she moves out, the phone company's going to retire her number!

Roger: Mom, look at the neat ninja sword Randy gave me!
Mother: Well, wasn't that nice of Randy! Why did he give it to you?
Roger: So I'd stop hitting him with it.

What time is it when the kids need a nap?
Whine o'clock.

Meryl: My little Horace insists on putting on his socks inside out, and it drives me crazy! What should I do?
Beryl: Turn the hose on him!

Sandy: My husband gave me a gift subscription to a science-fiction magazine.
Mandy: Oh, really? What's its name?
Sandy: Better Homes & Gardens!

Wife: You can't go to the golf course today.
Husband: Okay, I'll just putter around the yard then.

CRIME & PUNISHMENT

....

Jokes from the Big House

Judge: Are you guilty or not guilty?
Defendant: That's for me to know and you to find out!

Unsuccessful outlaw: There's a price on my head.
Sheriff: Take it!

I was arrested for purse-snatching, but it was a case of mistaken identity...I didn't know she was a cop.

Lucie: What's the difference between crime and politics?
Brucie: In crime it's take the money and run; in politics it's the other way around.

....

Witness: Well, I think the defendant was…
Prosecutor: Just tell me what you know, not what you think.
Witness: Sorry, but not being a lawyer, I can't talk without thinking.

What do you get if you cross a policeman with an alarm clock?
A crime watch.

Junior lawyer: Justice has triumphed!
Senior partner: Appeal at once!

Judge: You look familiar. Have I met you before?
Defendant: Yes, sir, I taught your daughter to play the trumpet, remember?
Judge (banging down his gravel): I certainly do…twenty years!!!

What did the policeman say to the lumberjacks?
Chop in the name of the law!

Policeman: Okay, buddy. Let's go to the station and take a breathalizer test.
Man: But Ossifer, I'm not drunk.
Policeman: Oh, yeah? Then why are you walking with one foot in the gutter and the other on the sidewalk?
Man: I'm so grateful you stopped me. I thought I was lame.

Crime victim: Oh, please don't take my wedding ring. It has only sentimental value.
Robber: That's okay. I'm a sentimental guy.

A photographer was hired to take pictures at a lawyers' convention. When he lined up his subjects he got them to look their best by shouting, "Okay everyone, say fees!"

Store manager: I'd just like to know one thing: Why do you always pick my store to rob?
Shoplifter: You always advertise such great bargains.

Mr. Oyster: What will you do if I don't pay my bill?
Mr. Hermit Crab: I'll take you to small clams court.

When does a newspaper get arrested?
When the comic strips.

Warden: All Prisoner 2228 does is draw cartoons all day.
Guard: That's why we put him in an animation cell.

Why did the lawyer fall asleep in court?
He was working on a pillow case.

Lawyer: Why did the cod go to court?
Judge: He had to appear for a herring.

What did the crow police shout to the jailbird?
Stop in the name of the caw!

Man: You did a terrible job on the title search for my house.
Lawyer: What do you mean?
Man: You deed me wrong.

Show me a court case about skimpy swimwear...and I'll show you a bathing suit.

Judge: Did you steal that lamp?
Crook: If I plead guilty, Judge, will you give me a light sentence?

Guest: I hit my head on your doorway and I plan to sue.
Lawyer: Forget about going to court. Will you settle for a lump sum?

Who says crime doesn't pay? Yesterday a mugger stole my wallet while his butler held a gun on me!

Prisoner No. 1: When do you get out of jail?
Prisoner No. 2: Who knows?
Prisoner No. 1: Now that's a questionable sentence.

Why did they arrest the dairy farmer with long fingernails?
Because he wasn't kind to udders.

Judge Carol: I can't go out with you, counselor.
Lawyer Bob: But why not?
Judge Carol: You don't appeal to me.

Attention counterfeiters! Never hold on to the first dollar you made. It could be used as evidence against you!

Bailiff: This man broke into a pet shop, your honor.
Judge: What's he charged with?
Bailiff: Pet-ty theft.

Why was the artist arrested for graffiti?
He had to draw the line somewhere!

Defendant: Your Honor, I'm being unfairly accused of robbery because I'm a locksmith by profession!
Judge: Can you explain what you were doing at the scene of the crime when the police arrived?
Defendant: Just making a bolt for the door!

An enterprising young man stood on a street corner with a stack of newspapers, shouting, "Extra! Extra! Scam Claims 50 Victims! Read all about it!" A passerby stopped to purchase a copy, and stood to one side as he paged though the entire paper. Then he spoke up: "Hey, I can't find anything in here about a scam."

"Extra! Extra!," shouted the young man, ignoring the passerby. "Scam Claims 51 Victims!"

Eb: Jake down at the flower shop was just held up at gunpoint!
Flo: I'll bet he was a petrified florist!

Prosecutor: Your Honor, my opponent is a liar!
Defense attorney: Your Honor, my opponent is a cheat!
Judge: Good, I'm glad to see you're acquainted with each other!

Bob: I have a guilty face.
Bill: You know that can't be true.
Bob: It must be true. Why, a jury of my peers just found me, an innocent man, guilty!
Bill: Really! I didn't know you were on trial.
Bob: I wasn't! I was the foreman!

Judge: Young man, you've got a lot of nerve smiling like that when I've just given you two years for forgery!
Defendant: Yeah, thanks, Your Honor: I oughta be able to pick it up in that much time!

Dan: Did you ever hear of Sherlock Holmes?
Van: No. But I bet burglars have a tough time getting into them.

Defendant: You're a terrible lawyer! I'll never win this case!
Attorney: Now, why do you say that?
Defendant: The court swears me to tell the truth, but every time I start to, you jump up and object!

Stranger: Excuse me, have you seen a policeman anywhere nearby?
Passerby: No I haven't.
Stranger: Then—stick 'em up!

Defendant: We'll never win the case!
Defense attorney: Now, don't be pessimistic. It's a complicated case...
Defendant: Yes, and it's in the hands of twelve people who couldn't figure out how to get out of jury duty!

Police captain: What do you mean, you can't ID these fingerprints! We know the robbery was committed by Lefty LaForge!

Fingerprint expert: Sorry, but these prints and Lefty's are whorls apart!

Lifeguard: Three hundred crooks at the beach just went surfing.

Policeman: Uh-oh! We'd better watch out for a crime wave.

Witness: Money can't buy my silence.

Gangster: If I offered you $10,000 not to talk, what would you say?

Witness: No comment.

Reporter No. 1: Did the police spokesman give a description of the missing bank teller?

Reporter No. 2: Yes. He was six feet tall and $50,000 short.

Criminal: I'm willing to pay for my crime.

Judge: That's fine.

Franklin: I'm looking for a new accountant.

Theodore: Get hold of mine, and you'll make a mint.

Franklin: He's really good, eh?

Theodore: No, there's a reward for his arrest.

Judge: Don't try any April Fool tricks in my courtroom.
Lawyer: Is that a gag order, your honor?

Prisoner: It took me five years to write this book.
Convict: Big deal. I'm working on a sentence that will take me 99 years to finish.

Robber: What do you say to a policeman who stands six feet tall and weights 280 pounds?
Crook: Hummm…I give up.
Robber: Right. Only you say it a lot faster.

Warden: I hear you're a very polite convict.
Convict #1828: Yes sir. And I beg your pardon.

Police officer: How could you hit that tree?
Driver: Don't blame me. I honked my horn but it didn't get out of the way.

Judge: Have you ever appeared before this court in any other suit?
Lawyer: Why, yes—the navy pinstripe!

Stacy: I just read in the paper the police want a middle-aged man for embezzling from beautiful young widows.
Stanley: Really? What's the salary?

Drunk: What do you mean I'm going to jail? I demand to know the charge!
Police officer: Oh, no charge. This one's on the government.

Pickpocket: Your honor, I demand that the court appoint a lawyer for my defense!
Judge: You were caught with your hand in someone else's pocket! What could a lawyer possibly say in your defense?
Pickpocket: That's what I want to find out!

Traffic cop: Do you realize this is a one-way street?
Motorist: Well, of course! I only drive one way!

Sherry: Why do escaped convicts always head for Canada?
Terry: Where else have they got Toronto?

In the days of the Berlin Wall, there was a little old man who crossed the checkpoint every week, pushing his bicycle and carrying a heavy sack. The border guard, suspecting him of smuggling, always searched the sack thoroughly but never found anything worthwhile.
One day, after the wall came down, the guard ran into the little old man.

"Look, I just know you were smuggling something all those years but I could never prove it," said the guard. "Tell me what it was."

The little old man chuckled, "Bicycles."

Convict: Writing your memoirs?
Cellmate: No, just a letter to myself so I'll get some mail.
Convict: What are you saying?
Cellmate: Don't know—mail call isn't until 3:30.

Crime is on the rise everywhere. There's an inner-city neighborhood that is so tough the local police station has a peephole on the front door just to be safe!

Guard: Nice suit boss. Did you buy it off the rack?
Warden: No. It's jailor made.

What do you get if you cross robbers with television producers?
Crime Time TV.

What do you say when your car's been stolen?
   "Rats!" cried the exterminator.
   "Dam!" cried the hydroelectric expert.
   "Blast!" cried the miner.
   "Darn!" cried the sock maker.
   "For the love of mike!" cried the radio announcer.

What do you call it when several cops get into a fight?
A policeman's brawl.

Crook: Your money or your life?
Scrooge: Humm....
Crook: What's taking you so long? Hand over your wallet!
Scrooge: I'm thinking it over.

What do you call five policemen wearing galoshes?
Cops in rubbers.

Jim: How many stupid crooks does it take to crack a safe?
Tim: I don't know. How many?
Jim: Six. One to hold the tumblers and five to spin the safe.

Two policemen went up to a young man selling pills he claimed would keep people eternally youthful. They slapped handcuffs on the quack and asked him if he had a prior record.

"Yes," he admitted. "I got arrested for the same offense in 1775, 1885, and 1995."

Judge: Why are you in my courtroom?
Man: I'm a camera enthusiast, your honor.
Judge: You mean you were arrested for taking pictures?
Man: No, your honor. For taking cameras.

A detective who spent his entire career in plainclothes quit the police force and bought a farm.

"What kind of crops do you plan to grow?" the police chief asked the farmer-to-be.

"Carrots and potatoes," the man replied.

"Why carrots and potatoes?" asked the chief.

"Because," answered the ex-detective, "I'm very fond of undercover crops."

Judge: Mr. Hunk, you're accused of losing a pro wrestling match on purpose. How do you plead?
Mr. Hunk: Guilty, your honor. And I'd like to throw myself on the mercy of the court.

A couple was walking home one evening when they were accosted by a crook who threatened, "Your money or your life," a robber who screamed out, "Hands up!" and a bandit who told them, "Fork over the cash!"

"Wow!" said the woman, "What a lot of hollering and yelling!"

"I know," said the man. "Talk about a din of thieves."

Clerk: A masked man came into the store with a shotgun and told me to give him all the pickles in the place.
Policeman: And what did you do?
Clerk: I let him have both barrels.

Did you hear the one about the farmer found guilty of selling rotten fruit?
He was judged by his pears.

Convict: I'm in jail just because I made big money.
Guard: How can they put you in prison for that?
Convict: I made it about a half inch too big.

Madge: My dog is a police dog.
Mindy: He doesn't look like a police dog to me.
Madge: That's 'cause he's in plainclothes.

Convict No. 1: I need to call my lawyer right away.
Convict No. 2: Here, use my cell phone.

News Flash!
In California today three criminals carrying surfboards held up the First, the Second, and the Third National Banks. Police fear it's the start of a bizarre crime wave.

Deputy: Why did the sheriff put glue on his hands before the showdown?
Marshall: He wanted to stick to his guns.

Judge: For your crime you're sentenced to perform one hundred hours of community service in Washington, D.C.
Man: Wow! Talk about capitol punishment!

Witness: I tell you the defendant robbed the bank while wearing a wig.
Defense attorney: I object, your honor. That evidence is hairsay.

Man: Help! Police! Someone stole my mongrel dog!
Policeman: Aha! Another case of cur jacking.

Cop: I need to know if you're going to snitch on your criminal pals.
Crook: It's too soon to tell.

I used to live in a high-crime area. I remember when I first moved in, a neighbor told me, "Keep your door closed and locked all night. Never open it until morning."

I followed his advice, and when morning came, the door was gone.

Traffic court judge: So you just drove right into the dress shop window. Why didn't you look where you were going?
Driver: I couldn't, your Honor. I was too busy going where I was looking!

Tom: You think New York is dangerous...why, right here in Hilldale a guy pulled a razor on me!
Dick: Were you hurt?
Tom: Nah—he couldn't find a place to plug it in.

Rinky: I'm reading a very interesting article on the makeup of the Supreme Court.
Dinky: Gosh, I didn't know they wore any!

Why are burglars so relaxed?
They like to take things easy.

New prisoner: I'm the toughest con in this cellblock.
Cellmate: Prove it.
New prisoner: I committed armed robbery.
Cellmate: Big deal. So did I.
New prisoner: With a bitten-off shotgun?

Traffic court judge: And when you crashed into the stop sign, what gear were you in?
Driver: The blue suit, red pumps, and matching handbag, your Honor.

Convicted criminal (on the scaffold): Well, you tried. I guess this is good-bye.
Lawyer: Don't worry! Tomorrow I'm suing for whiplash!

Lou: What happened to that fashion model we used to see on all the magazine covers?
Bud: She was deposed.

Jury foreman: Of the charge of first degree robbery, we find the defendant...not guilty!
Defendant: Does that mean I get to keep the money?

A little girl accompanied her father to the post office one day. She noticed the "Wanted" posters pinned to the wall and asked her father about them.

"Those are pictures of people the police would like to catch," explained her father.

"But, Daddy," said the little girl, "If the police wanted to catch them, why didn't they hold on to them when they took their pictures?"

Desk Sergeant: Any previous convictions?
Suspect being booked: Well, I used to think honesty was the best policy!

Buyer: Hey, you told me you had purebred police dogs for sale. This animal is the mangiest, dirtiest, scrawniest mutt I've ever laid eyes on! How can you get away with calling him a police dog!
Breeder: He works undercover.

HISTORY

Humor Through the Ages

What do Sir Galahad and Sir Lancelot watch at 6 o'clock?
The Knightly News.

Lucy: Christopher Columbus was famous for his memory.
Ethel: What in the world makes you think that?
Lucy: Well, they're always putting up monuments to it,
aren't they?

What did Paul Revere say when he finished his famous
ride?
Whoa!

Benny: I didn't know George Washington was an orphan.
Jenny: What makes you think he was?
Benny: It says in this book he's our country's foundling father.

How is the 16th President of the United States like an owl in the daytime.
They're both A-blinkin'.

Teacher: Was George Washington a sailor or a soldier?
Boy: He was a soldier.
Teacher: Right. But how do you know that?
Boy: I saw a picture of him crossing the Delaware and no sailor in his right mind would stand up in a boat like that.

What's green, leafy, and discovered America?
Christofern Columbus.

Joan: I'm studying ancient Roman history.
Mike: I'm studying the ancient Greeks. Let's get together and talk over old times.

What did King Arthur use to play golf?
Knight clubs.

Dad: Son, when Abraham Lincoln was your age he walked miles to school every day.
Son: Yeah? Well, when Lincoln was your age, Dad, he was President!

What do you get if you cross a canyon with a Revolutionary War hero?
Gorge Washington.

Professor: Every time I lecture about ancient Rome I get the hiccups.
Tess: I guess it just goes to prove that history does repeat itself.

Which cat discovered America?
Christopurr Columbus.

Teacher: Georgie, if April showers bring May flowers, what do May flowers bring?
Georgie: Pilgrims!

Security: See ya, Lancelot. So long, Galahad. Take care, Gawain.
Visitor: Who are those men?
Security: Those are the guys on the knight shift.

Jefferson: Why did you bring an interpreter for the hearing-impaired to this meeting?
Adams: She's going to sign the Declaration of Independence.

What union did Butch Cassidy and Billy the Kid belong to?
The World Rustling Federation.

Father: How did you do on your history test about the Allied invasion of Europe during World War II?
Son: Humph! It was D-Day all over again.

Lancelot: Why is King Arthur wearing a cowboy hat and boots?
Galahad: He's going to a squire dance.

Student: Why did the ancient Romans close down the arena?
Professor: It was the high overhead.
Student: What do you mean?
Professor: The lions were eating up the prophets.

Randy: George Washington threw a silver dollar across the Potomac River.
Andy: I bet he couldn't do that today.
Randy: And why not?
Andy: A buck just doesn't go as far these days.

Father: When Abraham Lincoln lived in Washington, he had a goatee.
Son: Gee, I didn't know they allowed pets in the White House.

King Arthur: Get on your horse. We're going out to kill a dragon.
Sir Mordred: Oh boy! I love a slay ride.

Where did King Tut go to ease his back pain?
To a Cairo-practor.

Name Game
Caesar: How did the Roman general do on his test?
Plato: I don't know. I still have to Mark Antony.

Which president of the United States hit a lot of home runs?
Babe Lincoln.

Little Julius: Boo-hoo! I fell down at the playground and hurt myself.
Soothsayer: I told you to beware the Slides of March.

Why were the Pilgrims' pants always falling down?
Because they wore their belts around their hats!

Jill: The person who lived in this apartment before us must've been an expert on Ancient Greece!
Bill: Did you find some scholarly tomes in the closet?
Jill: No, but the oven's never been cleaned!

Why is it so wet in England?
Because Kings and Queens have always reigned there.

Lucy: Mom, why is George Washington standing up in that boat crossing the Delaware?
Mom: Must've had the same travel agent as we do!

Father: Today is Honest Abe Lincoln's birthday.
Daughter: If he was so honest, why do they do they close all the banks?

King: We're giving you a medal because you've killed every giant dragon and ogre in the realm.
Knight: Gee, I don't know what to slay.

Captain Kidd: What do you get if you cross rodeo broncos with a corn field?
Captain Morgan: Buckin' Ears!

Who taught physical education at the Alamo?
Gym Bowie.

King Arthur: What are those apprentice knights doing?
Lancelot: It's a squire dance, Sire.

What did Paul Revere Octopus yell?
Two arms! Four arms! Six arms! Eight arms!

HOW HOT WAS IT?

....

So hot that at the beach we took turns sitting in each other's shade.

How cold was it?
It was so cold the snowman kept trying to get into the house.

Bettor No. 1: Boy, did my horse run slow.
Bettor No. 2: Really? How slow did he go?
Bettor No. 1: He was so slow, they timed him with a calendar.

Joe: Boy, was the show I went to last night bad.
Moe: How bad was it?
Joe: It was so bad even the empty seats got up and walked out.

....

How hot was it?
It was so hot, a dog chased a cat and they both walked.

How polite is she?
My mother's so polite, she won't open an oyster without knocking first.

Tom: My girlfriend is so modest.
Jack: How modest is she?
Tom: She's so modest, she goes into a closet to change her mind.

Susie: Boy, is my cousin Ferdy unlucky!
Annie: Yeah? How unlucky is he?
Susie: He's so unlucky he once went to see the Grand Canyon, but it was closed!

Madge: Boy, is Fred dumb.
Flora: How dumb is he?
Madge: He's so dumb, he planted a dogwood so he could raise a litter of puppies.

Joe: I have insomnia so bad.
Moe: Really? How bad is it?
Joe: It's so bad the sheep fell asleep.

How cold was it?
It was so cold, even the clock had to rub its hands together to stay warm.

   …so cold my overcoat was wearing a down jacket.

   …so cold the snowman made a down payment on a house.

Madge: Boy, is Fred absentminded.
Flora: How absentminded is he?
Madge: He's so absentminded he stood in front of the mirror for two hours trying to remember where he had seen himself before.

Customer: Excuse me, but is your milk fresh?
Farmer: I'll say it's fresh.
Customer: How fresh is it?
Farmer: Three hours ago it was grass!

Susie: Boy, is my father chintzy!
Annie: Yeah? How chintzy is he?
Susie: He's so chintzy, he's angry at the doctor because he got better before the medicine ran out!

Joe: When I was young we were so poor.
Moe: How poor were you?
Joe: We were so poor that when the wolf came to the door, he brought his own sandwiches.

How hot was it?
It was so hot, we had to feed ice cream to the chickens so they wouldn't lay hard-boiled eggs.

Mickey: What a traffic jam this morning!
Minnie: How bad was it?
Mickey: I was going so slow, an abandoned car passed me!

Lou: My apartment is really tiny.
Sue: Yeah? How tiny is it?
Lou: It's so tiny there isn't even room for improvement.

Susie: Boy is my brother lazy!
Annie: Yeah? How lazy is he?
Susie: He's so lazy, he had to hire a private investigator to find out what he did for a living.

How cold was it?
It was so cold, last winter they had to wait for the phone lines to thaw just to find out what folks had been talking about.

NATURE & THE FARM

....

Homegrown humor

Private Pork: Who are you?
Non-commissioned pig: My name is Sergeant Hog and I'm an expert in ham-to-ham combat.

Where does a pig leave its car when it takes the train?
In a Pork and Ride.

Tim: Why do you have a cow in your front yard?
Jim: It's mooing the lawn.

What do you do to a piggy who is bad in class?
Make him sty after class.

....

Mrs. Goat: I'm expecting a baby.
Mrs. Sheep: Are you kidding?
What happens when a black sheep crosses your path?
You have baa luck.

Mr. Pig: How did you enjoy the buffet?
Mr. Hog: It was swill.

What did the rooster say when he walked into the cow barn?
Cock-a-doodle-moo!

How does a family of turnips travel cross-country?
In a Rutabago.

First sheep: Baa.
Second sheep: Moo.
First sheep: What's the matter with you? Sheep don't say moo.
Second sheep: I'm learning a foreign language.

When does a gardener call a plumber?
When the leeks sprout!

Mr. Horse: Did you hear about the swine who bought a million acres of farmland for development?
Ms. Cow: Wow! What a ground hog!

What did one empty corn stalk say to the other?
I can't wait for a new ear to start.

Father: This rainstorm is ruining my topsoil.
Son: Blame it on mudder nature.

What did the redwood tree say when Old Faithful insulted it?
Quiet, you old geyser.

Man: Why is my grass making strange noises?
Gardener: Relax. It's just lawn cheers.

What do farmers in Tibet grow?
Lama beans.

Nellie: We had a little accident down on the farm. The cow knocked over a case of Scotch and got drunk.
Sue: Any ill effects?
Nellie: Not really. But the next morning...what a hangunder!

Why didn't Mr. Stallion ever get married?
He didn't want to be saddled with any responsibilities.

Cow: What are those lambs over there up to?
Goat: It's a meeting of Gambolers Anonymous.

What's a baby cow say to her mother?
There's no udder but you!

Mr. Elm: Don't trust that lumberjack.
Mr. Oak: Why not?
Mr. Elm: He tried to knife me in the bark.

What did the calf say to the haystack!
Are you my fodder?

Cow: I have an appointment with the vet today.
Sheep: Why? What's the matter?
Cow: Oh, I don't know. Lately I've been so moo-dy!

Why did the police arrest the crow?
He was caught making crank caws.

Farmer: Would you like a job working in my garden?
Rabbit: That depends. How much celery will you pay?

What do you use to dust a flower garden?
Ragweed.

Son: What do you get if you cross a rabbit with horse food?
Daughter: A hoppy fodder.

What do you call a pod of little peas?
Beanie babies.

Patty: That cow just got married.
Matty: I guess that makes her a honeymooer.

Why was the nanny goat so upset?
She had too many kids to take care of.

Man: Where can I read up on keeping my garden free of unwanted plants?
Librarian: Try the weeding resource room.

A city slicker was walking through a plowed field when he heard some frightening noises. "Ouch! Ooh! Ah! Ouch!!" The city slicker was amazed when he realized the sounds were coming from the ground beneath his feet. He ran over to a farmer who was standing nearby. "There's something wrong in that field," the city slicker shouted to the farmer.

"Nah," replied the farmer. "I planted that field last week and it's just experiencing growing pains."

Gardener: Why did you bring an alarm clock in the flower bed?
Lady: My psychologist told me to take time to smell the roses.

What do you get when you put overweight sheep in a steam cabinet?
Wool sweaters.

Mrs. Jones: How do you keep your flower garden so beautiful?
Mrs. Smith: I weed a lot in my bed.

Where does a sheep go for a haircut?
To a baa-baa shop.

Matt: Did you hear about the tree surgeon who ended up in the hospital?
Pat: No. What happened?
Matt: He fell out of one of his patients.

Why are horses lousy dancers?
They have two left feet?

Tree Surgeon: What's the trouble with the patient?
Lumberjack: Lower bark pain.

Why did the farmer teach his livestock to play poker?
He wanted to see the three billy goats bluff!

Cow: You silly hen, why are you sitting on that axe?
Hen: Shh. I want to hatchet.

What says "Oom, Oom?"
A cow meditating.

Farmer No. 1: Want to hear a really dumb joke about cows?
Farmer No. 2: No. Spare me any udder nonsense.

Who is the strongest sheep in the universe?
Hercufleece.

Hotel clerk: When do a mother hen's eggs hatch?
Farmer: At chick-out time.

Where do teenage pigs like to hang out?
At slopping malls.

Broker: What do bullish cows invest in?
Client: Mootual funds.

What alcoholic beverage made from grapes do pigs like to drink?
Swine coolers.

Jed: I'm going to buy a farm and raise ducks for their feathers.
Ned: How ya' gonna keep their down on the farm?

Where do cows go to have fun?
To a-moos-ment parks.

Zeke: I just bought a steer that weighs 5,000 pounds.
Clem: That's a lot of bull, pal.

Why did the farmer's cows go on a sit-down strike.
They wanted moo money.

Farmer Brown: I just crossed a flock of chickens with a herd of steers.
City slicker: What did you get?
Farmer Brown: Roost beef.

What does an alien tree do when it sees an earthling?
It saps him with a ray gum.

Urbanite: Can you make a mule laugh if you tickle him?
Farmer: Maybe, but you'll get a bigger kick out of it than he will.

What does a tree do when it doesn't feel like going to work?
It takes a leaf of absence.

Farmer: Never let a sheep drive your car.
City slicker: Why not?
Farmer: They make too many ewe turns.

What was the sloppiest prehistoric era?
The Messy-zoic Era.

Farmer: I ordered 50 baby chickens and you delivered 51.
Mailman: Don't complain. It must be a bonus chick.

Why did the evergreen tree go on a strict diet?
Because it was a porky pine.

Orange: You'd better get off of the beach.
Banana: Why?
Orange: You're starting to peel.

What did the angry farmer say to his immature plants?
He said, "Why don't you grow up already!"

News Flash!
The Ace Donkey Rental Company has been accused of using kickbacks.

Why should you take extra care of your metal items by the end of the week?
Because everyone knows Sunday is a day of rust.

Why did the alga and the fungus get married?
They took a lichen to each other!

Farm boy: My pa can't decide whether to buy a tractor or some cows.
City fella: Well, he'd sure look silly plowing his field on cows.
Farm boy: True. But he'd look even sillier milking a tractor!

Why was the weeping willow weeping?
Because he was so unpoplar.

Minnie: I have a green thumb.
Winnie: That means you're a good gardener.
Minnie: No, it means I'm a sloppy painter!

Which tree has nerdy white flowers on it in spring?
The dorkwood tree.

Farmer: That's my millenium cornfield.
Man: Why do call it that?
Farmer: It's a thousand ears long.

What did one farmer say to the other?
Let's get together for a plower lunch real soon.

Student: Where can I find a book about trees?
Librarian: Over at the branch library!

What do you get if you cross a summer vegetable with a chicken?
A corny yolk.

City slicker: How do you know how many baby hens you have?
Poultry farmer: I write it in my chick book.

What did the tree say in the fall?
It's time to leaf home.

Mrs. Smith: I collect foliage.
Mrs. Jones: What do you keep your collection in?
Mrs. Smith: A loose leaf binder.

A local businessman came to call on a farmer one day. He found him out in the orchard, hoisting an enormous pig in his arms so the pig could nibble an apple hanging from a tree.

"Sure takes a lot of time to feed a pig that way," cracked the businessman.

"Yep," replied the farmer, "but what's time to a pig?"

Farmer: What do you say when a sheep accidentally bumps into a skunk?
Herdsman: Ewe stink.

What kind of weapon does Captain Calf the Pirate use?
A *veal cutlass.*

Sheryl: Darling, we'll have to fire the new gardener.
Meryl: Why? I thought he was very experienced.
Sheryl: Doesn't look like it. He's out there watering the flagpole.

What floats, has big guns, and is covered with wool?
A *battlesheep.*

Cow: What did the vet say about your rash?
Pig: Just gave me some oinkment, and I feel better already!

Farmer: What moos and floats in the ocean?
Surfer: A cowbuoy.

What speedy mail service do hens use?
Nest day delivery.

Mr. Goat: I borrowed 10 bucks from a sheep.
Mr. Ram: Did you write her a promissory note?
Mr. Goat: No. I gave her and I.O.EWE.

Do turkeys have good table manners?
No. They always gobble up their food.

Mark: I always talk to my flowers, and I believe they'll
eventually talk back!
Megan: Don't waste your time: they're mums!

Why was the sheep so sad?
It had the winter baas.

Farmer: That sheep is a troublemaker.
Man: What makes you say that?
Farmer: It has a baa attitude.

What did the sailor say when he saw a boat loaded with ewes?
Sheep ahoy!

Slim: Why is the pig wearing cowboy boots?
Jim: He's going to do a country swine dance.

What kind of train do pigs take to Florida?
Ham Track.

Ralph: When it comes to planting a garden I'm too dumb to get anything to grow.
Alice: I always knew you were a blooming idiot.

What kind of cheese comes from a tree?
Limburger.

Father: You sure cleaned up the garden fast.
Son: I'm a speed weeder.

What do you get if you cross poison ivy with a four-leaf clover?
A rash of good luck.

Smokey: What did the romantic spruce tree say to the hemlock tree?
Ranger: You have kisses sweeter than pine.

*Overheard…*In the vegetable patch:
Oh, honeydew, don't be so melon-colly! You know we cantaloupe!

ANIMAL KINGDOM

Humorous goings-on from the natural world

Did you hear about the paranoid bloodhound?
He thought everyone was following him!

Al: Your bird's making fun of me.
Sal: Of course he is—he's a mockingbird.

What did Mr. Fox say when he tucked in his children?
Pheasant dreams.

What does a well-dressed bee wear to work?
A *buzzness suit.*

Where is the best place in the house to keep sled dogs?
In a mush room.

Man: I think my dalmatian has a rash.
Vet: Gosh! We'd better do a spot check.

Why did Ms. Shark kiss the ocean marker?
Because he was her lover buoy.

Producer: Where do you want the actor who is playing the skunk to stand?
Director: Scenter stage.

The gosling never believed a word his father said. As far as he was concerned…it was all papaganda.

Which dinosaur had radial wheels?
Tire-rannosaurus Rex.

Customer: Is that pooch a good watchdog?
Pet store owner: Absolutely. He'll raise a ruckus every time he sees a stranger.
Customer: How do I know you're not just making that up?
Pet store owner: The dog comes with a money bark guarantee!

Did you hear about the performing seahorses?
They got wave reviews!

How do you know if there's an elephant in front of you at the movies?
You can't see the screen.

Mr. Beaver: I'm starving. What's for dinner?
Mrs. Beaver: A tree-course meal.

Show me a bunch of rabbits who get holiday gifts they don't like...and I'll show you many hoppy returns.

Rose: Why do you love those talking birds so much?
Tom: They're my grand parrots.

What did one hungry spider say to the other at the end of the week?
Thank heavens it's Flyday.

Jack: What do you get if you cross a skunk with a big dog?
Mack: A Scent Bernard.

Why did the King of Beasts wear a cowboy hat and boots?
He wanted to do some country lion dancing.

Couch potato No. 1: I just watched a TV show about a family of skunks.
Couch potato No. 2: Was it a comedy?
Couch potato No. 1: No. A smellodrama.

What kind of crazy bird yells "Polly wants a cracker" when he jumps out of an airplane?
A parrot-trooper.

Tim: Do you know what the favorite sport of polar bears is?
Slim: Sure. Snow-pitch softball.

Show me some skunks in the Marine Corps...and I'll show you a phew good men.

Hunter: Why did the grizzly have to go on a diet?
Trapper: He had a big bear belly.

Why didn't the shark have to pay cash at the checkout counter?
He had a credit cod with him.

Mrs. Frog: Why is that little turtle crying?
Mr. Frog: I think he's a young weeper-snapper.
Why did Mrs. Antelope go to the beauty parlor?
She wanted a gnu hairstyle.

Mr. Turtle: My son just graduated from college with honors.
Mr. Toad: Really? What kind of honors?
Mr. Turtle: He was Phi Beta Snappa.

What do little fish watch on weekends?
Saturday morning carptoons.

Janet: I'm rich! I just bought fifty female pigs and fifty male deer!
Jeff: And just what do you expect to get from that?
Janet: Expect, nothing! I've already got a hundred sows and bucks!

What do you call a skunk who can predict the future?
A fortune smeller.

An alligator walked into a bar, seated himself on a stool, and ordered a beer.
Bartender: That'll be ten dollars for the beer, buddy. Say, we don't get many alligators in here.
Alligator: At these prices, I shouldn't wonder.

Did you hear about the talking birds concerned about population growth?
Yes, they're called Planned Parrothood.

What do you call a bunch of ill wolves?
A sick pack!

Mr. Cod: How do I become a flying fish?
Mr. Fluke: Join a flight school.

What's yellow, covered with feathers, and talks?
A gold myna.
Teacher: Wayne, what do we call the condition when a snake sheds its skin?
Wayne: Ssss-naked.

Why was the lion's neck all wet?
He had a leaky water mane.

Moe: The mosquitos this summer are the biggest I've ever seen.
Joe: Yeah? How big are they?
Moe: They're so big that the last one that bit me left footprints on my arm!

Why was Mrs. Rabbit so unhappy?
She had a bad hare day.

A seagull flies over the sea. What flies over the bay?
A bagel.

Nancy: It's raining cats and dogs outside.
Wayne: I'll say. Must've stepped in a thousand poodles.

What do you get when a cantaloupe and a dog have an offspring?
A melon-collie baby.

Kangaroo: Doc, I can't sleep at night, I'm so jumpy.
Vet: Here, take these pills and you'll be completely out of bounds.

Why do elephants have trunks?
No glove compartments.

Mama fish: Don't bite that hook!
Small fry: Why not?
Mama fish: You're too young to face the reel world.

How does an elephant get out of a tree?
He sits on a leaf and waits for the fall.

Customer: I'm returning this parrot you sold me. He absolutely will not talk.
Pet shop owner: Of course not!
Customer: But you told me he could talk!
Pet shop owner: Sure, but he was raised in a tough neighborhood. He won't talk without his attorney!

Why are elephants banned from public swimming pools?
They keep dropping their trunks.

First white rat: What's this Doctor Einstein like?
Second white rat: Oh, he's very bright. Whenever I ring the bell he brings my dinner immediately.

How do you get five elephants in a Honda Civic?
Two in the front, two in the back, and one in the glove compartment.

Kangaroo: I hate April!
Wallabee: Why?
Kangaroo: It rains so much, the kids have to play inside!

What do elephants have that no other creatures have?
Baby elephants.

First ant: Why are you running across the cracker box? What's the hurry?
Second ant: Can't you read? It says here, "Tear along dotted line."

What do you say to a two-headed crocodile?
Bye, Bye.

First worm: You're the most beautiful worm I've ever seen. Marry me, my darling.
Second worm: Cool it, Bozo. I'm your other end.

How do you cure a puppy who won't stop barking?
Give him a yappin' dectomy.

Boy: That giraffe swallowed the paper airplane I made.
Zookeeper: Oh no! Another plane in the neck.

How does an elephant get down from a ladder?
He doesn't get down from a ladder, he gets down from a goose.

Game warden: What are you doing with that trout at the end of your line, mister?
Off-season wrangler: Just teaching him to swim, Warden.

How do you stop a charging elephant?
Take away his credit cards.

Dad: So, how did Rover make out at the pet show?
Son: He was a sure thing for best of breed, but at the last minute another basset hound showed up.

What did the ram say to his girlfriend?
Ewe and I are finished.

Mrs. Rabbit: How can I stay cool in the summertime?
Mr. Bunny: Buy a good hare conditioner.

What do adult rabbits in Scotland drink?
Hop scotch.

Donald: What does the littlest duck in a family wear?
Daffy: Hand-me-down.

Which cartoon dog comes from a dysfunctional family?
Bark Simpson.

Visitor: I just saw a bluebird on the windowsill!
Host: Remember, we're in Los Angeles; with our smog, it was probably a sparrow holding its breath!

Customer: I'm looking for an exceptionally well-bred dog.
Pet shop owner: Madam, this puppy's pedigree is so long, if he could talk he wouldn't speak to either of us!

What do you get when you cross a rabbit with a skunk?
A furious rabbit!

Toad: The Lily Pad Players opened a new production of "The Frog Prince."
Trout: Good show?
Toad: Ribbeting!

What's black and white and black and white and purple?
A zebra rolling down a hill with a violet stuck in his hoof.

What happens when 50 rabbits hop backwards at the same time?
You get a receding hare line.

A flock of ostriches was startled by unusual noises coming from the underbrush.
"Quick, hide," said the ostrich leader.
The ostriches did what came naturally—they buried their heads in the sand. But the noise turned out to be only another ostrich, who emerged from the bushes, looked around, and said, "Hey, where is everybody?"

Ram: But why won't you marry me?
Ewe: Because we have mutton in common!

What happened when the bumblebee fell in love with the dinner bell?
They had a little humdinger.

Why couldn't the little lost elephant call his mother?
He forgot his elephone number.

Laura: Why are elephants so wrinkled?
Matt: Because they're too big to fit on the ironing board!

What grows down as it grows up?
A duck.

Dog owner: Doctor, I've tried everything to calm Rex down, but he's still a vicious beast.
Vet: Give him garlic. Lots of garlic.
Dog owner: Garlic?
Vet: Then his bark will be worse than his bite!

What's the difference between a cat and a comma?
One has its claws at the end of its paws; the other has its pause at the end of its clause.

Customer: I'd like to buy a parrot.
Pet Store Owner: This one's a dandy. If you pull on his left leg, he'll sing "Joe Hill." If you pull on his right leg, he'll sing "God Bless America!"
Customer: And what if you pull on both legs?
Parrot: I fall off the perch, you idiot!

What happened when the canary flew into the electric fan?
Shredded tweet.

Carnival patron: That's the most amazing act I've ever seen; a lion and a sheep performing together. Do they always get along so well?
Trainer: They argue now and then, but we don't let it bother us. We just buy a new sheep.

Harry: What did the vet say to the sick crow?
Larry: Take two aspirin and caw me in the morning.

Bill: Why is your dog making so much noise?
Sam: He's sitting on our bark porch.

Len: My Saint Bernard likes to eat fish.
Jen: What do you feed him?
Len: Holy mackerels.

Mr. Octopus: Why are you swimming so near the surface?
Little fish: I'm in high school now.

Two squirrels were living in an evergreen forest. One weekend the first squirrel turned to his mate and said, "Company is coming. Spruce up the house."

Mary: What do you get if you cross a whale with a kangaroo?
Barry: I don't know.
Mary: Neither do I, but you should see it ski jump.

What's purple, dangerous, and swims in the ocean?
A grape white shark?

Trainer No. 1: Did you kiss an aquatic mammal?
Trainer No. 2: Ugh! Yes. And now my lips are sealed.

Which animal is the best one to borrow money from?
A kangaroo, because it always has plenty of pocket change.

Man: My canary swallowed a gun.
Vet: Beware of cheep shots.

Mr. Tuna: Those sea mollusks told me you swallowed a whole ship.
Mr. Whale: Ah, that's just a bunch of abalone.

Pet owner: My dog is sick, but I can't pay for this visit.
Vet: Don't worry. Medicur will cover the bill.

What do teenage ducks worry about?
Getting goose pimples.

Matt: What's the best way to locate missing hares?
Pat: Comb the area.

What does a hungry termite say when it strolls into a tavern?
Hi! Is the bar tender here?

Joe: My dog's bark is worse than his bite.
Moe: Why is that?
Joe: He's been eating garlic.

What do you display when you see an antelope with a cigarette in its mouth?
A gnu smoking sign.

Errol: My cat is very cunning.
Cheryl: What makes you think that?
Errol: He eats a lot of cheese and then he waits near a mousehole with baited breath.

Why didn't the minnow go to lunch with the stork?
He was afraid he'd get stuck with the bill.

Mr. Bird Brain: I want to make a new movie. Find me some actors.
Mr. Crow: Okay. I'll send out a casting caw.

Al: There's a new instant breakfast drink for monkeys that has lots of vitamin C in it.
Cal: What's it called?
Al: Orangu-tang.

Sometimes bad things happen to good peepers, as on the day when the branch supporting the sparrow's nest snapped, sending a small but optimistic baby bird hurtling down from the tree top. As he passed a squirrel, the animal called out, "Are you all right?"

"So far," replied the sparrow.

Hunter: Why aren't those ducks flying faster?
Guide: It must be a slow-down zone.

What do you call a parrot in a raincoat?
Polyunsaturated.

Buck: I have hart-burn.
Jane Doe: Try drinking some elk-o-seltzer.

Where can you see a chorus line of cows?
At Radio City Moosic Hall.

Tourist: What do sea bass do in the winter?
Boat captain: They harbornate.

Why aren't there more elephants in college?
Because their SAT scores are terrible.

Baby polar bear: Mom, are you sure I'm not adopted?
Mama polar bear: Of course I'm sure! Why do you ask?
Baby polar bear: Because I'm c-c-cold!

What goes "Zub Zub"?
A bee flying backwards.

Customer: What've you got that'll cure fleas on a dog?
Druggist: Depends on what's ailing the fleas.

What do you get when you cross a teddy bear and a skunk?
Winnie the Peeyew!

First fish: My family has been swimming the Charles River for a hundred years.
Second fish: So what? My family swam over under the Mayflower!

What's big and gray and goes putt, putt, putt?
An elephant trying to play golf.

First barfly: I'll bet you a hundred dollars I can lift an elephant with one hand!
Second barfly: Hah! You're on!
First barfly: Fine! Get me a one-handed elephant!

How does an elephant sink a submarine?
He knocks on the door.

Mookie: Is it true your cat had a litter?
Cookie: Not really. Turned out she swallowed a ball of yarn and gave birth to mittens.

What do you get when you cross a mink and a kangaroo?
A fur coat with pockets.

Vinnie: What do you mean you got thrown out of the flea circus?
Minnie: I brought my dog and he stole the show!

Why did all the circus elephants go on strike?
They got tired of working for peanuts.

Eb: I'm in the circus parade, but I don't know how to lead the elephant.
Flo: It's simple. Just tie a rope around her neck, take hold of the other end...
Eb: Yes?
Flo: And then ask the elephant where she wants to go!

How do you make an elephant stew?
Keep it waiting at the doctor's office.

First goldfish: So I guess you're not dating that terrific-looking lobster anymore.
Second goldfish: It didn't work out. He was too shellfish.

What wears a coat in the winter and pants in the summer?
A dog.

Buyer: I just paid a fortune for a little parrot at this auction of yours. I suppose you'll guarantee that it can talk?
Auctioneer: Talk? Who do you think was bidding against you?

The zoo vet was carrying a thin ten-foot pole with a huge swab on one end.

"What are you going to do with that?" a visitor asked.

"The giraffe is ill," explained the vet, "and I have to take a throat culture."

A snake and a cat fell in love and got married. What did they put on their bath towels?
Hiss and Purrs.

Mr. Penguin: I sure am thirsty.
Mr. Seal: So am I. Let's go out for a polar beer.

Which newspaper do stockbrokers at the North Pole read?
The Walrus Street Journal.

What did Mr. Squirrel send his ex-girlfriend after they broke up?
Forget-me-nuts.

Baby snake: Mom, are we poisonous?
Mama snake: We most certainly are! Why?
Baby snake: I just bit my tongue!

What kind of insect jumps on a moon dog?
A *luna-tick.*

Henny: I see you got a new puppy. Does he have his papers?
Penny: Does he ever! They're all over the house!

What happens when an elephant steps on a grape?
The grape gives a little whine.

Mick: How do you converse with a crocodile?
Keith: By long-distance telephone!

What kind of fish has perfect pitch?
A *piano tuna.*

Little boy: Mommy, why do flamingoes stand on one leg?
Mommy: Because if they picked up the other leg, they'd fall over!

What do you do if your elephant squeaks?
Give it some peanut oil.

Mickey: My dog lost his tail. What'll I do?
Minnie: Guess you'll have to take him to a retail store.

What do you get when you cross a centipede and a parrot?
A *walkie-talkie.*

Mom: Don't be afraid of the dog, honey. He barks a lot, but see how he's wagging his tail?
Janey: But Mommy, I don't know which end to believe!

What has long tails, big ears, and lots of ice skating?
The Mice Capades.

Kerry: Someone I know thinks he's an owl.
Terry: Who?
Kerry: Now I know two people.

What do beavers like to drink?
Birch beer.

Mrs. Cod: Why aren't you swimming home, little fish?
Sardine: I'm staying for the after-school program.

What part of a fish weighs the most?
The scales.

What do you call naughty antelopes?
Bad gnus.

Why did the crow become a truck driver?
It couldn't resist the caw of the open road.

Mr. Cod: Why are you so sad, little fish?
Sardine: School season is just around the corner.

What do you call a baby kangaroo who does nothing but watch television?
A pouch potato.

How do you help an injured alligator?
Call for Gator Ade.

Melanie: There's a television program on tonight about an Arctic ox.
Marcia: Do you think I should watch it?
Melanie: Absolutely. It's musk-see-TV

Why do kangaroos make unreliable sailors?
Because they always jump ship.

Circus trainer: The elephants want to take a swim.
Ringmaster: How do you know that?
Circus trainer: They're wearing their bathing trunks.

How did the robber fish escape from the river bank?
They drove a getaway carp.

Penguin judge: To win this race you have to slide down the iceberg and dive in the icy water. Any questions?
Penguin contestant: Yes. What's the win chill factor?

What do you call a duck test pilot?
A flyer quacker.

Chester: I heard scientists are going to genetically splice owls with dogs in the year 2000. I wonder what they'll get?
Lester: Who-curs?

How did the beetle uncover the caterpillar's secret plans?
She bugged his phone.

Fisherman No. 1: After 3 hours, I landed this fantastic monster of the sea.
Fisherman No. 2: I saw the picture of your monster. It was barely 6 inches long
Fisherman No. 1: Sure. In 3 hours of fighting, a fish can lose a lot of weight.

Why don't lobsters share?
They're shellfish.

Mr. Roach: Mr. Centipede, why do you look so sad?
Mr. Centipede: I have ten children and school is about to start.
Mr. Roach: Most parents are happy when school starts.
Mr. Centipede: Not me. All of my children need new shoes!

What did the nitwit name his pet zebra?
Spot.

Captain: When I sailed from Australia, I took a dingo and a kangaroo with me.
Mate: And what happened?
Captain: The dingo proved to be an old sea dog, but the kangaroo jumped ship.

Where do thirsty apes go for a cold beer?
To monkey bars.

Father: The new dog can't sleep in the house.
Son: But he doesn't have a doghouse yet.
Father: We'll buy him a pup tent.

What's the best way to talk to a tarantula?
Long distance.

Animal Tamer: Don't let that lion scare you. He was raised on milk.
Trainee: So was I, but I'm eating meat now.

What do you get if you cross a little song bird with a big ape?
A chirpmonk.

Boy: My dog eats fish.
Girl: What kind of dog is he?
Boy: A Saint Bernard.
Girl: What kind of fish does he like?
Boy: Holy mackerels.

Where does a skunk go when the banks are closed?
To an automatic smeller machine.

Mr. Firefly: I'm starring in a Shakespearean play.
Mr. Glow Worm: Which one?
Mr. Firefly: A Midsummer Night's Gleam.

A man walking along a country road sees a car run over a rabbit. The driver stops, gets out, goes to the trunk of his car, pulls out an aerosol can, and sprays its contents on the rabbit. Miraculously, the rabbit gets up, hops 10 feet down the road, turns around, and waves. It hops another 10 feet down the road, turns around and waves, and continues doing this until it disappears from sight. The driver of the car tosses the aerosol can aside, gets in his car, and drives away. The astounded witness picks up the can and reads the label: "For hair restoration, and permanent wave."

Buck: We just had a baby antelope.
Rhino: Congratulations on being a gnu parent.

A lady went into a pet shop. "I'd like to buy two yellow canaries," she told the owner.

"We don't have any canaries, but we have these," the owner said. He showed the lady some pale green parakeets.

"That's not what I'm looking for," the lady stated. But the pet store owner refused to give up.

"Just think of them as yellow canaries that aren't quite ripe yet," he said.

Wife: Our pet dog is very friendly. Every time people come to visit, he licks their hands.
Husband: Yeah, he's a real welcome mutt.

Two caterpillars are sitting on a leaf when a butterfly zooms by, startling them. One turns to the other and says, "Boy, you'll never get me up in one of those things!"

Abe: What happens when lions play basketball?
Babe: They use mane-to-mane defense.

Granny Mouse was taking her two grandchildren for a walk when they spotted a cat coming toward them. The mice hid in some tall grass and waited anxiously. The cat didn't see them, but started over toward their hiding place. "Woof! Woof! Woof!" cried Granny Mouse loudly. "Woof! Woof! Woof! Bark! Bark!" The cat thought there was a dog lying in the grass and scampered away. "See children," Granny Mouse said to the little mice, "it's always handy to speak a second language."

Lady: Your dog seems to be in terrific shape.
Trainer: He should be. I make him do sit-ups every day.

Did you hear the one about the firefly who won the million-dollar lottery?
He's one happy-glow-lucky bug!

Why is the firefly so depressed?
It's Saturday night and he has no place to glow.

Mr. Mantis: Are you making a meal of those fireflies?
Mr. Spider: Yes. I'm having a light supper tonight.

Three polar bears were sitting on an iceberg floating in the ocean. "Well, since we're stuck here," said the father polar bear, "I have a tale to tell."

"Now that you mention it," said the mother polar bear, "I have a tale to tell, too."

Finally the shivering baby polar bear looked up at his parents, blew his runny nose, and said, "By tail's told!"

What kind of coffee does a T. Rex drink?
Jurassic Perk.

Two crows were sitting on a fence, amazed at how fast a jet with smoke pouring out the back was going.
First crow: Man, look how fast that guy is going,
Second crow: You'd fly that fast too if your tail was on fire!

What do you get if you cross dinosaurs and pigs?
Jurassic Pork.

Mrs. Jones: My spaniel likes to draw pictures with his paw.
Vet: Maybe he's a cockerdoodler.

What do frogs wear for a night out on the town?
Jumpsuits.

Visitor: Why are you crying?
Zoo attendant: The elephant's dead.
Visitor: You must really have loved him?
Zoo attendant: No. The boss just told me I have to dig his grave.

What do you call an exhibit stocked with wild bucking horses?
The Bronc's Zoo.

Boy: My father got me a turtle instead of a dog, and I hate it.
Girl: Why?
Boy: Do you know how long it takes me to walk my pet every day?

What do you use to fix a beehive hairdo?
A honeycomb.

What do you get if you cross a dog with a talking amphibian?
Kermutt the Frog.

Mel: How does the King of Beasts stay in good shape?
Nell: He jogs around the jungle?
Mel: Nope. He practices in-lion skating.

Why couldn't the antelope borrow money from the bank to buy an automobile?
They didn't give gnu car loans.

Ms. Beetle: Ms. Spider is getting married next month.
Ms. Cricket: Yes, and I hear she's making her own webbing gown.

How do pudgy bunnies get in shape?
They do harerobics.

Moe: I see you have a dog.
Joe: Yes. He used to be a pointer but my wife spoiled him.
Moe: How?
Joe: She taught him it wasn't polite to point.

How do you stop a skunk from smelling?
Hold its nose.

Jim: What do you call a gorilla with earphones on?
Slim: Anything. He can't hear you.

Why did the guppy join the Army's motorized division?
It wanted to be in a fish tank.

Mr. Hawk: That's one stupid bird in that tree.
Mr. Sparrow: Well you know what they say. There's no fool like an owl fool.

What do health conscious turtles eat?
A slow-calorie diet.

Caveman No. 1: What's the toughest part of hunting dinosaurs?
Caveman No. 2: Setting up the decoys.

Where do Arctic animals go for a cold beer?
A polar bar.

Camper: Last night I heard the cry of a depressed owl.
Ranger: How do you know it was depressed?
Camper: It kept calling, "Who cares! Who cares!"

How can you tell that you have a slow dog?
He brings you yesterday's newspaper.

How do you keep a dog off the streets?
Put him in a barking lot.

First turkey: As the days get shorter, I'm feeling more and more nervous.
Second turkey: Not me! Every time the farmer goes by I just say "MOOOO!"

How do you groom a rabbit?
You use a harebrush.

Hunter: What do you call that giant cat reclining on that tree branch over there?
Guide: I'd call him a lier and a cheetah.

What do you get if a bee falls in the meat grinder?
A *little humburger.*

John: Why is one polar bear attracted to another polar bear?
Ron: Animal magnetism.

What do you get if you light a duck's tail?
A *firequacker.*

Sally: I'm so excited. I found a panda.
Lynn: Why don't you take it to the zoo?
Sally: I took it to the zoo yesterday. Today we're going swimming.

Joey: I don't know what's wrong with me lately. I eat like a bird, work like a horse, but I'm tired as a dog.
Chloe: Sounds serious. Maybe you should see a vet!

Mrs. Bluebird: Honey, what happened? Did you have a hard day at work? You're a mess!
Mr. Bluebird: Work was okay, but on the way home I got caught in a badminton game!

Why were the little scrods thrown out of their school of fish?
They were always doing cod tricks.
Camper: I heard that grizzly bears won't bother you if you carry a flashlight.
Ranger: That depends on how fast you carry it.

A deer, a skunk, and a duck stopped at a bar for a drink. Who paid the tab?
Not the deer—she didn't have a buck. Not the skunk—he didn't have a scent. So they put it on the duck's bill.

What did the rabbit say when he fell into a hole filled with water?
"Oh, well."

Lucy: Have you read about these Africanized bees? They travel thousands of miles, and when they get where they're going, they're ready to kill!
Ricky: Yeah, I've had airline flights like that!

What do you get if you cross a cocker spaniel, a poodle, and a rooster?
A cockapoodledoo!

Why did the antelope read the classified ads?
He was looking for a gnu job.

Prospect: Are there any barking dogs in this neighborhood?
Agent: Oh, no. An extremely quiet neighborhood.
Prospect: That's good, because I've got a couple of dogs that bark constantly, and I don't think I could stand listening to any more!

Remsen walks into a bar and tells the bartender he's got something amazing to show him. From his coat pocket he pulls out a tiny piano and chair. From another pocket he brings out a little mouse. From a third pocket he lifts out a butterfly and sits it on top of the piano. Then the mouse plays the piano and the butterfly sings a Cole Porter medley. The bartender is truly amazed, but Remsen looks uncomfortable. He pockets his little act and starts to leave but turns back at the door.

"Look," says Remsen, "there's something I have to confess. This act isn't as amazing as you thought."

"Oh, a hoax, eh?" says the bartender.

"In a way," Remsen admits. "That butterfly can't sing at all. The mouse is a ventriloquist!"

Jim: Do you know why it's so noisy in Tibet?
Slim: No, why?
Jim: Because everywhere you go it's yak, yak, yak!

Did you hear the one about the snake who married an undertaker?
Their towels said "Hiss" and "Hearse."

Sandy: There's nothing to worry about. Here's a rabbit's foot for good luck.
Mandy: Now I'm really worried.
Sandy: Why?
Mandy: Because it wasn't so lucky for the rabbit!

What do you get if you cross a parrot with a huge emerald-colored man?
The Polly Green Giant.

AGING

Laughing as time goes by

Mrs. Fumpher: Why, when I was your age we never thought of doing the things you girls do today.
Young thing: So that's why you didn't do them.

Little Lucy: Mommy, why does Grandpa walk so slow?
Mommy: Because he's old.
Little Lucy: Will he walk faster when he's old-and-a-half?

Pearl: You'll live to be ninety.
Ruby: I am ninety.
Pearl: See?

I went to my high-school reunion. What a shock! Everyone had gotten so old and fat...they didn't even recognize me.

Caller: Congratulations, sir! You've just won a series of dancing lessons at Arturo's Temple of Terpsichore!
Grandpa: I'm much too old for dancing lessons. Why, I'm 90 years old!
Caller: Oh, no, we have many senior citizens here.
Grandpa: Well, in that case hold the line and I'll ask my father if he's interested.

Scoutmaster: Well, boys, did you do your good deeds for the day?
Scout #1: Yes, sir—we helped an old lady across the street.
Scoutmaster: It took both of you?
Scout #2: She didn't want to go!

Old man: My memory isn't what it used to be—would you mind telling me your name again?
Really old man: How soon do you have to know?

Susie: I've found a marvelous way to eliminate wrinkles!
Annie: Tell me!
Susie: I take off my glasses when I look in the mirror!

Rose: My dear, you really should eat only organic foods.
Violet: Honey, at my age I need all the preservatives I can get!

Rich old man: Ah, it's tough to grow old.

Very rich old man: Not at all! Why, I'm 10 years older than you are, and I play tennis every day of the year except for August.

Rich old man: Too hot to play in August?

Very rich old man: Oh, no, that's when the lad who swings the racquet for me takes his vacation!

Not-so-elderly lady: Well, Doctor, I guess I've reached that awkward age.

Doctor: What do you mean?

Lady: Too young for Medicare, and too old for men to care! Overheard in a beauty parlor: I'm so sick of my old hair color I feel like dyeing.

Mrs. Green: My children are driving me crazy.

Mrs. White: Yes. But children are a great comfort in old age.

Mrs. Green: True. The problem is they help you reach it faster than you want to!

Junior: Did they have TV when you were little, Great Grandpa?

Great Grandpa: Nope. They only things I saw on a 28-inch screen when I was your age were moths, flies, and mosquitoes.

Alice: Just how old are you?

Trixie: Oh, in the neighborhood of forty.

Alice: Are you planning on moving anytime soon?

Chuck: Boy, am I depressed! My doctor told me I was in great shape for a fifty-year old.
Chick: So why are you depressed?
Chuck: I'm only thirty-five!

Patty: How can I recapture my youth?
Matty: Try tying his shoelaces together.

Joey: I'm losing my hair!
Zoe: Really, I can't see it.
Joey: Of course not! I lost it!

Elderly patient: Help me, Doc. I'm ninety years old and I still chase women.
Doctor: If you're that old and you still chase women, you don't need my help.
Elderly patient: But I keep forgetting why I chase them!

Visitor: Have you lived here all your life?
Old-timer: Not yet.

Mr. O'Malley died and went to heaven. A week after the funeral, Mrs. O'Malley awoke to hear her husband's voice.
  "Mary, it's me. I'm up here in Heaven!"
  "How is it up there, John?" asked Mrs. O'Malley.
  "Wonderful, Mary! Golf every day, gin rummy every night, and I always win! Just think, if it hadn't been for that stupid oat bran, I could've been here ten years ago!"

Grandmother: I used to love to eat penny candy.
Grandson: Wow! I never knew you were a money hungry person.

An old man was wondering if his wife had a hearing problem. So one night, he stood behind her while she was sitting in her lounge chair. He spoke softly to her, "Honey, can you hear me?" There was no response. He moved a little closer and said again, "Honey, can you hear me?" Still, there was no response. Finally he moved right behind her and said, "Honey, can you hear me?" She replied, "For the third time, yes!"

Franklin: Another birthday...ah, it's hard to grow old alone.
Theodore: But you have your wife.
Franklin: Yes, but she hasn't had a birthday in fifteen years!

Elderly wife: You were more gallant when you were a boy.
Elderly husband: And you were more buoyant when you were a gal!

Why do grown-ups still put candles on their birthday cakes?
They like to make light of their age.

TV, MOVIES &
POP CULTURE

....

On famous faces and fleeting fads

Who do bucks and does write to for advice?
Deer Abby.

Old woman: When you die, where would you like to be
buried?
Very old woman: I'd like to be buried with Paul Newman.
Old woman: But he's not dead yet.
Very old woman: Neither am I!

What noisy piggy is a great movie director?
Steven Squealberg.

....

Weatherman No. 1: Compile the names of this season's hurricanes.
Weatherman No. 1: One gust list coming up!

What did Einstein drive when he was in the Army?
A think tank.

Astronomer: See that? It's a comet.
Little boy: A what?
Astronomer: A comet! Don't you know what that is?
Little boy: Nope.
Astronomer: Well, it's a star with a tail.
Little boy: It doesn't look like Lassie to me.

Which famous actress is great at altering suits?
Elizabeth Tailor.

Gloria: What are you watching on TV?
Jack: I'm watching lumberjacks demolish a cabin.
Gloria: What kind of program is that?
Jack: It's the home-chopping show.

Who is the greatest vegetable sleuth?
Celery Queen.

What lifeguard show do wolves howl at?
Bay Watch.

Mom: I thought you were going to watch TV?
Son: I am.
Mom: Then why are you dressed in a bathing suit?
Son: I plan to do some channel surfing.

What did Milton write one chilly winter morning?
Paradise Frost.

Ed: I'd like to be an actor when I grow up.
Fred: Why? Acting is hard work.
Ed: How can it be hard work when actors spend so much time in play groups?

Who has black feathers and anchors the nightly news?
Tom Brocaw.

Actor: Do you think my new hospital show will be a hit on TV?
Critic: Only if you doctor up the scripts.

What's the latest bombshell to hit Hollywood?
A Tom Cruise missile.

TV viewer: Do you think we should do away with showing violence on TV?
Critic: Definitely not! We need news programs.

Who is the handsomest movie star in the bakery?
Bread Pitt.

Anchorman: What do TV reporters wear under their pants?
Cameraman: News briefs.

What's totally silly and makes dogs itch?
The Flea Stooges.

Joe: Say, can anyone tell me which state Helena is the capital of?
Vince: The answer is Montana, Joe.

Which cable TV show do thunderstorms love to watch?
Rain's World.

Billie Jean: Hey! Who is that guy wearing a crown while he's playing tennis?
Referee: That's the King, Billie Jean.

What would you get if you crossed a famous opera singer with a hit TV show about rich teenagers?
Beverly Sills 90210

Bobby: Hey, Maurice, what do you call the bottom of a boat?
Maurice: That's called a Hull, Bobby.

What kind of TV show bubbles when you add water to it.
A soap opera.

Reporter: Is it true you drove a motorcycle off a cliff and didn't get hurt?
Daredevil: Nah! It was just a bluff.

A young man went to an interview for potential guests on a TV talk show. "What do you do?" the show's producer asked the young man.

"I imitate birds," the young man answered.

"What?" grunted the producer. "People who imitate birds are a dime a dozen. We can't use you."

"Okay," replied the disappointed young man. And he flapped his arms and flew out the window.

What do you get if you cross an electrician and an athlete?
A shock jock.

Did you know?
To a lot of modern writers, sex seems to be a novel idea.

What do you call a film fan who's willing to do a nude scene?
A film buff.

Pippen: What kind of sandwich would you like?
Jordan: Ham and cheese.

Pippen: American cheese?
Jordan: No. "Swish" cheese.
What do you get when you cross Jay Leno and a lizard?
A *stand-up chameleon.*

Hollywood name game
   Gregory, Peck on someone your own size.
   Kathy Bates her hook with worms.
   John Hurt himself when he fell.
   Martin Short-changed me when I paid my bill.
   Kevin, Bacon and eggs taste great with hash browns.
   Whitney, Houston is a large city in Texas.

Video review
Rocky: A boxing movie that really rings the bell when it comes to delivering punch lines. Watch it and see lots of stars. It's a knockout!

Mr. Spock: Let me explain the unusual shape of my ears.
Bones: Only if you get to the point quickly.

Which space villain from Star Wars is also a famous country western singer?
Garth Vader.

C3PO: Why are you afraid to go outside today, R2D2?
R2D2: Hey! Don't you know that Sunday is a day of rust?

What has wheels and eats spinach?
Popeye the Trailer.

Deion: How do you get this wood so smooth?
Tex: We use Sanders, Deion.

What do you call a short plump branch?
Porky Twig.

What did Beavis say to Butthead when they got hired to husk corn?
Heh! Heh! This job shucks!

Consumer: Hello, Ralph Nader? I'm calling about an automobile that absolutely must be recalled!
Ralph Nader: Oh, really? What part of the car is defective?
Consumer: The nut behind the wheel!

What company spokesman would you get if McDonald's merged with Disney?
Ronald McDonald Duck.

Who styles Bugs Bunny's fur?
A Hollywood haredresser.

Wizard: What is you favorite TV show?
Witch: The Hex-Files.

Who wears a sailor suit and has wrinkles and feathers?
Don Old Duck.

TV listings we'd like to see
   Third Rock from the Sun...guest-starring Sharon Stone.
   Seventh Heaven...guest-starring Jason Priestly.
   Home Improvement...guest-starring M.C. Hammer.
   Sister, Sister...guest-starring Dr. Joyce Brothers.

What's hard-boiled and can bench-press 300 pounds?
Arnold Schwarzenegg.

Mickey: Minnie, will you marry me?
Minnie: No way! Why should I give up a career in show business to become an ordinary mousewife.

What did Cinderella wear to the undersea ball?
Glass flippers.

Which cartoon character spends most of his time in a basement?
Popeye the Cellar Man.

News Flash!
Little Miss Muffet's spider couldn't change his pattern of behavior because he was too set in his whey.

What does Superman eat for lunch?
A *hero sandwich*.

Which instrument does Bugs Bunny play?
The *haremonica*.

Ms. Doe: What do you do for a living?
Mr. Stag: I just sold Bambi some life insurance and Rudolph some flight insurance.
Mr. Doe: Oh, you're a deer-to-deer salesman.

What do you get if Batman and Robin get smashed by a steam roller?
Flatman and Ribbon.

What is Ronald McDonald's favorite dance?
The *Big Macarena*.

Theatergoer: Is that new Broadway play Broken Vases any good?
Ticket scalper: Yes! It's a smash hit!

What's blue and used to ride waves?
A *smurfboard*.

What teenage superheroes are very helpful when it snows?
The *Plower Rangers*.

What comes in a six-pack and causes Superman to lose his strength if he drinks it?
Krypto-lite beer.

Trapper: I just saw a ghost that looked like Bambi.
Woodsman: It was probably just a deer haunter.

What do you call a small bathroom in Robin Hood's house?
The Little John.

Which fairy story is about a princess and seven short wimpy guys?
Snow White and the Seven Dorks.

Hans: Which lovely princess pushed a broom around tirelessly because a witch put a spell on her?
Christian: That was Sweeping Beauty.

What did Bambi call his father?
Deer old dad.

Why was Bambi too embarrassed to leave the thicket after he was born?
Because he was buck naked.

Why did Bambi get a job as a Hollywood stuntman?
Because he was a deerdevil at heart.

Tom: What kind of shirts does Robin Hood like to wear?
Jake: Arrow shirts.

Two billy goats were nosing around the back lot of a Hollywood movie studio. One goat found a spool of film, managed to unroll a few feet of it, and started munching. The other goat joined him, and pretty soon the film was consumed.

"What did you think of that stuff?" asked the first goat.

"Frankly," replied the second goat, "I liked the book better."

Convict: Mr. Joker! Mr. Penguin! Mr. Freeze! How did you guys end up in jail?
Mr. Joker: You might say we all had a stroke of bat luck, fella.

Which of Groucho's brothers got the best grades in school?
Hy Marx.

What kind of program is Oprah Parrot the star of?
A TV squawk show.

Why weren't Larry and Curly upset when they went broke?
Because they still had Moe money.

Bud: Do you know what they feed horses and cows?
Lou: Hay, Abbott!

What idiot started painting the Mona Lisa but couldn't finish it?
Leonerdo Duh Vinci.

Which western marshall only came out at night?
Bat Masterson.

What do you do when a blizzard hits Walden Pond?
Use a snow Thoreau-er.

Mickey: Hey, Yogi! What do you call that big wooden thing over your fireplace?
Yogi: Why that's a mantel, Mickey.

What do you get when you cross the New York Times Book Review with Professor Indiana Jones?
A movie called Readers of the Lost Ark.

Which elephant is a millionaire who owns a hotel and casino?
Donald Trunk.

What do you do if you cross Oprah, Phil, Geraldo, Ricki, and Sally Jesse with footwear?
TV talk shoes.

Which Muppet is green and made out of wood?
Kermit the Log.

Arnie: Is your brother a man or a woman?
Lou: What a dumb question! Don't tell me you know any female brothers!
Arnie: Sure—Dr. Joyce Brothers!

Who's chocolatey and draws Mickey Mouse?
Malt Disney.

RELIGION

May the good Lord save us—from these jokes

Disciple: Oh, Holy Vessel of Universal Wisdom, what is the secret of eternal life?
Guru: Lie about your age.

What two religions originated in San Francisco?
The Quakers and the Shakers.

Millie: What's an insomniac, dyslexic, agnostic?
Willie: Someone who stays awake all night wondering if there's a dog.

Who are the patron saints of vacations?
St. Thomas, St. Croix, and San Juan.

Minister: My new assistant minister is a real spendthrift.
Minister's wife: Why do you say that?
Minister: Whenever he's out of town he phones me parson-to-parson.

Why did the dumb farmer plant prayer books?
He wanted to be a church grower.

Sinner: Father, I've been bad. My conscience is bothering me.
Priest: Are you seeking a way to strengthen your willpower?
Sinner: No, I'd like a way to weaken my conscience.

What do you call it when a rabbi, a priest and a minister hold a service together?
A triple pray.

Pessimist: Boy, the world's in terrible shape. I don't think things could get any worse.
Optimist: Well, at least you're happy.

If Noah were alive today he probably couldn't float a construction loan to build his ark.

Teacher: Georgie, why did you write in your essay that you're Jewish? I happen to know your father's a minister.
Georgie: But I can't spell Presbyterian!

How do ministers get paid for their work?
They fill out pray vouchers.

John: Did you hear about Ugly Jim? He says he's "born again."
James: That's good, but did he have to come back as himself?

What do you get if you cross an American homeowner with a minister?
A taxprayer.

Minister: Do you spend much time wondering about the hereafter?
Old-timer: I'll say! Whenever I find myself in front of the refrigerator with the door open, I have to ask myself "What am I here after?"

How does one angel greet another?
She says, "Halo!"

Noah: Okay, all of you animals, go forth and multiply.
Snakes: Not us.
Noah: And why not?
Snakes: We're adders.

An elderly clergyman died and went to Heaven. Upon his arrival, he saw Father John, his lifelong mentor, stretched out on a chaise lounge next to a swimming pool. An unbelievably beautiful woman in a bathing suit was dropping grapes into his mouth.

"Father," exclaimed the clergyman, "I'm so glad to see you here! Of course I never doubted you would be here, but...well, frankly, I never once thought of all this"—the clergyman waved his hand at the pool, the woman, the grapes—"as your idea of Paradise!"

"You've got it all wrong, George," replied Father John. "This isn't my idea of Paradise. This is her idea of Purgatory!"

Minister: And how did you like your first church service, Billy?
Billy: Well, the singing and stuff was okay, but the commercial was way too long!

What holiday do monks get off from work?
Every Friarday.

John: Reverend, is it a sin to play bridge on Sunday?
Minister: John, the way you bid, it's a sin any day of the week!

What do you call a craft show put on by monks?
A friar works display.

Moe: Boy, was I a fat baby!
Joe: Yeah? How fat were you?
Moe: I was so fat that instead of baptizing me they launched me!

Who was the first man mentioned in the Bible?
Chap. One.

What's that?
Overheard in Heaven, between two angels:
"Do you believe in the Heretofore?"

Which government agency does St. Peter work for?
The Eternal Revenue Service.

Billy: Why does your great grandmother read the Bible so much?
Lilly: She said that she's cramming for her final exam.

In the Garden of Eden Eve was very upset. "I'm worried about Adam," Eve told the serpent in the tree. "He's absent without leaf."

Minister: Now, Mary, do you pray before dinner?
Mary: Nah, my mom's a great cook!

What do you call a team of ministers who play a game in Yankee Stadium?
Baseball prayers.

Minister: Faith can move mountains.
Boy: I believe you, but I think dynamite works faster.

How much fruit did Noah take on the Millennium Ark?
Two thousand pears.

Sunday school teacher: The Three Wise Men followed a big star.
Little girl: Oh, they were kind of like the world's first groupies.

A group of scientists has found a way to cross a praying mantis with a termite.
They've come up with an insect that says grace before it eats your house.

After hearing a bible lesson about miracles, a little girl went up to her religion teacher.

"In my house," said the little girl, "when handwriting appears on the wall it's not a miracle, it's the work of my little brother."

Man in church: Why isn't that pastor praying in English?
Lady in church: I don't know. Maybe he's a foreign minister.

What did the Zen master say to the New York City hot dog vendor?
Make me one with everything.

Director: I want to make a religious movie.
Author: Okay. I'll write a screen pray.

Did you hear the one about the man who quit the CIA to become a bishop?
Now all of his files are marked "Sacred" and "Top Sacred."

Preacher: Dust we were, and dust we shall be...
Preacher's boy: Gee, Dad, there must be someone under the bed either coming or going!

Did you hear the one about Little David?
He delivered a slingin' telegram to Goliath.

Minister: I'm now going to pray over the meal before we eat dinner.
Boy: Relax, Reverend. Mom's cooking isn't all that bad.

Why did the Israelites wander for 40 years in the desert?
Because Moses refused to ask for directions!

Mr. Smith: I'd like to speak to Mr. Jones, please.
Receptionist: Mr. Jones is no longer with us. He's gone to the United Kingdom.
Mr. Smith: I'm so sorry; is it too late to send flowers?

How did Moses part the Red Sea?
He used a sea saw.

Adam: I was made from dust.
Eve: Humph! Another dirty old man story.

What's brown and lives in a cathedral in Paris?
The Lunchbag of Notre Dame.

Optimist: This is the best of all possible worlds.
Pessimist: You're right!

How does St. Patrick enter a church?
He walks down the Emerald Aisle.

Wacky weather report
For long-winded priests—a mass of hot air expected.

Show me a monk with a temperature of 104 F°…and I'll show you a burning hot friar.

POLITICS

···

(no explanation needed)

Moderator: We'll open this debate with a question for the Republican candidate.
Candidate: I refuse to answer on the grounds that it may eliminate me.

What are the three great American parties?
Democratic, Republican, and Tupperware.

Senator: I stand on my record.
Heckler: Yeah—to keep us from taking a good look at it!

···

James: George Washington must have been coldhearted.
Mother: What makes you say that?
James: My teacher said he was the frost president.

Hotel clerk: I'm sorry, sir, but we're completely full.
Traveler: If the President of the United States were standing here, you'd have a room for him, wouldn't you?
Hotel clerk: Naturally.
Traveler: Well, he won't be coming tonight, so how about letting me have his room?

What's the biggest problem politicians suffer from in Washington?
Truth decay.

John: My dad went to a $100-a-plate political dinner.
June: Wow! If the plate cost that much, how could he afford to pay for the food on it?

Which president of the United States was very destructive to the White House Rose Garden?
Blight D. Eisenhower.

Jack, Jr.: Politics must be a lot of fun.
Mary: What makes you say that?
Jack, Jr.: A politician came to our house yesterday and asked my parents to join his party.

Which baby chick is a big shot at the White House?
The Cheep of Staff.

Senator: What's the worst thing a bachelor politician can do?
Judge: Take a June bribe.

Which U.S. president was always in a rush?
Hurry Truman.

What did Honest Abe drive when he joined the circus?
A *Lincoln Clown Car.*

Politician: It's a small world, my friend.
Taxpayer: Really? Then why does it cost so much to run it?

Annie: Know what I hate about political jokes?
Fannie: What?
Annie: They keep getting elected!

A young man was running for the Senate in New York State. His political advisor heard some news that really upset him. "Look," he said, "you've got to go to Albany right away or you'll lose a lot of votes. They're telling lies about you there."

"I've got to go to Buffalo first or I'll lose more votes," the candidate replied.

"What's going on in Buffalo?" the advisor asked.

"They're telling the truth about me there," the candidate replied.

Politician: America is the land of promise!
Heckler: Only during election years!

Candidate: And if elected, I know just what to do to get our city's industry moving again!
Voter: Yeah—if you win, we're moving!

Senator: With the new weapons installation in my state, we'll be able to hit targets as far away as Anchorage, San Diego, or Guadalajara!
Journalist: How about enemy targets—can you hit them?
Senator: Of course! As long as they're in Anchorage, San Diego, or Guadalajara!

Reporter: What's that minister doing out on the ice?
Coach: He's a hockey prayer.

What ship did the American president sail on?
The electoral boat.

Mr. Brown: I'm going on a fact-finding trip.
Mr. Green: Are you a politician?
Mr. Brown: No. I write encyclopedias.

Reporter on the campaign trail: "After all is said and done, more is usually said than done."

Candidate: Why shouldn't I run for president?
Reporter: You had a lousy track record in the Senate.

Mike: I wish politicians had more horse sense.
Spike: If they did maybe they could stabilize the economy.

Congressman: Which fish is the most at home in Washington, D.C.?
Lobbyist: The Senate herring.

Constituent: Vote for you? Hah! I wouldn't vote for you if you were St. Peter himself!
Candidate: If I were St. Peter, you wouldn't be living in my district!

Reporter: Senator, were you surprised when you were nominated for the vice-presidency?
Senator: Was I! Why I was so startled my acceptance speech fell right out of my hand!

Abe: There are two sure things in life—death and taxes.
Gabe: Yeah, but death doesn't get worse with every session of Congress.

Candidate: ... And in conclusion, I want to thank you for your kind attention. Now, are there any questions?
Heckler: Yeah...who else is running?

Society lady: Oh, Mayor Smith, I've heard so much about you!

Mayor Smith: But you can't prove any of it!

Obstetrician: Well, Senator, you're the father of triplets!

Senator: I demand a recount!

Why do politicians like kangaroos to make campaign contributions?

Because they have deep pockets.

Republican: What made George Washington such a great President?

Democrat: He never blamed any of the country's problems on the previous administration.

School principal: Do you know what happens to little boys who continue to tell big lies?

Boy: Yes. They grow up to be elected to Congress.

Reporter: Is it true diplomats tend to be evasive even when they answer simple questions?

Diplomat: Not necessarily.

Reporter: Well suppose I asked you what your favorite color is. What would you say?

Diplomat: Plaid.

Moe: If you were elected president, what would you do about defense?
Joe: I would paint it de same color as de house.

Three friends—a surgeon, an engineer, and a politician—were discussing which of their professions was the oldest. The surgeon said, "Eve was created from Adam's rib—a surgical procedure." The engineer replied, "Before Adam and Eve, order was created out of chaos, and that was an engineering job." The politician said, "Yes, but who do you suppose created the chaos?

Little girl: Daddy, do all fairy tales begin with, "Once upon a time....?"
Father: No, there is a whole series of fairy tales that begins with "If elected, I promise..."

Politician: Vote for me and I promise you the pie in the sky you've been hearing about for years.
Voter: Big deal. And whose dough will you be using?

Some guests were at a Washington party. "Have you heard the latest dumb White House employee joke?" one guest asked another.

"No," replied the second guest. "But I must warn you, I work at the White House."

"That's okay," said the first guest, "I'll tell the joke very slowly."

Politician: Just remember it's a small world.
Taxpayer: Then why does it cost so much to run it?

Did you hear the U.S. government is going to issue three new kinds of bonds?
The Clinton bond has no principle, the Dole bond has no interest, and the Gingrich bond has no maturity.

Reporter No. 1: Did you hear? A Democratic senator and a Republican congressman just went into business together and opened a bakery in Washington.
Reporter No. 2: Well they say politics makes strange breadfellows.

Sal: I know a carpenter who is now running for Congress.
Hal: Is he a good politician?
Sal: No, but he built a great campaign platform.

Overheard on Capitol Hill
"The trouble with dark horse candidates is you can't find out about their track records until you're saddled with them."

Reporter: What happened to the mouse who was sent to Congress?
Senator: He was just named Squeaker of the House.

Politician: It's no disgrace not to be able to run a country economically today.
Voter: I agree. But it is a disgrace to keep on trying when you know you can't do it.

Did you hear the one about the ex-NFL-quarterback who was elected to the Senate? He went to Washington to pass a lot of Bills.

What is the most powerful fish in Washington, D.C.?
The Congressional Herring.

Reporter: Did you hear about the nudist who won a seat in Washington?
Lobbyist: No. What happened?
Reporter: He was named Streaker of the House.

What nationality are most politicians?
They're members of the Congressional race.

Senator: The United States has made a lot of progress over the last 120 years.
Reporter: It sure has. President Washington couldn't tell a lie and now every politician in Washington can.

Reporter: What's the first thing you'll do if elected?
Politician: Demand a recount!

First bird: So, who do you like in the next election?
Second bird: I'm for Smith.
First bird: Smith? Why would you be for him?
Second bird: Because I hear he's for us.

Candidate: My campaign is picking up speed!
Campaign manager: Yeah, that's what happens when you're going downhill!

Politician: Re-elect me for a second term! In spite of what the House Ethics Committee investigation concluded, my conscience is clean.
Heckler: Yeah, because in the last six years you never used it!

Teacher: Can anyone tell me why the Capitol has a rotunda?
Student: So the politicians can run around in circles?

Attention Workers: *Remember, President Abe Lincoln was a union man!*

Cindy: I've been calling and calling the City Council to do something about these terrible potholes! After months of badgering, they finally took action!
Mindy: And now are the potholes filled?
Cindy: No, now the City Council has an unlisted number!

Skeptical Student: It's pretty hard to believe that George Washington never told a lie!
Teacher: Well, remember that American politics hadn't been perfected yet!

Felix: I don't think George is going to succeed as a politician.
Oscar: Why not?
Felix: Well take that speech he gave yesterday... when he asked if they could hear him in the back and the answer was "no," everyone in front moved to the back!

Which vegetable lives in the White House?
Celery Clinton.

Which president had a hard shell?
Abraclam Lincoln.

STOP ME IF
YOU'VE HEARD THIS ONE

....

Often-told tales and variations on the classics

Maisie: My brother is so dumb!
Daisy: Why do you say that?
Maisie: He read in a magazine that most accidents happen within two miles of the home.
Daisy: So?
Maisie: So, he moved!

Albert had just read a book on ice fishing, and was eager to try it. He followed the book's instructions carefully and had just finished cutting a hole in the ice when a voice out of nowhere boomed, "There are no fish here!"

"God, is that you?" asked Albert, his voice trembling.

"No," boomed the answer. "It's the rink manager!"

....

Larry: I hear you went to the fights last night—how was it?
Barry: Lousy! Right in the middle, a hockey game broke out!

What did the corn chip say to the potato chip?
Hey! Let's go in for a quick dip!

Patient: Help me, doctor, my husband thinks he's a refrigerator and I can't sleep a wink.
Doctor: I see; stress-induced insomnia.
Patient: No, he sleeps with his mouth open and the light keeps me awake.

One day a mailman was greeted by a boy and a huge dog. The mailman said to the boy, "Does your dog bite?"
    "No," replied the boy.
    Just then a huge dog bit the mailman.
    "Hey," he yelled, "I thought your dog doesn't bite!"
    "He doesn't," replied the boy, "but that's not my dog!"

Sandy: Why is Six afraid of Seven?
Randy: Because Seven Eight Nine.

Why did the chicken cross the road?
That's where he parked his coup.

Susie: Did you know you're wearing one black shoe and one brown shoe?
Sallie: What a coincidence. I have another pair at home just like this.

Car salesman: You say you want a customized sportscar?
Sam the snail: That's right. I'd like it painted with a big capital "S" on every side.
Car salesman: So people will know the car belongs to Sam Snail?
Sam the snail: No. So people who see me race by will say, "Look at that escargot!"

Did you hear about the restaurant on the moon?
The food is great, but there's no atmosphere.

Moe: What animal can jump higher than a house?
Joe: Any animal—houses can't jump!

Did you hear about the tornado who married a twister?
It was a whirlwind romance.

Patient: Help me doctor, I think I'm a set of expensive drapes.
Doctor: Oh, for heaven's sake. Pull yourself together!

Golfer: Notice any improvement since last year?
Caddy: Yes sir, you bought a new golf bag.

What made Babe Crow a famous baseball slugger?
He cawed his shot before hitting a home run.

SEASONAL LAUGHS

....

Timely jokes for special occasions.

Christmastime

Madge: Did you hear about Fred? He was arrested for doing his Christmas shopping early.
Flora: What do you mean early? It's almost Christmas.
Madge: Before the store opened.

Why did Santa visit his doctor before Christmas?
Because he always gets a flue shot before he slides down chimneys.

What did the antelope shout on January 1st?
Happy Gnu Year!

....

Blake: Why are you shivering so much?
Louise: It's the frost day of the week.

What did Santa Claus say to the lumberjack?
There are only 23 chopping days left until Christmas.

Ghost No. 1: What kind of Christmas tree is that?
Ghost No. 2: It's a boo spruce.

Why did Santa Claus send for a barber?
He needed someone to trim his Christmas tree.

Jenny: Do you know why snowmen get cold feet in bed?
Lenny: Sure. They sleep on sheets of ice.

What did the little monster hope to have on December 25th?
A very scary Christmas.

Father: They know when you're sleeping. They know when you're awake. They know if you've been bad or good.
Mother: Are you telling Junior about Santa's elves?
Father: No. I'm telling him about the CIA and FBI.

Who is Santa's nastiest reindeer?
Rude-Often the Red Nose Reindeer.

Mary: Are we going to exchange Christmas presents this year?
Harry: I don't know about you, but I always exchange mine.

Why does Santa's sled get such good mileage?
Because it has long-distance runners on each side.

Karate instructor: Why is your hand in a cast? Have you been practicing on boards or bricks at home?
Karate student: No, just Aunt Harriet's Christmas fruitcake!

Marty: Are you making any New Year's resolutions this year?
Mel: Yes. I plan not to be so insulting to people.
Marty: Ha! Knowing your temperament, how long do you expect to keep that resolution?
Mel: The whole year, you stupid idiot!

Why don't kangaroos visit Times Square on New Year's Eve?
They're afraid of pickpockets.

Hester: I took the kids to pick out a Christmas tree.
Lester: Was it fir?
Hester: No, just a few blocks away.
Lester: No! I mean...cedar tree?
Hester: Well, naturally we cedar tree.
Lester: No, no! Juniper!
Hester: Of course not! We paid for it fair and square!

Why did the pig farmer rush off in such a hurry?
He had to do some last minute Christmas slopping.

Elf No. 1: What did Santa say to his toys on Christmas Eve?
Elf No. 1: Okay everyone, sack time!

What does a deep sea fisherman send to his friends in December?
Christmas Cods.

Judy: What did the ghosts say to Santa Claus?
Mike: We'll have a boo Christmas without you.

Which number wears ornaments and flashing lights?
The Christmas Three.

Hunter: Why are you putting trout in the river this time of year?
Game warden: It's our Christmas stocking.

Why does Scrooge love Rudolph the Red-Nosed Reindeer?
Because every buck is dear to him.

Gina: This time of year is good for gossip.
Tina: Why do you say that?
Gina: Because it's time for the winter blah, blah, blahs.

Why did Santa Claus go to a workshop that builds self-confidence?
Because he no longer believed in himself.

Swinger: I went to the wildest New Years party! Even the butler was totally nude!
Nerd: Oh yeah? Then how did you know it was the butler?
Swinger: Well, it sure wasn't the maid!

How did the Abominable Snowman know he had dandruff?
There were Frosted Flakes on his shoulders at breakfast.

Tillie: Is that natural snow on the ski slope?
Lillie: No. It's man-made.
Tillie: I didn't know this resort used snow fakes.

How does Santa Claus take instant pictures?
He uses a North Pole-aroid camera.

Jack: I work as a substitute Santa at a department store.
Mack: What's your job title?
Jack: Subordinate clause.

When does the New Year begin at the North Pole?
January Frost.

Child: Daddy, Christmas is the day Santa brings me lots and lots of presents!
Father: And he leaves me holding the bag the rest of the year!

Ernie and his dad ventured into the woods to bring home a Christmas tree. They walked for hours in the snow, examining every tree they found. As the afternoon turned into evening, the temperature dropped ten degrees and the wind began to blow. Still no tree. Finally, Ernie piped up:

"Listen, Dad, I really think we'd better take the next tree we see, whether it has lights on it or not!"

Mrs. Santa Claus was seeking a divorce from an incredulous judge who asked her to explain her marital problems.

"It's that happy, jolly stuff, all year long," she said. "It drives me crazy!"

"All year? Why, I thought Santa's work was only in the winter," said the judge.

"Sure, but in summer he takes up gardening," Mrs. Santa replied, "and then it's hoe, hoe, hoe, all over again!"

What do you get if you deep fry Santa Claus?
Crisp Cringle.

Holiday Grab Bag

Why does the 9th letter of the alphabet like St. Patrick's Day?
Because it's when all the Irish "I's" are smiling.

Sean: What kind of cologne do you wear on March 17th?
Danny: Scent Patrick.

First Moth: Have a bite of this delicious sweater, old boy.
Second Moth: Sorry, old chap, I've given it up for lint!

What pantomime game do you play on the last Thursday in November?
The Thanksgiving Day charades.

Melanie: I was born on Flag Day.
Marty: No wonder your hair is so wavy.

Nick: Have you decided on costumes for the Halloween party?
Nora: Well, since I'm overweight and my husband's crazy, I think we'll go as a horse and buggy!

How can a person be five on her last birthday and seven on her next birthday?
Today's her birthday.

Why is March the shortest month of the year?
Because the wind blows a few days out of every week.

NOT FOUND IN WEBSTER'S

....

Humor that defies definition.

Actor: a person who works really hard at never being himself

Nudist: a person who is never clothes-minded

Sauna bath: a slimming pool

Tightrope walker: a top of the line performer

Shepherd: a person all kids flock to

Playground: the stuff kids use to make mudpies

....

Bracket: a shelf-help gadget

Bargain basement: a place where what you seize is what you get

Infantry: a day-care center

Khakis: a necessity for automotive ignition

Tension: what the sergeant shouts to the troops

Zinc: what you do if you can't zwim

Amnesia: a disease often occurring in people who borrow your books

Twins: womb-mates

Bigamist: a heavy fog

Secret: what we tell everyone not to tell anyone

Hospital: where you might wind up if you get run down

Fan mail: an air-cooled suit of armor

Seersucker: someone who spends a lot of money on fortune-tellers

Beauty contest: the lass roundup

Bathmats: small dry rugs children like to stand next to

Lemonade: a benefit rock concert for destitute citrus fruit

Beehive: a sting ensemble

Zounds: noizes

Egoist: someone who wants to die in his own arms

Paralyze: a couple of fibs

Gossip: a person with a great sense of rumor

Polygon: a runaway parrot

Grudge: a place to keep your car

Surgeon: a student who was the class cut-up at medical school

Health nut: a person the bullies will never pecan

Recipe book: thought for food

Meal time gossip: a dining rumor

Bacteria: rear entrance to a cafeteria

Theater school: a place where you can find some class acts

Correspondence college: an institute of flyer knowledge

TV Ministry: another cable pray channel

Bulldozer: someone who can sleep through a campaign speech

Flower shop: a budding enterprise

Seamstress: a real material girl

Diploma: the person you call when you toilet backs up

Operetta: an employee of the phone company

Eclipse: what a gardener does to a hedge

Masseurs: people who knead people

Mistletoe: a kiss miss plant

Calculator: a product you can count on

Mall shopper: someone who loves to go buy-buy

Medal: an award heroes get stuck with

Tree surgeon: a branch manager

Microwave: a head full of tiny curls

Obstetrician: a person who specializes in labor management

Jail cell: a bar room

A *baby chicken coop:* cheep housing

Classical Music Recital: a Bach party

Charge Card Company: a place that gives everyone else all the credit for its success

Mine owner: a coal-hearted individual

Retirement fund: money put aside in case your car gets a flat

Dog obedience school: a make-rover class

Door to door salesman: a real pain in the knock

Skeletons: stacks of bones with the people scraped off of them

Golf cart: a vehicle with a fore cylinder engine

Goblets: little sailors

Psychologist: a person who encourages you to speak freely and then charges you for listening

Dr. Frankenstein: the first champion body builder

Swing set: a place where you hope push will come to shove

Rollerblading: a new fall sport

Minister: a man who is the soul support of his family

Cashew: the noise a nut makes when it sneezes

Massage therapist: a cramp counselor

Microwave: the smallest movement of the ocean

Life insurance fraud: a case of mistaken identity

Diet plan: fast thinking

Enlistment papers: a service contract

Stupendous: advanced stupidity

Hurricane: What Abel said to his brother when he was late for school

Teepees: past tents

Tap: a beer barrel poker

Miser: a Commander-in-Cheap

Little Miss Muffet: a lady who knows how to make her way in the world

Hangover: The Wrath of Grapes

Bore: someone who talks about himself when you'd much rather talk about yourself

Doctor: someone who suffers from good health

Exhausted lover: someone who is temporarily out of ardor

Flypaper: what kites are made of

Television: a medium that's neither rare nor well done

Gallery: a girls' dormitory

Oscillator: something to say when taking leave of a friend (see *Abyssinia*)

Paradox: a couple of physicians

Stucco: what many homeowners are getting this year

Auction: where you get something from nodding

Stopwatch: what a cop yells to a runaway Timex

Apple turnover: command given by an apple trainer

Gardener: someone who's sure that what goes down must come up

Fortification: two twentifications

Cauliflower: what grows on a dogwood tree

Gerbil: a rat with a good press agent

Dieting: the punishment for exceeding the feed limit

Infantry: a sapling

Digital computer: someone who counts on his fingers

Optimist: someone who thinks things can't get any worse— after they just got worse

Stalemate: your ex-husband

Antique furniture: what you get from living with children

Perfectionist: someone who takes infinite pains…and then gives them to everyone else

Kleptomania: the gift of grab

Exercise: droop therapy

Icicle: a stiff upper drip

Naval Destroyer: a hula hoop with a nail in it

Outpatient: someone who faints in the doctor's office

Pessimist: someone who's always building dungeons in the air

Parapets: a dog and a cat

Protein: favoring young ladies and gentlemen

Nudity: a one-button suit

Think: what you do when you can't thwim

Hangnail: a hook for your jacket

Hotel: a place where you trade dollars for quarters

Girdle: a pot holder

Sunbathing: a fry in the ointment

Artery: a painting studio

Myth: a female moth

Fireflies: mosquitos with flashlights

Fief: a robber with a speech impediment

Monotony: having only one spouse

Europe: what the umpire calls when it's your turn at bat

Consultant: someone who gets $100 an hour to tell you the same thing your assistant told you last week

Aardvark: difficult labor

Pinochle: the very tippy-top of a mountain

Tumor: an extra pair

Steering committee: two backseat drivers

Cauterize: got her attention

Fjord: a Swedish automobile

Privatize: Sam Spade, Philip Marlowe, and Mike Hammer

Graffiti: street grime

Prison graffiti: animation cells

Bowling alley: a place where pin pals meet

Policeman's ball: a coptail party

Geologist: a scientist with rocks in his head

Dogma: a puppy's mother

Pelican: a bird who's way down in the mouth

Baby chick exhibit: a real peep show

Woolly caterpillar: a worm in a fur coat

Thongs: what Thinatra things

Ventriloquist: a person who enjoys talking to himself

Bee: a real buzz word

Wind: air that's late for work

Astronomer: a night watchman

Marriage: a union that defies management

Psychiatrist: a person who never has to worry as long as others do

Tirade: a cruel breeze

Theory: a college-educated hunch

Wimbledon Tennis Tournament: the supreme court

Cindy Crawford: a model citizen

Cloud bank: a place to save money for a rainy day

Pastry chef: a bake-up artist

Southpaw: a dad from below the Mason Dixon Line

Fitness trainer: a person who lives off the fat of the land

Sheep farmer: a person who runs a business with ewe in mind

Diet doctor: a man whose patients are wearing thin

Hair colorist: a dyeing breed

Snowball fight: an old-fashioned cold war

Pioneer: early American who was lucky enough to find his way out of the woods

Ring announcer: a minister at a wedding

Football center: a guy who makes snap decisions

Millennium ale: a thousand beers of good taste

Credit card: a debt charger

Meteorite: a space chip

Valiant steed: a knight mare

Snowplow: a mechanical device used to fill in the end of your driveway as soon as you finish shoveling it

Bachelor of Science: one who has mastered the science of remaining a bachelor

Drawers: artists

Greyhound: a stock cur racer

Traffic light: apparatus that automatically turns red when your car approaches

Megahertz: what you feel when a computer drops on your foot

Archeologist: a scientist whose career lies in ruins

Vampire: hemo-goblin

Tears: remorse code

Time-out chair: a sit calm

Ski jump: a soar spot

Minimum: a very tiny mother from England

Constitutional debate: star-spangled banter

Proofreader: a book marker

Computer gossip: chat rumors

Fishing net: a lot of little holes tied together

New Year's resolution: something that goes in one year and out the other

Kindred: fear of relatives

Bunions: spicy breakfast rolls

Censor: someone who tells artists to paint scenery instead of obscenery

W. C. Handy: a famous musician whose mother delivered him in a nearby washroom

Braggart: someone who always puts his feats in his mouth

Well adjusted: being able to make the same mistake over and over and over and over without getting upset

Barbells: pretty young ladies who like to hang out in saloons

Dilate: to live a long, long time

Counterfeit money: pseudough

Ambience: what you go to the hospital in

Coincide: what you should do if it starts to rain

Krakatoa: what can happen when you walk into a wall

Born-again Christian: a person benefiting from a faith lift

Drive-in movie: a theater with wall-to-wall car-petting

Efficiency: putting Murine in your grapefruit

Prison: the place you'd go only in a pinch

Alimony: 'bye now, pay later

Sleeping bag: a nap sack

Canadian bacon: a heat wave in Montreal

Gossip: words that go in one ear, and in another...

Atrophy: what you get for winning the Boston Marathon

Optimist: someone with little experience

Nostalgia buff: someone who finds the past perfect and the present tense

Miser: someone who earns money the hoard way

Skeleton: bones with the people off

Windbag: a person who's hard of listening

Minnehaha: a very, very small joke

Millennium: a centennial with more legs

Claustrophobia: fear of Santa

Acoustic: what you shoot pool with

SILLY SIGNS & SLOGANS

....

Used with pride by all the best businesses

Acme Picture Frames: We want to hang around your house.

Acme Clothespins: Our products are top of the line.

Acme Rope Company: If you can't afford a clothes dryer, ask us about a credit line.

Acme Thermostats: Install one of our thermostats and you'll never have to worry about your home cooking.

Acme Paste Company: Customers always stick with us.

....

Acme Pantyhose: We promise to give you no runs for your money.

Acme Bounty Hunters, Inc.: We always reward our employees.

Acme Sneakers, Inc.: Tie us, you'll like us.

Acme Furnace Company: We're proud to be full of hot air.

Acme Pager Company: We're at your beep and call!

Acme Sports Canvas Company: We cover all the bases.

Acme Shoelace Company: We are truly fit to be tied.

Acme Rope, Incorporated: Knot your ordinary company.

Silly Signs...

On a honey farm: You'll like our grade of honey—it's bee plus!

In a bankrupt bakery: No dough!

On a rodeo gate: bronc riders needed immediately—big bucks possible!

Near a prison exit for paroled convicts: From now on, keep right.

In a country prosecutor's office: If at first you don't convict, try, try again.

In a flexibility class: Think of us as your local limber yard.

In the window of a pillow company: For sale—all it takes is a small down payment.

Over the taps in a bar: One pitcher's worth a thousand words.

In the window of a health food restaurant: All you should eat: $3.50.

In the window of a bodybuilding academy: The weak ends here!

In the window of Acme Rabbits: When you've been in business as long as we have, you can't help but have a few gray hares.

In a discount store: Our prices are so low, why risk shoplifting?

In the window of an employment agency that specializes in domestic help: Maids to order.

On an egoist's door: Gone fishing for compliments.

On an optometrist's school: We're concerned about our pupils!

In a vegetarian restaurant: All we are saying is give peas a chance.

In a dog biscuit company: Caution! We bake for animals.

In a suspender factory: We specialize in hold-ups!

In a barber shop: Beware of falling locks.

In a pottery plant: We make clay while the sun shines.

In a taxi cab company: Our goal is to drive away all of our customers.

In a fish factory: Many are cod, but few are frozen.

In a cheese plant: We never lie about our aging.

In a gambling casino: We care where the chips fall.

In a post-office: Come to our year-end show—it's an all-mail review.

In a bowling alley: Sign up for our cash prize tournament and win some pin money.

In a beehive: Winter is coming so get buzzy!

In a scuba diving school: Our charges are in depth.

On a barbecue restaurant: This is a house of grill repute.

In a theatrical agency: We guarantee our products will perform well.

On the door of a police detective: Out to hunch.

In a staircase manufacturing plant: To keep your jobs, watch your steps!

In an optometrist's office: If you don't see what you're looking for, you're in the right place!

In a doctor's office: We know how to treat you right.

On a submarine: When we fight, we're not ashamed to take a dive!

On a print shop: Walk right in, don't wait for an engraved invitation.

On a tire company: Our tires will give your car good traction on wet roads. We skid you not!

On a travel agency: We mean it when we say we want you to go away.

On a home building company: Ask about our bargain basements.

On a tackle shop: "Get reel!"

On a fence company: Let us picket your house or place of business.

On an oil rig: We always do a fuel day's work.

Welcoming customers to the Deep Ravine Restaurant: We have valley parking.

On a diaper factory: Let us pamper your newborn baby.

Backstage of a nudie review: Undress rehearsal today.

In an exotic bird pet store: Caw us and we'll tweet you right.

On a poultry farm: Don't be offended if you hear a lot of fowl language.

At a chalkboard factory: We promise to give you a clean slate.

At a sleigh towing company: Payment is expected when service is reindeered.

On a pastry truck: We deliver the goodies.

At a fried chicken restaurant: All employees must wash their hens before cooking.

On a cafeteria trash bin: Junk Food Here.

At a retirement home for school principals: We've lost our faculties.

On a golf course: School around the bend—drive carefully!

At a sewing shop: Pin Cushion Sale—Low Sticker Price.

At a calculator company: We'll help solve your problems.

At a match-making company: We want to light your fire.

At a pastry shop: Come to us for your just desserts.

At a restaurant: Eat now—pay waiter.

At a broom factory: Rest assured you can sweep easy.

At a Scottish pawn shop: Join our fife-swapping club.

At a golf country club: Putt an end to your troubles.

At an atomic research center: Gone Fission.

At a skunk ranch: We love being in this stinkin' business!

At a pickle factory: Welcome dilly beloved!

In a bakery window: Cakes, $.66 Upside-down cakes, $.99

At Happy Farms Vegetables: Eat our corn on the cob and you'll smile from ear to ear!

CLASSIFIEDS

··

We're looking for a few good jokes.

Work for the Acme Perfume Factory.
It's a job that makes scents.

Wanted: Counterfeiter wants to form partnership with
print shop owner.
Object: Money making opportunities.

Wacky ad: Pre-Millennium Sale—Good Buy 1999

For Sale: Antique ashtray shaped like classic car. You'll
park your butt in it.

··

Wanted: Jelly maker wants to practice with professional jazz band.
Object: Jam sessions.

For sale cheap: Double-barrel shotgun. Slightly used, but only half shot.

Wanted: Intelligent watchmaker wishes to contact clockmaker with a high I.Q.
Object: Timely discussions.

Help Wanted

Mail Sorters—Must be letter perfect.

Camera salesman—Picture yourself working for us!

Drama school needs acting principal.

People needed to work in a clothesline factory—We'll teach you the ropes!

Success-oriented people to drive cement trucks—Only individuals with concrete plans for the future need apply.

Foot soldiers—Lots of chances to advance.

Tester at playground equipment factory—Must work the swing shift.

Dishonest carpenter—To help frame houses.

Comic book artist needed to finish stories—Draw your own conclusions.

Construction company needs man to dig holes—Ground level position available.

Secretary needed to work in lamp factory—Requires some light typing.

Man needed to pack new mittens in small crates—Must have experience boxing gloves.

Live-in custodian needed to sweep up dusty mansion—Broom and board included.

Secretary good with shorthand needed by music composer—To take down notes.

Astronomer needed by Hollywood gossip columnist—To watch movie stars.

Oak door tester—Must be a graduate of the School of Hard Knocks.

Jellymakers needed to form band—Opportunity for a jam session!

People urgently needed to work at Armed Forces Installation—Base pay to start.

Fitness room installers needed immediately—On the job training provided.

Top executive needed to take charge of mousetrap company—Must be able to make snap decisions.

Employee needed to test tongue depressors—Applicants must be willing to stick it out.

Newspaper needs freelance writer to cover zoo story about a mother bear about to have babies—Applicant must be willing to start as a cub reporter.

Farm hands needed—Take a job on our sheep farm and learn about profit-shearing.

Carpet installers needed to lay down rugs—Good pay. No tacks.

Tailors needed to make western rawhide jackets—Job includes lots of fringe benefits.

Fast food restaurant needs a chicken cook—We offer a frequent fryer bonus plan.

Writer needed to plagiarize novels—Job includes work as a copy editor.

Diner needs waitress for busy lunch hour rush—Applicant must be counterproductive.

Odd job descriptions

Lamp designer: A person who is light-headed.

Mail carrier: A person whose goal it is to be letter perfect.

Dance teacher: A job that allows you to really put your foot down.

Roof repairman: A person who likes to stay on top of things at work.

Army barber: A guy who knows all the short cuts in fast hairstyling.

Audio technician: A person who can tape the words right out of your mouth.

Swimming instructor: A job where all the employees are still wet behind the ears.

Real estate agent: A person whose job it is to put you in your place.

Geometry teacher: An instructor who definitely knows all of the angles.

X-ray technician: A health-care specialist who knows how to see through people.

KNOCK KNOCK

....

Who's there?

Knock, knock
Who's there?
Winnie.
Winnie who?
Winnie finally shows up for work, tell him he's fired.

Knock, knock
Who's there?
Freddy.
Freddy who?
Freddy or not here I come!

....

Knock, knock
Who's there?
Annapolis.
Annapolis who?
Annapolis a juicy fruit.

Knock, knock
Who's there?
Hugh's.
Hugh's who?
Hugh's cars aren't brand new.

Knock, knock
Who's there?
Texas.
Texas who?
Texas are high in this country.

Knock, knock
Who's there?
Hank.
Hank who?
You're welcome.

Knock, knock
Who's there?
A.C.
A.C. who?
A.C. come A.C. go.

Knock, knock
Who's there?
Luke.
Luke who?
Luke out the window and see.

Knock, knock
Who's there?
Armageddon.
Armageddon who?
Armageddon tired of all this cold weather.

Knock, knock
Who's there?
Recycle.
Recycle who?
Recycle around town on our bikes.

Knock, knock
Who's there?
Thelma.
Thelma who?
Thelma I went out for pizza.

Knock, knock
Who's there?
Armageddon.
Armageddon who?
Armageddon outa here!

Knock, knock
Who's there?
Kenya.
Kenya who?
Kenya give me a hand?

Knock, knock
Who's there?
Avis.
Avis, who?
A visitor from Mars!

Knock, knock
Who's there?
Sari.
Sari, who?
Sari I was sarong!

Knock, knock
Who's there?
Sikkim.
Sikkim who?
Sikkim and you'll find him.

Knock, knock
Who's there?
Olive.
Olive, who?
Olive me, why not take olive me...

Knock, knock
Who's there?
Ammonia.
Ammonia who?
Ammonia bird in a gilded cage...

Knock, knock
Who's there?
Samoa.
Samoa, who?
Samoa coffee, please!

Knock, knock
Who's there?
Uganda.
Uganda who?
Uganda come in without knocking!

Knock, knock
Who's there?
Chuck.
Chuck who?
Chuckago, Chuckago, that wonderful town...

Knock, knock
Who's there?
José
José who?
José, can you see?

Knock, knock
Who's there?
Amazon.
Amazon, who?
Amazon of a gun!

Knock, knock
Who's there?
Ptolemy.
Ptolemy, who?
Ptolemy that you love me.

Knock, knock
Who's there?
Wanda Way.
Wanda Way, who?
Wanda Way, and you'll be lost!

Knock, knock
Who's there?
Jewel.
Jewel who?
Jewel know who when you open the door.

Knock, knock
Who's there?
Toots and Theresa.
Toots and Theresa who?
Toots Company and Theresa Crowd!

Knock, knock
Who's there?
Fido.
Fido who?
Fido known you were coming, I'd've baked a cake.

Knock, knock
Who's there?
Wooden shoe.
Wooden shoe who?
Wooden shoe like to know?

Knock, knock
Who's there?
Irish.
Irish who?
Irish you a merry Christmas!

Knock, knock
Who's there?
Atlas.
Atlas who?
Atlas the sun's come out. I'll just stay out here.

Knock, knock
Who's there?
Eileen.
Eileen who?
Eileen too hard on this door and it'll break—better open
up!

Knock, knock
Who's there?
Marjorie.
Marjorie who?
Marjorie found me guilty and now I'm in jail.

Knock, knock
Who's there?
Theodore.
Theodore who?
Theodore is locked and I can't get in.

Knock, knock
Who's there?
Your maid.
Your maid who?
Your maid your bed, now lie in it.

Knock, knock
Who's there?
Euell.
Euell who?
Euell miss out on a big opportunity if you don't open the
door soon.

Knock, knock
Who's there?
Irish.
Irish who?
Irish I could carry a tune.

Knock, knock
Who's there?
Freeze.
Freeze who?
Freeze a jolly good fellow.

Knock, knock
Who's there?
Tarzan.
Tarzan who?
Tarzan stripes forever!

Knock, knock
Who's there?
Gnu.
Gnu who?
Gnu Zealand is a cool place to visit.

Knock, knock
Who's there?
Amish.
Amish who?
That's funny. You don't look like a shoe!

Knock, knock
Who's there?
Sweden.
Sweden who?
Sweden the lemonade, it's bitter.

Knock, knock
Who's there?
Decanter.
Decanter who?
Decanter at my temple is almost eighty years old.

Knock, knock
Who's there?
Dishes.
Dishes who?
Dishes the end of the world. Good-bye to all!

Knock, knock
Who's there?
Amanda.
Amanda who?
Amanda fix your TV set!

Knock, knock
Who's there?
C.D.
C.D. who?
C.D. badge I'm holding? This is the police. Open up!

Knock, knock
Who's there?
Aussie.
Aussie who?
Aussie you later, mate.

Knock, knock
Who's there?
Candice.
Candice who?
Candice be true love at long last?

Knock, knock
Who's there?
Hour.
Hour who?
Hour you today? I'm pretty good myself.

Knock, knock
Who's there?
Marie.
Marie who?
Marie Christmas to all!

Knock, knock
Who's there?
Water.
Water who?
Water our chances of winning the lottery?

Knock, knock
Who's there?
Hatch.
Hatch who?
Bless you.

Knock, knock
Who's there?
Army.
Army who?
Army and my friends invited to your Halloween party?

Knock, knock
Who's there?
Demure.
Demure who?
Demure I get, demure I want.

Knock, knock
Who's there?
Whale.
Whale who?
Whale meet you in the bar around the corner.

Knock, knock
Who's there?
Cairo.
Cairo who?
Cairo the boat for awhile?

Knock, knock
Who's there?
Hugo.
Hugo who?
Hugo and see for yourself.

Knock, knock
Who's there?
Wooden.
Wooden who?
Wooden it be nice to have Mondays off?

Knock, knock
Who's there?
Abby.
Abby who?
Abby Birthday to you!

Knock, knock
Who's there?
Manicures.
Manicures who?
Manicures the sick is a doctor.

Knock, knock
Who's there?
Thesis.
Thesis who?
Thesis a stickup!

Knock, knock
Who's there?
Ale.
Ale who?
Ale! Ale! The gang's all here.

Knock, knock
Who's there?
Ox.
Ox who?
Ox me for a date and I may say yes.

Knock, knock
Who's there?
Mary.
Mary who?
Mary me, my darling.

Knock, knock
Who's there?
Frosting.
Frosting who?
Frosting in the morning brush your teeth.

Knock, knock
Who's there?
Sheila.
Sheila who?
Sheila be coming around the mountain when she comes.

Knock, knock
Who's there?
Gnats.
Gnats who?
Gnats not funny! Open up.

Knock, knock
Who's there?
Knoxville.
Knoxville who?
Knoxville always get an answer if you bang long enough.

Knock, knock
Who's there?
Vericose.
Vericose who?
Vericose knit family. We stick together.

Knock, knock
Who's there?
Police.
Police who?
Police open the door. I'm tired of knocking.

Knock, knock
Who's there?
Dee.
Dee who?
Dee-livery. Open up—your pizza's getting cold!

Knock, knock
Who's there?
Zeus.
Zeus who?
Zeus house is this anyway?

Knock, knock
Who's there?
Ivan.
Ivan who?
Ivan to come in. It's cold out here.

Knock, knock
Who's there?
Asia.
Asia who?
Asia father home? He owes me money.

Knock, knock
Who's there?
Selma.
Selma who?
Selma shares in the company. The stock is going down.

Knock, knock
Who's there?
Harriet.
Harriet who?
Harriet too much. There's nothing left for me.

Knock, knock
Who's there?
Dewey.
Dewey who?
Dewey have to go to the dentist?

Knock, knock
Who's there?
Stan.
Stan who?
Stan up straight and stop slouching!

Knock, knock
Who's there?
Irving.
Irving who?
Irving a good time on vacation. Wish you were here.

Knock, knock
Who's there?
Maryanne.
Maryanne who?
Maryanne and live happily ever after.

Knock, knock
Who's there?
Mandy.
Mandy who?
Mandy lifeboats. The ship's sinking!

Knock, knock
Who's there?
Wayne.
Wayne who?
Wayne are we gonna eat? I'm starving!

Knock, knock
Who's there?
Wiley.
Wiley who?
Wiley was sleeping my wife packed my things and moved
me out of the apartment!

Knock, knock
Who's there?
Boo.
Boo, who?
Don't cry, sweetie pie.

Knock, knock
Who's there?
Watson.
Watson, who?
Nothing much. Watson who with you?

Knock, knock
Who's there?
Radio.
Radio who?
Radio not, here I come!

Knock, knock
Who's there?
Olive carrots.
Olive carrots who?
Olive carrots in the springtime; olive carrots in the fall...

Knock, knock
Who's there?
Little old lady.
Little old lady, who?
Hey, I didn't know you could yodel!

Knock, knock
Who's there?
Sahara.
Sahara who?
Sahara you dune?

Knock, knock
Who's there?
Shannon.
Shannon who?
Shannon, Shannon harvest moon, up in the sky...

Knock, knock
Who's there?
Iowa.
Iowa who?
Iowa lot to my mother.

Knock, knock
Who's there?
Hugh.
Hugh, who?
Hi, there.

Knock, knock
Who's there?
Hair combs.
Hair combs who?
Hair combs the judge! Hair combs the judge!

Knock, knock
Who's there?
Annapolis.
Annapolis who?
Annapolis red and round!

Knock, knock
Who's there?
Wallabee.
Wallabee who?
Wallabee sting if you sit on it?

Knock, knock
Who's there?
Lemon juice.
Lemon juice who?
Lemon juice you to my friend!

Knock, knock
Who's there?
Catch.
Catch, who?
Gesundheit!

Knock, knock
Who's there?
Shelby.
Shelby who?
Shelby comin' round the mountain when she comes...

Knock, knock
Who's there?
Yah.
Yah, who?
Gosh, I'm glad to see you, too!

Knock, knock
Who's there?
Elsie.
Elsie who?
Elsie you later!

Knock, knock
Who's there?
Annie.
Annie who?
Annie body home?

Knock, knock
Who's there?
Dots.
Dots who?
Dots for me you know, and for you to find out!

Knock, knock
Who's there?
Demons.
Demons who?
Demons are a ghoul's best friend!

Knock, knock
Who's there?
Stopwatch.
Stopwatch who?
Stopwatch you're doing and open this door!

Knock, knock
Who's there?
Surreal.
Surreal, who?
Surreal pleasure to to be here, folks...

Knock, knock
Who's there?
Harmony.
Harmony, who?
Harmony times do I have to knock before you let me in!

Knock, knock
Who's there?
Detail.
Detail who?
Detail-a-phone man!

Knock, knock
Who's there?
Don Giovanni.
Don Giovanni who?
Don Giovanni come out and play?

Knock, knock
Who's there?
Pencil.
Pencil who?
Pencil fall down without suspenders.

Knock, knock
Who's there?
Wayne.
Wayne who?
Wayne dwops keep falling on my head...

Knock, knock
Who's there?
Avoid.
Avoid who?
Avoid to the vise is sufficient.

Knock, knock
Who's there?
Avenue.
Avenue who?
Avenue met me somewhere before?

Knock, knock
Who's there?
Cargo.
Cargo who?
Cargo honk, honk.

Knock, knock
Who's there?
Tarzan.
Tarzan who?
Tarzan tripes forever!

Knock, knock
Who's there?
Henrietta.
Henrietta who?
Henrietta grasshopper.

Knock, knock
Who's there?
Sam and Janet.
Sam and Janet who?
Sam and Janet evening, you may see a stranger...

Knock, knock
Who's there?
Goliath.
Goliath who?
Goliath down. Thou lookest tired.

Knock, knock
Who's there?
I, Irma.
I, Irma who?
I Irma keep by working hard.

Knock, knock
Who's there?
Phyllis.
Phyllis who?
Phyllis in on the office gossip.

Knock, knock
Who's there?
Myron.
Myron who?
Myron around the park made me tired.

Knock, knock
Who's there?
Rice.
Rice who?
Rice and shine, Sleepyhead!

Knock, knock
Who's there?
Oil.
Oil who?
Oil change just give me a chance.

Knock, knock
Who's there?
A vet.
A vet who?
A vet ya vant to come in.

Knock, knock
Who's there?
Esau.
Esau who?
Esau you come in late last night.

Knock, knock
Who's there?
Thermos.
Thermos who?
Thermos be someone home, I see a light on.

Knock, knock
Who's there?
Yule.
Yule who?
Yule hear from my lawyer about this!

Knock, knock
Who's there?
Saddle.
Saddle who?
Saddle be the day when I die.

Knock, knock
Who's there?
Wylie's.
Wylie's who?
Wylie's on vacation, we don't have to work so hard.

Knock, knock
Who's there?
Al B.
Al B. who?
Al B. back.

Knock, knock
Who's there?
Turnip.
Turnip who?
Turnip the stereo. I love this song.

Knock, knock
Who's there?
Canada.
Canada who?
Canada boys comma over to play poker?

Knock, knock
Who's there?
Recent.
Recent who?
Recent you a bill the first of the month.

Knock, knock
Who's there?
Sonny and Cher.
Sonny and Cher who?
Sonny and Cher to cloud up later.

Knock, knock
Who's there?
Heavenly.
Heavenly who?
Heavenly met somewhere before?

Knock, knock
Who's there?
Omar.
Omar who?
Omar darling Clementine.

Knock, knock
Who's there?
Barn.
Barn who?
Barn to be wild!

Knock, knock
Who's there?
I, Hoyt.
I, Hoyt who?
I Hoyt myself. Boo-hoo!

Knock, knock
Who's there?
Tamara.
Tamara who?
Tamara I have an important meeting.

Knock, knock
Who's there?
Oscar.
Oscar who?
Oscar for a date and maybe she'll go out with you!

Knock, knock
Who's there?
Otto.
Otto who?
Otto theft is a serious crime.

Knock, knock
Who's there?
I'm Helen.
I'm Helen who?
I'm Helen wheels. VAROOM!

Knock, knock
Who's there?
Vision.
Vision who?
Vision you a happy New Year!

Knock, knock
Who's there?
Rabbit.
Rabbit who?
Rabbit up nice. It's a Christmas gift.

Knock, knock
Who's there?
I, Felix.
I, Felix who?
I Felix-cited!

Knock, knock
Who's there?
Urn.
Urn who?
Urn your keep by finding a job.

Knock, knock
Who's there?
Venice.
Venice who?
Venice pay day. I'm broke.

Knock, knock
Who's there?
Market.
Market who?
Market paid in full.

Knock, knock
Who's there?
Laurie.
Laurie who?
Laurie, Laurie hallelujah!

Knock, knock
Who's there?
Butcher.
Butcher who?
Butcher arms around me and give me a big hug.

Knock, knock
Who's there?
Ferris.
Ferris who?
Ferris fair, so don't cheat.

Knock, knock
Who's there?
Ammonia.
Ammonia who?
Ammonia lost person looking for directions.

Knock, knock
Who's there?
Midas.
Midas who?
Midas well sit down and relax.

Knock, knock
Who's there?
Gopher.
Gopher who?
Gopher a swim. It will refresh you.

Knock, knock
Who's there?
Cairo.
Cairo who?
Cairo the boat for a while?

Knock, knock
Who's there?
Jonas.
Jonas who?
Jonas for a cocktail after work.

Knock, knock
Who's there?
Turnip.
Turnip who?
Turnip the TV. I can't hear the news.

Knock, knock
Who's there?
Ken.
Ken who?
Ken you open the door already?

Knock, knock
Who's there?
Barn.
Barn who?
Barn to be wild!

Knock, knock
Who's there?
Rita.
Rita who?
Rita good book lately?

Knock, knock
Who's there?
Ida.
Ida who?
Ida written sooner, but I lost your address.

Knock, knock
Who's there?
Menu.
Menu who?
Menu wish upon a star, good things happen.

Knock, knock
Who's there?
I'm Cher.
I'm Cher who?
I'm Cher I don't wanna be standing out here—open up.

BONUS ONE-LINERS

Quick and efficient humor for joke-telling on the fly

My wife's as cold as marble...she says I take her for granite.

My father was a dentist and my mother was a manicurist...for most of their married life they fought tooth and nail.

My wife's always saying our poodle is just like one of the family...but which one?

My wife said we just had to hold down our grocery bills...so I bought her a paperweight.

They finally invented a computer as smart as a person...it blames all its mistakes on another computer.

I was up all night wondering where the sun went when it set...finally, it dawned on me.

I always have lunch at this Japanese fast-food place...you only have to take off one shoe.

My kid's such a bad student, his grades are always underwater...they're below C-level.

Senator Clagshorn's a real cowboy politician...he shoots from the lip.

Did you hear about the day the computer at the office broke down and everybody had to think?

The therapist told my wife to put some magic in our marriage...so she disappeared.

Our son wrote home from college that he's grown another foot...so my wife knitted him a third sock.

People are always calling me a hypochondriac, and let me tell you, it makes me sick.

My neighbor's got such a big mouth her name ought to be Ms. Issippi.

My ex-husband and I just weren't compatible—I'm a Capricorn and he's a jerk.

I read in the paper that Xerox merged with Wurlitzer...now I guess they'll be selling reproductive organs.

My brother's so conceited, he sent Mom and Dad a congratulations card on his last birthday!
Not only does he have a one-track mind...it's narrow gauge!

I used to run a doughnut shop, but I got tired of the hole business.

My husband's so dumb, when the TV set was broken he went in the other room and watched the radio.

My husband tests train whistles—that's why he's always out on a toot.

Did you hear about the comedian who told the same joke three nights running? He wouldn't dare tell it standing still!

I was so out of shape, when I went to the beach all the men dressed me with their eyes.

My sister's so self-centered, she takes a bow when she hears a clap of thunder.

My girlfriend's so conceited, she goes to the garden to let the flowers smell her.

You read in the papers about trade relations...Well, I'd like to.

I almost got married a few times, but fortunately, they were only near-Mrs.

I know I'll never find another man like my first husband...but then, who's looking?

I won't worry about the energy crisis as long as I have electricity in my hair and gas in my stomach.

My daughter plays the piano by ear...only problem is, she gets her earring caught between the keys.
I've always had my feet on the ground—but it sure makes it tough to take off my pants.

I don't mind running into debt...it's running into my creditors that's embarrassing.

My doctor told me I was iron-deficient...so I took up nail-biting.

I'm so unlucky I get paper cuts from get-well cards!

My uncle's so dumb, he went into the used-car business and turned back all the fuel gauges!

My mother's a woman of rare gifts—hardly anyone ever gets one from her!

My girlfriend's so selfish, she won a trip for two to Paris, and went twice!

I told my wife she'd have to make my paycheck go farther, so she took it to Hawaii!

My sister's so lazy, she puts popcorn in the batter so the pancakes flip themselves!

The church I belong to is so classy even the bingo game uses unlisted numbers!

With all the deductions from my paycheck, my take-home pay barely survives the trip!

Did you hear the one about the guy who opened a school for horseback riding, but business fell off?

Did you hear the one about the golfer who always brings an extra pair of trousers in case he gets a hole in one?

My brother's so stiff, when he visits a wax museum he needs a note to get out.

With these new microwave TV's, you can watch a half-hour sitcom in only 5 minutes!

The town I live in is so small, the road map is actual size!

I used to live the life of Riley. Until Riley discovered his credit cards were missing!

Last week I flew on an airline so small you had to have exact change to board the plane!

My brother is so hostile, he visits a fortune teller to have his fist read!

I'm so overweight I tried dieting—but all I lost was my temper!

I saw a terrible play last night, but I have to admit the conditions were poor—all the seats faced the stage!

My brother's the meanest acrobat in the circus—he's always got a chap on his shoulder.

You know the economy's really in a slump when even the wages of sin are frozen!

My husband's so dumb, he saves burned-out light bulbs to use in his darkroom.

I know a guy so dumb, he went to a dentist to have some wisdom teeth put in.
My neighbor's so dumb...he planted bulbs in his yard so the garden would get more light.

I knew a guy so dumb he locked his keys in his car...took him three hours to get his family out.

I was such a loser in school...girls sent back my love letters marked "Fourth Class Male."

Talk about your boring parties...the one I went to last night was a fete worse than death!

My tailor didn't have my pants ready when he said he would...so I sued him for promise of breeches.

I'd tell you the joke about the broken pencil...but what's the point?

I spent the night at my sister's house...their sofa was so uncomfortable I had to get up every so often to rest.

I suffered for months with this ringing in my ear...until I got an unlisted ear.

My father came to this country from Russia and made a name for himself...he named himself Smith.

I took up gardening as a hobby...but I only grew tired.

My son just got his B.A. and now he wants to go for a Ph.D. Frankly...I think he should get a J.O.B.

Show me a good loser...and I'll show you a fellow playing golf with his boss.

Did you hear the one about the award-winning farmer? He was outstanding in his field.

I wrote a book about watchmaking...everyone said it was about time.

We went to a seaside resort for a change and a rest...the maid got the change and the hotel got the rest.

Did you hear about the European tour guide? Taught his clients French in three easy liaisons.

I was a near-great athlete in school. I used to put the shot...but I always forgot where I put it.

I know a matador who's met over 200 bulls...he's the envy of every cow in Spain.

I had to move all my plants away from the telephone...they kept making obscene fern calls.

I went to a restaurant the other day and had a businessman's lunch...the businessman was furious.

I'm writing a screenplay about a seaside romance...it's a classic buoy-meets-gull story.

Last night my daughter's school orchestra played Beethoven...Beethoven lost.

Some mornings I wake up grouchy; other mornings I just let him sleep.

My brother is so vain, he joined the Navy so the world could see him!

Did you hear about the boxer who lost every bout? He had to go in for jab counseling.

Did you hear about the jester who lost his job? He was nobody's fool!

My husband's such a hypochondriac, he puts cough syrup on his pancakes.

My husband's so vain, he glued a mirror to the bathroom ceiling so he could look at himself while he gargled.

My husband's so thin, when he wears a red necktie he looks like a thermometer.

Lots of people thought Barbara was spoiled, but it was just the perfume she was wearing...

There's nothing wrong with Joe that reincarnation won't fix.

Did you hear about the Gouda, the Roquefort, and the Cheddar who ran away to France? It was a fromage à trois!

It rained so much on our vacation, instead of a sunburn we came back with rust!

The whole world is angry with me. Just yesterday, the tire of a used car kicked me!

My brother's an outdoorsman. He's been thrown out of more doors than anyone I know!

My wife went to the beauty parlor and had a mud pack treatment. She looked great for a few days...then the mud fell off!

My aunt ought to be on the Parole Board—she never lets anyone finish a sentence!

My mother's such a fitness freak, she tries to feed low-cal charcoal to her potbellied stove!

Did you hear the one about the amateur fisherman? He did it just for the halibut.

All the stores in town are pestering me to pay my bills, and it makes me mad. If they keep it up...I'll just take my debts somewhere else!

Last night I saw a movie with a happy ending. Everybody was glad it was over!